YALE STUDIES IN RELIGIOUS EDUCATION

XXI

ALEXANDER CAMPBELL AND NATURAL RELIGION

ALEXANDER CAMPBELL AND NATURAL RELIGION

BY

ROBERT FREDERICK WEST

Chairman, Department of Religion, Wabash College

28630

NEW HAVEN

YALE UNIVERSITY PRESS

LONDON · GEOFFREY CUMBERLEGE · OXFORD UNIVERSITY PRESS

1948

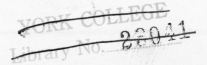

To my wife Mary Lewis, whose love of scholarship inspired this work—and to our little daughter Mary Margaret, who endured it.

PREFACE

DURING the last three decades of the eighteenth century the religious faith of America was challenged by the vogue of deism—the natural religion of the Enlightenment. Advocates upheld deism as the only true religion. They appealed to the freedom-loving Americans in the name of "freethought"; but the churches, prizing freedom just as much, called the movement "infidelity."

Basic to deism was its attack against all organized religion within the Hebrew-Christian tradition based upon divine revelation. The deists tried to promote what they regarded as a new religion by substituting reason for faith and nature for the Bible as ultimate sources for religious truth and inspiration.

By the first few years of the 1790's deism had become fashionable in certain academic and sophisticated circles in American society. In some circles atheism was welcomed as the more logical type of free thought. To say the least, both deists and atheists found it popular to denounce traditional Christian beliefs in revealed religion and to proclaim the universe as a self-sufficient machine.

However, during the last few years of the 1790's and during the early part of the nineteenth century, America experienced a marked recovery from the threat of deism and atheism. Three Christian movements have been customarily described as contributing greatly to this recovery in terms of a lasting interest in and commitment to revealed religion. These three movements were the "Second Great Awakening" in the Eastern States, the "Great Revival" on the Western frontier, and the Methodist movement under Francis Asbury.

But a fourth distinct movement, although later and not entirely unrelated to the others, needs to be stressed for its contribution to the recovery of America from the threat of deism and unbelief. This is known as the primitive gospel movement. The primitive gospel movement included a new variety of communions which arose in the nineteenth century in efforts to restore New Testament Christianity. Among the leaders of this movement Alexander Campbell (1788–1866) was the most noted figure. He was the most influential leader of the movement in meeting the challenge of natural religion and in arousing a nation-wide commitment to revealed religion.

This contribution of Alexander Campbell to American life has never been studied from this point of view. As distinct from the other three movements, Campbell began his religious leadership in America with a predisposition to the philosophy of the Enlightenment. In fact, he sympathized with most of the criticism which the natural religionists raised against the established churches and their views of revealed religion.

Alexander Campbell was so much influenced by the philosophy of the Enlightenment that it has been possible for some of his followers to overlook his commitment to revealed religion. Some have maintained that he placed reason above faith and nature above the Bible in seeking to understand Christian truth. But in his own day Campbell was known as an opponent of deism and of any form of naturalism which attacked revealed religion. Although he concurred with many of the criticisms of the natural religionists against traditional views of revealed religion, Campbell's watchword was liberty, not free thought. The liberty which he treasured was derived from his own commitment both to the Christian gospel and to American citizenship.

Previous studies have pictured Alexander Campbell chiefly as the main organizer and apologist of the Disciples of Christ and as a controversialist among Christian fellowships. He has been the subject of biographies and of the histories of the Disciples of Christ. Certain facts gathered about his life and his relation to the history of the Disciples of Christ are contained in the Appendix of this book. But the purpose of the book is not to duplicate studies which already have been made about Alexander Campbell and the history of his movement.

The purpose is to examine the relation of Alexander Campbell to the issue of natural and revealed religion on the American scene. This study will show that in the nineteenth century, at least, Alexander Campbell was known equally well as an apologist of the Christian faith in reference to the claims of natural religion. In this sense he was a churchman and not a mere sectarian; and in this light his changing program and apparent paradoxes can be understood more adequately.

The scene of the first major section of this book begins with Alexander Campbell's "Christian Baptist" type of antiecclesiasticism.[1] Hitherto, he had rather pacifically attempted to restore primitive Christianity in the limited form of specific local congregations from 1809 to 1823 on the American frontier. Now his enterprise has become more nation-wide in scope and American in emphasis.

1. We shall omit the abbreviation *op. cit.* in reference to the works of Alexander Campbell, for he wrote so many that we want no possible ambiguity as to the sources quoted. The years, the contexts, and the specific publications make crucial differences in interpreting his thought as a whole.

When the name "Campbell" is used without a prefix, it refers to Alexander Campbell. Also, for convenience, we shall not insert a (*sic.*) after every grammatical error in quotations, if the meaning is obvious and the readability would be otherwise hampered. Some misspellings were typographical and colloquial; others were efforts to be original.

ACKNOWLEDGMENTS

The author is grateful for the generous aid of those who have made available primary source materials from the libraries of Yale University, Bethany College, Butler University, the Christian Standard Publishing Company, Lynchburg College, Wabash College, and Texas Christian University. He is highly indebted to Dean Luther A. Weigle, whose guidance and encouragement in the study have made this book possible; to Professor Kenneth Scott Latourette of the Yale Divinity School and Professor Ralph H. Gabriel of Yale University for friendly counsel and helpful suggestions; to Professor Paul Dinkins of Texas Christian University for reading the manuscript; to Mrs. Banta for typing the manuscript; and, finally, to Mary Lewis West for constantly reviewing the work and enabling her husband to finish it.

R. F. W.

CONTENTS

PREFACE   vii

ACKNOWLEDGMENTS   xi

PART ONE: ATTACK UPON ECCLESIASTICISM

I. THE NEW REVOLUTION OF JULY 4   3

II. THE CLERGY AND THEIR KINGDOM   7

III. THE TYRANNY OF THEOLOGY AND TRADITION   29

IV. CONCURRENCE WITH OPPONENTS OF REVEALED RELIGION   45

PART TWO: DEFENSE OF REVEALED RELIGION

V. CLASSICAL SKEPTICISM   57

VI. THE OWEN DEBATE AND THE PLIGHT OF MAN   66

VII. CAMPBELL'S THEORY OF KNOWLEDGE   90

VIII. OTHER THEORIES OF KNOWLEDGE   105

IX. "NEW PHILOSOPHIES" AND "SCIENCES"   123

X. CHRISTIANITY AS A DIVINE INSTITUTION   136

XI. CHRISTIANITY IN HISTORY   151

PART THREE: PHILOSOPHY OF HISTORY

XII. THE MILLENNIUM   163

XIII. THE INTRODUCTION OF THE MILLENNIUM   185

XIV. THE POSTPONEMENT OF THE MILLENNIUM   211

XV. CONCLUSION   218

APPENDIX   223

BIBLIOGRAPHY   231

INDEX   241

PART ONE

ATTACK UPON ECCLESIASTICISM

A corrupt theory will never yield a correct and pure practice. . . . if Christianity was persecuted by its enemies, it was corrupted by its friends.

Alexander Campbell

well as political freedom. As a frail old man, he derived special vigor and strength in that hour of summoning the young gentlemen of Bethany to their respective callings in order that they might best serve conscience and country.

The 1830 "Oration in Honor of the Fourth of July" is a typical example of the lifelong trend of his approach to his American contemporaries as he raised his cry against ecclesiasticism. He declared that July 4, 1776, is "a day to be remembered as was the Jewish Passover." Every American citizen and philanthropist of the world should regard it gratefully. Praises of Washington, Franklin, and Jefferson will resound increasingly "in proportion as men are prepared to taste the blessings to result from the next revolution." Posterity will only "mingle regrets" that they, like Moses, "died short of the promised land."

A more glorious work is reserved for this generation—a work of as much greater moment, compared with the Revolution of '76, as immortality is to the present span of human life—the emancipation of the human mind from the shackles of superstition—to deliver them from the melancholy thraldom of relentless systems . . . This revolution, taken in all its influences, will make men free indeed. . . .[2]

The principles of this final revolution to make all men truly free were expounded during his editorship of the *Christian Baptist*. Characteristic of the magazine was its extremely negative attack upon ecclesiasticism. The attack was against every form of absolutism which enslaved mankind in individual or institutional life. If the people could see their real enemies exposed, the revolution would be won.

How were the people to find the real suppressors of their rights and liberties? One *"purely religious"* magazine which would advocate religious liberty by practicing religious liberty was his answer. Perfect freedom would be granted to all parties of the church and to all opponents attacked. They would be invited to defend and establish their own viewpoints against any assertions of the *Christian Baptist* editor. Thus the battle for liberty would bring the dark issues into the clear light of this day of plain speech and reason; the people would be given equal opportunity

2. Alexander Campbell, *Popular Lectures and Addresses* (Philadelphia, James Challen & Son, 1863), pp. 374–375. Also Alexander Campbell, ed., *The Millennial Harbinger* (Bethany, Va., Alexander Campbell), 1830, pp. 306–307.

to examine the evidence and to decide for themselves the fate of their oppressors.[3]

As a result of this policy, many of the most effective criticisms of Alexander Campbell's ideas are found in his own magazines.

In order to analyze the antiecclesiastical program of this campaign in its proper perspective, it is necessary to isolate the characteristic emphases of his attack upon the institution of the church and churchmen. But this undertaking is merely for the sake of convenient and organized reporting. As Campbell himself discovered, he never found time to express himself as systematically and as extensively as he wished, although he published about sixty volumes in the forms of collected essays, addresses, debates, magazines, and books. He frequently expressed this disappointment; for example, in the "Concluding Remarks" of the *Christian Baptist:*

Many subjects introduced into this work have not been fully and systematically discussed. General views have been submitted, rather than full developments and defences. Not a single topic has received that finish, or that elucidation which it is in the compass of our means to bestow upon it. . . .[4]

In this same apology, he noted that so many demands were made upon his time that even his series of essays were shorter and less frequently published than were originally contemplated. His articles were "almost universally written in the dispatch of ordinary letter writing, the half of an essay being often in type, or in the press, before the other half was conceived or written." While editing the *Christian Baptist,* he published two debates and two editions of the New Testament; consequently, "more was done than could be well done." Partly because of this problem the *Millennial Harbinger,* a larger project in which he hoped to "rally and concentrate our energies upon one work," was undertaken.

But the *Millennial Harbinger* did not rid him of this ghost which haunted him the rest of his life, as the same specters— other publications, correspondence, travel, and speaking engagements—increased rather than decreased.

Nevertheless, the spontaneity of his editorial presentations is important as an accurate account of his antiecclesiastical temper

3. *The Christian Baptist,* I, 8, 268; II, 5; III, 12.
4. *Idem,* VII, 284–285.

since they were written in the atmosphere of practical needs and developing expediencies. They unveil him in action as he unguardedly reflected upon "the current reformation," [5] as he termed the movement which generated under his leadership.

Ecclesiasticism to Campbell meant the institutionalism, the traditionalism, and the speculation of established churches which were filled with human absolutism that deprived the nineteenth-century layman of his natural and acquired rights and liberties. These objectionable tendencies were singled out in terms of the clergy, the union of church and state, the religious sectarianism, the superstitions, the orthodoxies, and the elements of Roman Catholicism which were inherent in ecclesiastical organizations and machinery.

As a result, defenders of the established churches did not permit his assertions to go unchallenged. It is no accident that he was called such names as infidel, freethinker, and deist. The method, content, and timing of his attack reveal a certain familiarity with the minds and spirits of the traditional enemies of orthodox Christianity which cannot be ignored. Before we analyze how far he concurred with them, let us examine his campaign against ecclesiasticism.

5. Campbell's immediate followers were often called "Reformers," "Disciples of Christ," and "Campbellites." He was frequently called "the Reformer"; they often referred to themselves as the "Reformers" as late as the first part of the twentieth century.

CHAPTER II

THE CLERGY AND THEIR KINGDOM

IN exposing the evils of ecclesiasticism, Alexander Campbell's first task was "to unmask the clergy and their kingdom." He accused the clergy of being the cause of "all division, superstition, enthusiasm, and ignorance of the people."

Consequently, he concentrated upon five types of clerical unmasking: exposing the clergy as a pretentious power-seeking "priesthood"; undermining any basis for special ministerial calling and authority; depicting all organization of clergymen as corrupt; describing traditional ministerial training as debasing; and denouncing clerical ranks and honorary titles as symbols of vanity.

Beginning with the nineteenth-century American scene, he appealed to the sense of independence and democratic spirit of his fellow Americans. He avowed that the "pretensions to authority" of Protestant clergy stand in the same light as "the arrogant pretensions of the Papist clergy to infallibility" at which the former have laughed when it suited their own interests.[1] The motive behind such pretensions is the claim of divine right in order to make the people afraid not to pay the clergy.

But, he insisted, the United States itself proves the fallacy of the doctrine that a nation cannot exist without kings or nobles at its head. Similarly, in things Christian, a church can exist without such structure. However, it would be as difficult to persuade the laity of that truth as to convince loyal subjects of an Eastern monarch that a nation could exist without kings and nobles at its head.

This favorite analogy was pressed home repeatedly. The details had the sting that suited his style and purposes in arousing the laity, for he insisted that there is a greater resemblance between the holy alliance of kings and the holy alliance of clergy than would appear at first thought:

1. *The Christian Baptist*, II, 3, 5.

In the first place, kings and clergymen of this day find themselves pretty much alike. They have both got upon thrones by the common consent of the people. The king upon a golden throne, or gilded one—the priest upon a wooden one, sometimes gilded, and sometimes crimson-cushioned too. The king wears a crown, and the priest a mitre . . . The king is high in honor and lives upon the toils of the people—the priest is high in honor too, and lives upon the sweat and sacrifices of his people. . . . The king pleads his divine right to rule . . . the priest pleads his divine right to instruct. . . . In this country we have no kings, and no king craft. We are not afraid to laugh at the impious and vain pretensions of the allied sovereigns. But in this country we have priests and priestcraft.[2]

During his early editorial years, Campbell had more in mind than individual clergymen who would abuse their public powers. He held that "the priesthood" as a system was inherently corrupt and its motives could be reduced to will to power and personal wealth. Its roots lay in the historical development of the clergy in which "no class or order of men" ever "obtained so much influence, or acquired so complete ascendency over the human mind." They held sovereign dominion over the Bible, the consciences, and the religious sentiments of all nations professing Christianity for about fifteen hundred years; and, though much impaired, their dominion still exists to an alarming extent and their same old eagerness for unrivaled control, haughty pretensions, and arrogance remains.

Their personal interest and greed for money are gratified once the dominion of power is obtained; and the vicious circle is never broken, for wealth gives them more power. Once the feelings and consciences of mankind were dominated, it was easy "to slide the hand into the purses of the superstitious." Thus the clergy enriched themselves enough to become "as powerful in the state as in the church." Proof of this interpretation is afforded, Campbell asserted, in the "history of France before the Revolution and Spain under the establishment of the Constitution and the Cortes."[3]

Money is the bond of union of the popular establishments, he concluded. Ministers are hired among congregations in such manner that "the strong become stronger, and the weak, weaker."[4]

2. *Idem*, I, 109–112.
3. *Idem*, I, 61–71.
4. *Idem*, I, 159.

As a proof of this, observe the familiar example of two men coming from the same "divinity school": the one of slender talents is placed as pastor of a local church paying a salary of three hundred dollars a year; the other, of considerable talents, is placed in the city over a church paying two thousand dollars annually.[5]

Money is not only the bond of union of the popular religious establishments but it is the rock on which they are built. "The modern clergy say that they do not preach for money. Very well; let the people pay them none, and they will have as much of their preaching still. Besides, there will be no suspicion of their veracity."[6]

Little imagination is needed to picture the effectiveness of such selected illustrations addressed to the lay frontier mind of nineteenth-century America! Satire, irony, simplicity of speech, and the analogy of kingcraft and priestcraft were choice weapons which he used to arouse the frontier folk of the Jacksonian era of American democracy.

Another ground on which he concurred with the popular spirit of that robust day is the offering of simple solutions to the complex problems confronted. Money is the basis on which the popular churches are built and the means of adding to a greedy priesthood; therefore, get rid of the problem by getting rid of money! Refuse to pay the clergy anything. To that simple solution he added another—get rid of the clergy. "Let us have no clergy at all, learned or unlearned—let us have bishops and deacons, such as Paul appoints, such as he described. 1st Timothy 3:14, Titus 1:5–9."[7]

As a logical outcome of this, Campbell found it necessary to undercut the basis on which he conceived clerical authority to be built. He defined the priesthood of the East and West as "those who claim a *Divine right of* teaching *authoritatively* the Christian religion."[8] He claimed that they invest themselves of such

5. *Ibid.*

6. *Idem*, I, 161. Benjamin L. Smith, in *Alexander Campbell* (St. Louis, The Bethany Press, 1930), claims that the ironical fact in this position is that, while helping to establish a tradition of underpaid clergy in America, Campbell died the richest man in the West Virginia of his day. He married a well-to-do woman, obtained revenues from his magazines, and was a successful sheep raiser and businessman. He was economically self-sufficient while advocating no pay for ministers.

7. *Idem*, I, 138.

8. *Idem*, II, 1.

authority by two grand means: "the alleged special call of God" to the ministry and the "necessity of consociation of these called ones for better administration of their government." [9]

He granted that there are many good men who believe both of these positions. But if he could not prove that "their pretensions, right, and authority to act as they do, is given them, *not from heaven,* but from men," to the satisfaction of "every umpire," he could not prove any point.[10]

In doing so he appealed to the social contract, one of the most familiar doctrines of the Enlightenment, and to the Bible to establish his position that a modern minister is called by a religious denomination or local congregation, on one hand, and by his own desires and qualifications, on the other. The only way in which a minister can demonstrate his authority is to produce a license or certificate from Papists, Episcopalians, Presbyterians, Methodists, or Baptists, to show that they consider him "competent and authorized to preach and teach Christianity." This is absurd, for it would mean that God calls people to preach different gospels and kinds of Christianity.

Neither these certificates nor the clergyman's swearing that he is called by the Holy Spirit can prove that he is so called. Only the evidence of a miracle could prove that he possessed such a call and that he cannot produce. Therefore, the basis of the call is a social contract and the minister need not fool others and himself, for he does speak and minister fallibly. Moreover, such pretensions are based upon the assumption that men need a new revelation and message from God for their salvation other than that which they have already been given through the Bible. "In short, there is no *need* to have men amongst us professing to be 'called and sent by God.' " [11]

Campbell held this position for the rest of his life, denying any special operation of the Holy Spirit directly upon the "naked spirit" of man either in ministerial calling or conversion.[12]

9. *Idem,* I, 63.
10. *Idem,* II, 2.
11. *Idem,* I, 65–69.
12. In regard to conversion, he maintained that the spirit of God operates through the word of truth, rejecting what he called both the *"Word alone* system" and the "Spirit alone system," which, he held, went all the way from a lifeless rationalism to an irrepressible enthusiasm. *A Debate between Rev. A. Campbell and Rev. N. L. Rice, on the Action, Subject, Design, and Adminis-*

With the authoritative claim of the priesthood to divine right by the special call of God undercut, his next logical blow for the religious freedom of the laity was to sever the final prop on which clerical power rests. Thus the whole organization around which the priesthood had built its power and interests was to feel the sharpness of Campbell's ax. Then the total ecclesiastical system would tumble. With the Bible as the ax, and innumerable proof texts to keep it sharp, he went to work.

In the first article of the *Christian Baptist* entitled "The Christian Religion," he set the framework for his attack against every conceivable institution of the modern church. He took his readers on a tour of the religious world and pointed out what he described as "the most glaring inconsistencies" of organized Christians as compared with the churches of the New Testament. After each stop he paused with the taunt, "Where is the Bible?"

Speaking of the Apostles he pointedly observed: "How freely, how cheerfully, how laboriously they performed the ministry which they had received! They look for no applause, for no stipend, no fixed salary, no lucrative office, no honorable title among men." [13]

The primitive Christian churches had as their only bond of union faith in Christ and admission to his will. They did "all they could for the glory of God and the good of men" in their church capacity alone, without delegating their obligations of social character to organized societies which are but the "in-

trator of Christian Baptism; Also on the Character of Spiritual Influence in Conversion and Sanctification, and on the Expediency and Tendency of Ecclesiastic Creeds, as Terms of Union and Communion (Lexington, Ky., A. T. Skillman & Son, 1844), p. 614. Hereafter this will be referred to as the Campbell-Rice Debate. "The Holy Spirit works in a Christian man and not upon him." *The Millennial Harbinger*, 1857, p. 182.

The debate between Alexander Campbell and the Reverend Nathan L. Rice, a Presbyterian, of Paris, Ky., was held in Lexington, Ky., from November 15 to December 2, 1843, with Henry Clay serving as president-moderator. It consisted of a total of one hundred thirty speeches for the eighteen days. In published form it contains 863 pages plus 37 pages of the correspondence which led up to the public discussion. As was customary with the debates in which Campbell participated, the published form carries a signed certificate of approval by both debaters authenticating it as a full and accurate report of the facts, documents, and arguments used on the disputed questions. By mutual agreement, the debaters chose neutral stenographers before the discussion began to take down its contents and proceedings.

13. *The Christian Baptist*, I, 14–26.

ventions of men." It was a literal priesthood of all believers about which Campbell was speaking:

Instead of the divinely established order of bishops and deacons, or as they are sometimes called, elders and deacons . . . we have popes, cardinals, archbishops, metropolitan bishops, diocesan bishops, rectors, presbyteries, deans, priests, arch deacons, presiding elders, ruling elders, circuit preachers, local preachers, licentiates, class leaders, abbots, monks, friars, &c. &c.[14]

The variety of doing good was expressed in all and by all without transforming themselves into any other kind of association and without dividing into missionary, Bible, and educational societies.

The head of a believing household was not in those days a president or manager of a board of foreign missions; his wife, the president of some female education society; his eldest son, the recording secretary of some domestic bible society; and his eldest daughter, the corresponding secretary of a mite society; his servant maid, the vice-president of a rag society; and his little daughter, a tutoress of a Sunday School. They knew nothing of the hobbies of modern times. They dare not transfer to a missionary society, or bible society, or education society, a cent or a prayer, lest in so doing they should rob the church of its glory, and exalt the inventions of men above the wisdom of God. . . .[15]

Also their devotional obligations were met by all on a day-to-day basis. Unlike the elastic and porous type of modern organized Christianity, the religious life of primitive Christians was so constant and consistent that special days and festivals were not set aside to be compressed into cold formalities at times and expanded into prodigious zeal and warmth at other times. All meetings were "at all times alike solemn, joyful and interesting." All days of the calendar alike were good—preparation and thanksgiving—for they had no "Easter Sunday, Thanksgiving Monday, Shrove Tuesday, Ash Wednesday, Holy Thursday, Good Friday, nor Preparation Saturday."[16] No ecclesiastical machines and accommodations had evolved to grind out their devotion and morality.

The strangest of all glaring inconsistencies of the established

14. *Idem*, I, 19–22.
15. *Idem*, I, 21.
16. *Idem*, I, 19–21.

churches, declared Campbell, can be seen in the following paradoxes: the *"Reverend Inquisitor"* dooming the heretic to destruction for the good of his soul; the Christian general and chaplain, with the Bible in one hand and the sword in the other, exhorting Christian warriors to fight valiantly the battles of God and country to make enough widows and orphans to afford others the opportunity of manifesting the purity of their religion; and enslaving and condemning a man, on the principle that might makes right because "his skin is a shade darker than the standard color of the times." [17]

This is the view of the outside surface showing the inconsistencies of established Christianity today as compared with the pure love and consistency of the ancient Christian community. Now, what lies underneath these strange appearances?

Underneath the cloak of all these modern ecclesiastical organizations, "priestly ambition"—the same old clerical combination of will to power and personal material greed—remains. A constant refrain of nervousness concerning the potential alliance of church and state runs throughout this cry of Campbell. He regarded "Missionary, Bible, Sunday-School, and Tract Societies, as great religious engines, fitted and designed for predominance of the leading sectaries who set them a-going, and ultimately tending to a *national creed* and a religious establishment." [18]

He appealed to the common people to beware of the clergy and their schemes which do "mischief to the temporal and eternal interests of men" and rob them of their civil liberties and "inalienable rights." [19]

Many clergymen, sympathetic with Campbell's charges, were not sure how the ancient church could be restored without organization. One minister, signing his name "Faithful," wrote Campbell that he agreed with his principles but wanted to know how to go about "restoring the ancient simplicity and glory of the gospel without making matters worse." It is easy "for you, my brother, to theorize on this subject; but how to reduce it to practice I have not yet found."

Perhaps the inquirer was surprised to receive the information, in the Reformer's reply, that "this happy circumstance" is already found among the congregations with which the man was

17. *Idem*, I, 25.
18. *Idem*, III, 59.
19. *Idem*, II, 4.

already connected, although some of them might have made their obeisance

to something called the Constitution of Alkhorn or Licking Associations, or something surnamed after the fishponds or millseats of your county. . . . But in all those congregations which have recognized that Christ's kingdom is not of this world and not composed of all born into the world by natural regeneration, methinks, it were easy, if the hearts of the people are regenerate, to have the ancient order of things restored.[20]

Then followed his advice for all members individually and collectively to search the Scriptures for the apostolic doctrine.

After all, it was a rather simple problem! But his solution appeared too simple for some of his readers and his complete atomism was challenged. When his *Christian Baptist* principles were accused of "pulling down everything, and building up nothing," his reply was, "There is nothing to build up." [21] He considered the charge a compliment, for all that had to be done was to remove the walls, the buttresses, and the rubbish of ecclesiasticism that men might have a clear view of the New Testament. This answer was typically entitled, "Potent Reply to a Weak Objection." [22]

It is important to note that during this period he was allied with the Baptists. Significantly, in February, 1826, an "Independent Baptist" questioned Campbell's consistency in remaining in full communion with Regular or Associated Baptists and yet professing to restore primitive Christianity. He stated that he did not doubt Campbell's honesty of conviction but he felt that it was only a "time-serving expedient." "If associations are scriptural, why then, say so—if not, 'come out from among them.' . . ." [23]

This hit Campbell where it hurt. He wiggled out of the problem to some extent by the ingenious distinction that consistency con-

---

20. *Idem*, III, 46–48.
21. *Idem*, IV, 274.
22. *Idem*, IV, 274.
While allied with the Baptists, this was Campbell's attitude: "The Baptist system is capable of being reformed or brought back again to the constitution of the kingdom of Heaven; the Paido-Baptist cannot. It must be destroyed. The one system carries in its bosom the means of its purification; the other, the fire that must consume it. The foundation of the former needs but to have the rubbish cleared away; the foundation of the latter must be totally razed." *Idem*, II, 51.
23. *Idem*, III, 221–224.

stitutes acting according to one's own professed sentiments and principles and not those of others, including the Independent Baptists. The only bond of union that Baptists ever professed "is the sincere and hearty conviction, expressed or confessed by the lips, *that Jesus is the Christ.*" He doubted that Paul, on the Independent Baptist's principles, could have broken bread with the congregation in Rome, Corinth, Thessalonia. or Galatia at the time he wrote his letters to them; or that the Saviour could have instituted the supper amongst the twelve on that basis. Thus the Bible helped Campbell in defending full fellowship with the Associated Baptists as long as he interpreted that fellowship to mean joint participation in social acts of worship but that was only part of the issue at which the Independent Baptist was driving. Campbell failed to deal with the problem of organization and association of the group in his reply but he well realized that he was being questioned in regard to his connection with "the Mahoning Baptist Association and the whole Baptist society." [24]

The shaft of the Independent Baptist was well aimed. At that time Campbell was not interpreting the Baptist conception of the church in terms of an associated cooperation between local churches but by Biblical references, in terms of mere local congregations of saints. He cited the example of Roger Williams' founding the first Baptist church in America, in which the leaders were chosen and called voluntarily by the people and from the people, as "a pretty good illustration of this principle." [25] He believed that the Baptist society and platform had more liberty of inquiry, "freedom from ecclesiastical tyranny," and independence of congregations than any other. He assumed that "confession of faith and authority of associations" were esteemed only by a few "rigid 'regulars.'" [26]

Consequently, since he held these views, it is not surprising that Baptist associations were attacked by Campbell before he finally withdrew his alliance from that denomination. Nearly two years after his exchange of letters with the Independent Baptist, he published an account of complaints which had come to his office from different parts of the country "of certain great stretches after dictatorial power, on the part of some leading members of

24. *Idem*, III, 224–227.
25. *Idem*, II, 49–50.
26. *Idem*, III, 230.

Regular Baptist Associations, within the last two years." He was not prepared to decide whether it came from Satan's wrath because his time is short, or whether "it is owing to the natural operation of the heretical principles on which such bodies are generally built." [27]

Earlier he had bewailed the tendency of Baptists to mock the principles of "once humble and unassuming people" by violating the custom of having "Bishops" or "overseers" of respective local congregations appointed and well approved by the congregation.[28] Tickled by the love of novelty and lured by the false majesty of Presbyterianism, some few Baptists, he had said, have compromised their distinctive features and grand peculiarities by joining the ranks of "the Clergy" and following the principle of leadership choices being made *by the few, rather than by the many*. They are thus exhibited

. . . in a classified priesthood, of ordinates, coordinates, subordinates, priests and Levites; ruling elders, licentiates, Reverends, and Doctors of Divinity . . . and have palmed themselves a species of demagogues, who, while they have all the airs, hauteur, and arrogance of some Paido-Baptist priests, have neither their erudition, nor their talents, nor their policy. They can neither wear the gown decently, nor conceal the cloven foot.[29]

By August, 1828, he was almost ready to abandon the Baptists as hopeless in the cause of reformation and to "come out from among them." (The "Independent Baptist" critic had had excellent insight into Campbell's underlying difficulties.) Campbell charged that "a few Doctors of Divinity" within the United States had done more to divest the Baptists of their ancient simplicity and love for the Bible "than all the Doctors of modern Divinity among them will restore in a century." [30] Hardly a relic of those traits of Waldenses and Albigenses from whom Baptists in this country are so proud to reckon their descent and to identify themselves as "fellow-professors of the same gospel" remains, he complained:

27. *Idem*, V, 93.
28. *Idem*, II, 49–50. Campbell did not rank the "bishop," "deacon," or "overseer" among "the clergy" or "priesthood." The bishop is merely a layman selected by all the other laymen to oversee the congregation. Whereas the clergy is set off from the laity by the claim of divine right, order, and authority.
29. *Idem*, II, 50.
30. *Idem*, VI, 5.

These modern, good, and wise, and *leading* men, being intoxicated with titles and worldly respectability, have cooperated to become imitators of their more respectable neighbours, the Presbyterians and Episcopalians. They have . . . actually got the whole machinery of the popular establishments in full employment to build up great meeting houses, parsonages, and colleges; to have a learned priesthood, tithes, and offerings; conventions, missionaries, tracts, and education societies, with all the "benevolent schemes" of the day. And those who will not say *Amen* to the whole paraphernalia, are heretics, unregenerated sinners, like myself. . . .[31]

Especially severe was he upon organized Presbyterianism, which exhibits "a countenance" like all other religious systems but is distinguished from them by its lofty "soul and spirit." "It cannot, like a Roman chief, bear an equal, or a superior. It aims for the chief place in the nation and views every other system as an impudent intruder upon its own rights and liberties." [32]

With this conception of Presbyterianism, he pounced eagerly upon anything which he could find to illustrate his point. An example is his review of the General Assembly's report of 1824 which happened to be entitled, "A Narrative of the State of Religion within the Bounds of the General Assembly of the Presbyterian Church and Its Corresponding Churches, in the United States of America." "Within the bounds of the General Assembly" was the only phrase Campbell needed to show their ambitious and aspiring spirit. He imputed that to mean that they wished to include the whole United States within their bounds, including Arians, Socinians, Arminians, Deists, Quakers, Methodists, Episcopalians, Papists, Baptists, Shakers, New Jerusalemites, and others.

The underlying evil of ecclesiastical organizations (Bible societies, Sunday schools, and missionary societies), reiterated Campbell, is that they are cunning devices of the priesthood to fill the ranks of their respective *competing sects* which take the lead in employing them. Inevitably, this competition means the attempt to dominate the political and economic aspects of the national life as a result of clerical will to power and personal interests.

31. *Idem*, VI, 6.
32. *Idem*, II, 6–10. See also I, 113–119; II, 143, 164; and III, 36–38, as mere samples.

The bulk of illustrations to back this contention was gathered during his travels as he observed the competition of religious sectarianism. In his early reform, he confessed that a three months' tour greatly clarified his reflection upon "the kingdom of the clergy, the necessity of the *restoration* of the ancient order of things, and the proper method of accomplishing it." [33] Freedom of speech, religious and political belief, and earning a living were at stake in supporting the ambitious clerics' drive for power.

The editor of the Times failed to continue his paper, more than six months, in the country of Knox, because of his editorial remarks on the avarice of a clergyman in his neighbourhood, who sued at law, through the trustees of his congregation, three widows and four paupers, for seven and six pence a piece. Having failed, and made his hegira to the country of Hopkins, he commenced with some encomiums on a sermon of the *Rev. Bene Placit:* his subscription lists were speedily enlarged, and by frequenting three meeting houses in town, in due succession, and by giving a little stipend to the three parsons in town, he got rich by his editorial labors. The motto to his paper is very apropos. It reads, *"Experientia docet."* His former motto was "Principes non homines." [34]

Commenting upon the same type of influence upon politics of the nation, he remarked that the time was when any candidate, supported by Pesbyterianism in western Pennsylvania, regardless of character or ability, would win over any opposition. And in "the agonizing struggle for the next President" some have alleged that the wife of General Jackson is a pious Presbyterian and the General himself is about to be "a ruling elder," whereas the friends of Mr. Adams "say he is a congregational saint." Yet "Messrs. Crawford and Clay" are neither "sanctified themselves nor their wives" and see how far they are behind!

Indeed, sectarian pride, ambition, and avarice, evidently threaten the continuance of our present free and beneficent institutions. . . .
    The clergy have ever been the greatest tyrants in every state, and at the present they are, in every country in Europe, on the side of the oppressors of the people who tramp on the rights of men. Nor are we to suppose this an accidental, but an essential characteristic of their assumptions. . . . We know that there are

33. *Idem,* II, 4–7, 141–143.
34. *Idem,* II, 142–143.

some exceptions; but these occur only where the spirit of the man preponderates over the spirit of the system.[35]

This distrust of potential political and economic power in the organization of the clergy remained with Campbell throughout his life. Typical were his observations on a tour of the South in 1839. To his disgust, he concluded that the South was in as bad a state as the West had been twenty years previously.

The people are safely lodged in the hands of the priesthood. . . . They seem to think it is their duty to pay the pastors for thinking and praying for them. . . . Demagogues in religion and politics are a more respectable and influential class in the South. . . . They are the sovereign of the sovereign people.[36]

Associated with the deceitful claims of special call and organization of the kingdom of clergy are the seminaries which are the "manufactories" of modern priests. Many people, Campbell asserted, falsely associate clerical training with the grace of God. For example, a parent educates his three sons, A, B, and C, to become a divine, a carpenter, and a doctor of medicine, respectively. Why should A, the divine, possess the grace of God or the faith of the gospel rather than B or C? Is there anything in the training of a divine that gives a special grace of God which does not exist in the education of the others? If so, it is the duty of every father to educate every son for the priesthood. But his money might run out and the father would not be able to educate the other two sons as the divine has been educated.

Then the gift of God is purchased with money! ! ! . . . Indeed, we would cheerfully undertake to prove that the training of a carpenter or mason is more *innocent* and less *injurious* to the human mind, than the training of a clergyman in the popular course, and that there is more in the education of the latter to disqualify him to enter the kingdom of God, than there is in the education of the former. . . .[37]

35. *Idem*, II, 143.
36. *The Millennial Harbinger*, 1839, pp. 185–186.
37. *The Christian Baptist*, I, 136–137. It is interesting to note that Campbell concurs with Martin Luther's taking the element of *special calling* from monastic and clerical life and putting it on the same basis as other vocations. But, whereas Luther describes a "devout prince" as a "rare game in heaven," Campbell claimed that "it is easier to be a good and pious king, than a good and pious clergyman." Constitutional principles must be trampled upon be-

The nature of popular ecclesiastical training for the ministry is degrading. Divinity schools train students in the arts of deceiving the people. In general, the training of all clergymen, Romanists, Episcopalians, Presbyterians, Congregationalists, and others is alike in spite of some specific differences.

Campbell reasoned that the divinity schools must be the cause of this degradation. Candidates for law, medicine, and divinity accompany each other in the same basic academic subjects and discipline until they receive their Bachelor of Arts' degrees and enter their particular fields of specialization. Then there is a marked contrast between the young priest and his fellows in other callings.

His former classmates, with whom he was once so jovial, retain their former jocularity or sobriety—there is no alteration of their visage. But my young priest gradually assumes a sanctimonious air, a holy gloom overspreads his face, and a pious sedateness reigns from his eyebrows to his chin. . . . His words flow with a heavenly cadence. There is a kind of angelic demeanor in his gait, and a seraphic sweetness in all his movements. With his sunday coat, on a sabbath morn, he puts on a mantle of deeper sanctity, and imperceptibly learns the three grand tones—the sabbath tone, the pulpit tone, and the praying tone—these are the devout, the more devout, and the most devout.[38]

In the meantime, he reads volumes of scholastic divinity, obtains skeletons of sermons from sermon books, studies sectarian dogmas carefully and the Bible carelessly, and becomes partially acquainted with church history and fully informed on the laws and proceedings of his respective ecclesiastical courts. Within a year or two, he is ready to appear before his ecclesiastical tribunal. After spending two or three months on his sermon which he has written, he has only to adjust

. . . the proper attitudes of the body, tones and gestures suited to the occasion; and, above all, he endeavors to conceal all art, that it may appear to flow with unfeigned sincerity. The sermon is pronounced and approbated, with a small exception or two. On the whole, it was a finished piece of mechanism.[39]

fore he can become a priest but not so with his advancement to the throne as president or king. The exceptions are few within the ranks of the clergy. *Idem,* I, 63.

38. *Idem,* I, 135.

39. *Ibid.*

Throughout his career, Campbell despised the artificial mechanism of sermon construction and delivery by the typical seminary product. Laziness and lack of genuine creativity he attributed to this training and to the young minister's licentiate preaching in which he could repeat the same discourses to strange congregations without the toil of preparing new sermons.

Nothing illustrated this "artful hypocrisy" to him more than certain prayers of clergymen. He recalled the subjective character of prayers which he had heard among pious Highlanders in 1808 in Scotland. He concluded that, as a rule,

. . . when two or three ministers of the same party happened to be present in the same pulpit, in which every one prayed, he made particular supplications for his ministering brethren. Thus the parson A prays very ardently for his brothers parson B and C, when they were present; but when B and C were absent, A asked no blessings for them. I do not recollect that I ever saw it otherwise in any sect or in any country.[40]

In Scotland he made this observation in his memorandum book under the head "Complimentary prayers, or prayers addressed to human beings not yet deified."

Whenever the opportunity came, he used his descriptive powers to belittle young clergymen fresh from the divinity schools. For example, he assailed a young divine of Washington, Pennsylvania, who had acquired the cane, assumed the black coat, but who had "not yet got the long face." He had practiced prayer before the mirror "that he might obtain a *graceful* appearance." This particular young divine "who was obliged to wear spectacles, either because of weak eyes or fastidious taste," once suddenly lost his notes, spectacles, and balance while preaching his sermon. Now just imagine this young priest spending some time in public prayer, before the sermon, asking

. . . to be *directed* to a suitable portion of Divine word, and that he might be *enabled* to make a seasonable discourse, which at the moment was in *writing* predetermined, premeditated, and committed to memory. O how long will they succumb to be thus mocked and insulted, by every boy, who has the hardihood to profess to teach a religion which he knows no more, feels less, than his

40. *Idem*, I, 259–260. Campbell emphasizes that he does not mean to censure a person or church's praying for another upon request or need but such intercessory prayers are different from "complimentary prayers."

blank book, when scrolled with one of Burder's sermons, or Rowland Hill's harangues! [41]

Thus the seminaries instill into students the motions, customs, and popular devices of displaying religious convictions but their mistake is to send the unconverted to convert others! Campbell compared the average trained clergyman in the pulpit with the lawyer at the bar, for the former could meet the requirements of the popular and orthodox sermon as easily as the latter could plead the case of his client without any grace.[42]

In this light, he ridiculed any plea of organized denominations for more ministers and for the support of seminaries. A typical example of this is his scathing series of articles entitled, "The Clergy," in Volume I of the *Christian Baptist,* in which he reviewed an "Extract of a Narrative of the State of Religion within the Bounds of the Synod of Kentucky," published by the Presbyterians in the *Pittsburgh Recorder* of November 6, 1823. The first paragraph of the report innocently states: "It is with pleasure the synod presents to the people a view of the state of religion within our bounds. From some points this view is dark; from others, encouraging."

The extract laments the death of four ministers, the lack of spirituality in the region, the lukewarmness in many churches, the vacancies within their bounds, and the subsequent need for more ministers and financial support of seminaries. It rejoices that prayers have been answered, in that pastors have been sent, and that "vacant congregations," in conjunction with those that have regular pastors, have cheerfully and liberally supported the poor and pious youth in the theological seminary.

But it becomes something else to Campbell, who concludes that the synod inconsistently takes pleasure in presenting a view,

41. *Idem,* II, 191.
42. *Idem,* I, 136. This is a favorite analogy of Campbell. The artificial fervor of the traditional lawyer on the stand bore the height of his contempt. In 1835 he related: "As a Pennsylvania Lawyer said to a client who wanted his advice for nothing, 'My tongue, sir, . . . is in your pocket'—so these accommodating ministers say to the candidate, 'My conscience is at your will, or in your election!'" In 1854, when interrogated as to the propriety of Christians engaging in law practice, he responded that a Christian man or minister might practice law with a good conscience and character, "providing only *that he will never knowingly and willingly defend a villain or a lawbreaker, nor make the worse appear the better reason.*" *The Millennial Harbinger,* 1835, p. 19; *idem,* 1854, p. 70.

dark or light. It reminds him of King George IV who, with heart-rending grief, told the citizens of Dublin in a speech that he had just heard of the death of his beloved spouse Queen Caroline while, with crocodile tears streaming down his cheeks, he expressed the great pleasure he then felt to be surrounded with his Irish subjects.

A vacant church! O for a new dictionary! . . . O your poor! who are not able to hire a faithful pastor, pray to the *rich* that you might be saved! . . . . Yes, yes, support the Theological Seminary . . . Give money to make poor pious youths learned clergy, or vain pretenders of erudition; and then pray that they may preach to you; yes, and pay them too. Was there ever such a craft as priestcraft? No, it is the craftiest of all craft! It is so crafty that it obtains by its craft the means to make craftsmen, and then it makes the deluded support them! . . .[43]

In the same manner, he seized upon the report of a missionary, published in the *Pittsburgh Recorder,* of a tour he had made through New Jersey and Pennsylvania in which he described the "total ignorance of Divine things" which he had seen within sight of a theological school of nearly one hundred students and also within the sight of Philadelphia. Writing in the wide expanse of the Virginia frontier, Campbell took the report for all he could squeeze out of it:

Mark it well— In sight of a theological school [Princeton Theological Seminary] in the vicinity of the annual meeting of the supreme court of the United States—a tract of country "70 miles long and 40 wide," the inhabitants are now in a worse state than the Pagans in Asia!! *Query*—what has this theological school, and this general assembly been doing for years, when their nighest neighbours have been so long without every thing they call Christian? . . .

How much is one hundred such students of Divinity worth?— One Benjamite with his sling and his stone could put a thousand such to flight.[44]

In fact, lay preaching was commended, especially when it concurred with his views and criticisms. He thought few regular clergymen could have done so well as the erudite layman Mr. Church of Pittsburgh who, on the banks of the Allegheny, appeared like Sampson among the Philistines. "He stripped the

43. *The Christian Baptist*, I, 113, 115–116.
44. *Idem*, II, 8–10.

clergy of all their exorbitant claims and pretensions, and fully expatiated on the devices of the clerical system." [45]

In the report of the Presbyterian General Assembly of 1824 he found ideal grist for his mill. Grinding upon its words and language for all the play he could get out of them, he reprocessed the phrase, "unanswered calls of our vacant territory." He declared that he had heard "in the cant phrase of Presbyterian tactics of a call from a *vacant church,* but not before of a *vacant territory* calling for the word of life, i. e., a preacher from Princeton!!" [46]

However, more than a play on words is involved here. He did not believe that the youthful clerics obtained real religious learning [47] in the seminaries from which they picked up smatterings of meaningless ecclesiastical jargon, customs, and ideas. He felt that the seminaries in the East, in spite of the assumed culture in that section, sent out ministers to the West with less "general information" and "Biblical knowledge" than the limited clergy of the West had. He supposed that the really learned clergy of the East stayed on their side of the mountains.[48]

At this stage in his reformation, Campbell had no patience with the secularized training which the ministerial students underwent. Whenever he could take a jab at the seminaries for this he did so. For example, in an "Address to Christian Mothers," he has much to say about the importance of women in religious history but, between the lines, he secures the opportunity for his blows:

You preach the gospel to them better than any Doctor of Divinity that ever lived. . . . Your example and your prayers, and your authority, and your well proved affection and sincerity in all that you say, are worth more than all the logic, mathematics, algebra, and rhetoric, which ever were collected in all the seminaries upon earth, to give efficacy to your sermons. . . .[49]

There is no question about Campbell's sincerely holding such sentiments about Christian mothers. But he had in mind, pri-

45. *Idem,* II, 22.
46. *Idem,* III, 37.
47. Campbell never advocated the abandonment of all learning even when he concluded that we must have no clergy. He warned that ignorance is not the mother of devotion any more than of "superstition" and "enthusiasm," although superstition and enthusiasm are equivalent to devotion "to many people." *Idem,* I, 139.
48. *Idem,* II, 51 (footnote).
49. *Idem,* I, 266.

marily, the contrast between their humility, sincerity, and simplicity of thought and life and the arrogance, artificiality, and secularized learning of the current seminary graduate.

To add to the shame of this seminary training the laymen, he scornfully thought, encourage the whole process. The wealthy and polite congregations sit too uneasily before the "sing-song monotony, and sawing gesticulation" of the homespun and awkward mechanic. He empties their pews and has to go West where he is accepted as John the Baptist in the wilderness. "His disgusting elocution, his awkward figure, and his frightful gestures are all unsullied sanctity, unfeigned devotion. The rural saint is full of his praise." [50]

On the other hand, the young divine of fine talents "is admired, is adored, where his class-mate would not be heard." In spite of all his polish, he is often "a mere retailer, a mere reader."

> "He grinds divinity of other days
> Down into modern use, transforms old print
> To zigzag manuscript, and cheats the eyes
> Of gallery critics by a thousand arts."
>
> Cowper [51]

Campbell concluded that the training of the priesthood is as corrupting as the claim of divine right and the organization of the clergy.

So far, we have seen that Campbell held that the priesthood as a system was based upon deceit. Three basic motives were behind its claims: will to power, material greed, and pride. We have dealt chiefly with the first two of these motives. Now we shall examine his contention that the priesthod was based upon conceit.

In this sense, the whole complex nature and structure of the organized priesthood could be pictured simply in terms of the quest after rank and title. Campbell's analysis of this can be reduced to three groups of symbols which reveal this competition after the chief seats in the synagogue: sectarianism, church office, and honorary titles.

The word sectarian to Campbell became a collective symbol of all that was odious in the conceit of the priesthood. It represented the organized efforts of competitive groups to see which

50. *Idem*, I, 160.
51. *Ibid.*

group could become the greatest among the kingdom of clergy. Much of that battle was centered around the search for new recruits, as we have already shown; thus missionary, tract, and Bible societies were the weapons with which they fought.

To this list he added another, the seminary. It was more than a training ground for young ministers to learn deceitful methods to delude the people. It was a means of domination by each sect to swell the ranks of its own leadership. In this context, Campbell ridiculed the report on the "State of Religion within the Bounds of the Synod of Kentucky," of November 6, 1822, issued by the Presbyterians, in which infidelity was described as on the increase around Lexington:

But the fact is, that the prevalence of infidelity in Lexington, means, that the synod having lost the management of the Transylvania University, and this seminary having, since it was by the state put under the management of others, flourished exceedingly, it has become exceedingly mortifying to the synod, which is about to get up another, for synods have always aimed at the sovereignty of colleges as subservient to their designs; consequently, whenever those lose the sway in any seminary, infidelity begins to rear its odious brow in the place.[52]

Aside from the competition of sectarian groups for the title of the greatest among all religious groups, all individuals in the kingdom of the clergy aspire for the highest status among the variety of offices within each respective ecclesiastical system. The kingdom of the clergy could be compared to the endless variety within the kingdom of nature; as from the mighty elephant to the clinging oyster, so from the haughty pontiff on the throne of an imaginary St. Peter to the poor curate who sells his fifty-two sermons per annum for the starving advance of 20 per cent on the first cost. "The class-leader would become a local preacher; the local preacher, a circuit rider; the circuit-rider, a presiding elder; and the presiding elder, a bishop. Then the highest round of the ladder is possessed." [53]

He viewed all sectarian groups as the same, although some maintained a greater variety of "gifts" than others. The bishop, for example, in some groups is an inferior dignitary and he views the archbishops "with envious eyes." [54]

52. *Idem*, I, 114.
53. *Idem*, I, 63.
54. *Idem*, I, 62–65.

Clerics are not satisfied with battling for highest titles between and within religious groups on a graded scale but also they seek special religious honors and titles, such as the "D.D." and "Reverend," which will sufficiently set them off from the common laity to satisfy their pride. Throughout Campbell's early attack upon the church, these clerical designations remained as symbols of the vanity of religious leaders.

He never missed a chance to poke fun at those titles. The title page of each monthly issue of the *Christian Baptist* bore the significant quotation: "Style no man on earth your Father; for he alone is your father who is in heaven; and ye all are brethren. Assume not the title of Rabbi; for ye have only one teacher:— Neither assume the title of Leader; for ye have only one leader— the Messiah." (Mat. xxiii, 8–10 *Campbell's Translation.*)

Whenever he heard of some one's refusing the award of D.D., he let his readers know it. Usually such special news items were headed, "Honourable Title of D.D. Refused." Then followed his commendation of the humility of the prospective candidate. On the other hand, whenever an article was captioned, "Religious Honors," the reader could anticipate a reproach for those who accepted such degrees.

A fair example of numerous instances of this kind is Campbell's informing his readers that *Reverends* Heron and Bruce received the degree of Doctor of Divinity at Jefferson College.

There is no country in Christendom, with which we are acquainted, which is more congenial to the growth of distinguished Divines than the regions of Canonsburgh and Washington. It is apprehended that owing to the peculiar influence of this climate, in a short time, all our Divines will grow into Doctors of Divinity. It is fairly presumable that the Doctors themselves will take a second growth, and shoot up into Metropolitans and Cardinals. But as it has been said, every new Baronet, Earl, and Duke, under a monarch, makes a few scores of ignorant dupes, who admire and fawn upon these Doctors proportionately to their ignorance and credulity. . . . It is an honorable army, where there are no privates, or subalterns; but in which every man is a Captain, or a Colonel, or a General— And how will Satan tremble when attacked by a whole army of Doctors of Divinity! ! ! ! [55]

His sense of humor and irony, which were particularly strong in so long as he, himself, was not attacked by such satire, would

55. *Idem*, II, 72.

not allow his title-bearing opponents to go to their graves in peace.

There has been, within a short time, a great mortality amongst the Doctors of Divinity in the Baptist denomination—Dr. Rogers, and Dr. Holcome, of Philadelphia, Dr. Furman, of South Carolina, and Dr. Baldwin, of Boston are dead. "Blessed are the dead that die in the Lord—for they rest from their labours; and their works," but not their *titles* "do follow them." [56]

His jesting was in its glory when he could uncover grammatical or theological errors or vanity among Presbyterian D.D.'s. " 'HOW are the mighty fallen, and the weapons of war perished!' " is the introduction he gives to such satire on "An Oration for Christian Missions" which was delivered before the General Assembly of the Presbyterian Church in the United States by William Craig, D.D., of Basking Ridge:

This is the golden age of Presbyterianism. . . . D.D.'s spring up as by a magic rod; and more especially in this warm climate where gourds, camp-meetings, theological schools, and pumpkins flourish with uncommon rapidity. But really if we advance one step farther in our profusion of literary honors we shall have D.D.'s like the popes of olden time, who can neither read nor write. We are just on the verge of such an era, now in the year of grace '25. [57]

56. *Idem*, III, 120.
57. *Idem*, III, 121.

CHAPTER III

THE TYRANNY OF THEOLOGY
AND TRADITION

CAMPBELL employed the same method of attack upon conventional theology and traditions of established churches as he did upon the priesthood. The priesthood, he avowed, is as presumptuous of religious knowledge as it is of power and authority. He was thinking of more than the call, the organization, the training, and the pride of the clergy. He was directing his attack against sectarian orthodoxies and clergy who he thought sought to enforce their own human and limited opinions in every realm of life.

For example, commenting upon the "anti-republican principle" of the Ohio legislature's granting a charter for the erection of Western Reserve College, he assailed the oration of the Reverend Stephen J. Bradstreet on the laying of the cornerstone, April 26, 1825. He suspiciously examined the orator's statement in regard to "this political-ecclesiastico literary institution" planning to "lay the foundation so broad and deep that a glorious superstructure may be raised upon it hereafter." Such language is understandable "when a Presbyterian divine so speaks." [1] Naturally, he refers to a preference to the creed of the mother country; this would gladden the hearts of the pious Covenanters in the reign of Scotch terror. " 'Knowledge is power,' says the orator, and he speaks the truth; and Presbyterian and Congregational power to oppress the uncharactered ignoramuses which constitute the fearful majority." [2]

He asserted that such charters historically have made the rich more powerful and the poor more miserable by putting in the hands of the few the means of tyrannizing the many. If public money is to be appropriated, it should be "a way of giving education to those who cannot otherwise obtain it." However, when the legislature of Ohio allots twenty thousand dollars in cash or

1. *The Christian Baptist*, IV, 9.
2. *Idem*, IV, 10.

public land, it makes the poor pay for the education of the rich man's son and the Baptist, Methodist, and Quaker pay for making Presbyterians or some other sect.[3]

The title of Campbell's blasting article reads, "Chartered & Legalized Priestcraft, Or Notes on an Oration on Laying the Cornerstone of a Sectarian College."

This clerical presumption that "knowledge is power" is not only seen in encroachments upon the minds, money, and liberty of the many but also in persecuting orthodoxies which condemn their dissenters as heretics. They seek to make their position more secure by cunningly devising ecclesiastical traditions and customs for church membership through which the laity are led to look to them for their temporal and eternal interests. Creeds and sects, he concluded, are inseparably connected with such thought and practices.

As one might suspect, on the basis of his solutions to other problems, the natural way for him to conquer this one was to abolish all orthodoxies and traditions. He would expose and abolish them through reason, common sense, and the Bible. To the cry of the priesthood of the East and West, who say that the church and souls of his readers are being endangered by his attacks, Campbell said that he would let the people read, examine, and judge for themselves. If they have really been instructed soundly in truth, the priests should have no fear. No teacher of grammar or arithmetic, after "teaching his pupils those sciences" for years, would greatly fear their reading any treatise in those fields.

If Campbell, himself, had a genuine coin and its genuineness were questioned, he would welcome its testing. But if he wished counterfeit money to pass as genuine "amongst the ignorant and unsuspicious," he would "fearfully avoid examination." [4]

Orthodoxies

Undermining conventional theology and speculations was his first step toward eliminating orthodoxies. Again, the tour of the ecclesiastical world with his readers in the first article of the *Christian Baptist,* "The Christian Religion," paved his way.

In it he maintained that the churches of the New Testament

3. *Idem,* IV, 11.
4. *Idem,* II, 1.

received and acknowledged Jesus as Lord Messiah and the Saviour of the world and put themselves solely under His guidance. The "only bond of union" for that "holy brotherhood" was faith in Jesus and submission to His will.

"But alas! 'how is the fine gold become dim!' " Just look at the present appearance of the Christian religion over the world:

Instead of the Apostles' doctrine, simply and plainly exhibited in the New Testament, we have got the sublime science of Theology, subdivided into Scholastic, Polemic, Dogmatic and Practical divinity. Instead of the form of sound words . . . , we have countless creeds, composed of terms and phrases, dogmas and speculations, invented by whimsical Metaphysicians, Christian Philosophers, Rabbinical Doctors, and Enthusiastic Preachers. . . .[5]

One of the surest signs of the corruption of the whole ecclesiastical structure of modern times, he contended, is its corrupt speech. Two of his favorite sayings were "the Saints are still in Babylon" and "more than half the language of Ashdod is mingled with less than half the language of Canaan." The way out of this confusion of language is to take the corrupt vocabulary of the established church and purge it of all Babylonish terms and phrases before the saints can understand the language which they profess.[6]

Today, orthodox zeal burns the brightest when it contends for its tenets and "a sort of technical language rendered sacred, and of imposing influence by long prescription." These misleading and arrogant distinctions distort the once simple teachings of Christianity into enough mystery to "employ linguists, philosophers, doctors of divinity, all their leisure hours, at a handsome per annum, in studying and then in giving publicity to their own discoveries, or in retailing those to others." [7]

However, Campbell did not confine to generalities his disgust

5. *Idem,* I, 21–22.

6. Alexander Campbell tried to solve this problem by publishing *The Sacred Writings of the Apostles and Evangelists of Jesus Christ, Commonly Styled the New Testament, Translated from the Original Greek by James Macknight, George Campbell, and Philip Doddridge, Doctors of the Church of Scotland, With Prefaces to the Historical and Epistolary Books, and an Appendix, Containing Critical Notes and Various Translations of Difficult Passages* (Alexander Campbell, Buffaloe, Virginia, 1826). He published a second edition in 1828 and a third edition in 1832. These and later editions became popularly called *The Living Oracles, The Sacred Writings,* or *Campbell's New Testament.* Hereafter, we shall refer to the work as *The Living Oracles.*

7. *The Christian Baptist,* I, 22.

toward a corrupt and technical language. Characteristic of his lifelong writings are frequent catalogues of specific theological word vices. To illustrate the sting and inclusiveness of his proscription lists, we need only to sample a few:

. . . the Covenant of works, the Covenant of Grace; the active and passive obedience of Christ; Legal Repentance; the terms and conditions of the Gospel; the Gospel offer; the Holy Sacraments; Ministerial, Sacramental, and Catholic communion; the Mediatorial kingdom of Christ; the millennium—Historic faith, temporary faith, the faith of miracles, justifying faith, the faith of Devils, the faith of assurance, and the assurance of faith; Baptismal vows; kirk sessions; fencing the tables; metallic tokens . . . experimental religion [8]

. . . "the Eucharist"; "Testament"; "Trinity"; "the first, second, and third person"; "Eternal Son"; "Original Sin"; "Christian Sabbath"; "effectual calling"; "merit of Christ"; "general atonement"; "free grace"; "free will . . ." [9]

. . . "The Holy Trinity," "Three persons of one substance, power and eternity." ". . . Humanity and divinity of Christ"; ". . . God out of Christ . . . ," "Satisfy divine justice . . ."; "justifying and saving faith"; "Evangelical Repentance"; "Perservance of the Saints"; "Falling from Grace"; Church "Government"; "The power of the keys." [10]

The Holy Ghost eternally proceeding from the Father and Son— God's eternal decrees— Conditional and unconditional election and reprobation— . . . Liberty and necessity . . . Total depravity— . . . Sovereign grace . . . —Reconciled God— . . . Common and special operations of the Holy Ghost— . . . Visible and

8. *Idem*, I, 20.

9. Alexander Campbell, *Christian Baptism, With Its Antecedents and Consequences* (Bethany, Alexander Campbell, 1851), p. 20.

10. Alexander Campbell, *The Christian System in Reference to the Union of Christians, And a Restoration of Primitive Christianity, As Plead in the Current Reformation.* 3d ed. (Pittsburgh, Forrester & Campbell, 1840), pp. 124–125. Hereafter this will be referred to as *The Christian System*. It was first published as *A Connected View of the Principles and Rules by Which the Living Oracles May Be Intelligibly and Certainly Interpreted, of the Foundation on Which All Christians May Form One Communion, and of the Capital Positions Sustained in the Attempt to Restore the Original Gospel and Order of Things, Containing the Principal Extras of the Millennial Harbinger, Revised and Corrected* (Bethany, Va., M'Vay & Ewing, 1835).

Invisible church— Infant membership . . . —Consubstantiation . . .[11]

All such words have no foundation in the realm of certainty and pure speech. He counted it a virtue to forget all "the scholastic jargon and even the names of the dogmas which have convulsed Christendom." All the words of Ashdod must be abandoned. This also includes all the work which church councils have done in their history, for no person has ever been known to have become wiser, sanctified, or converted by any of the "controversies about human dogmas, nor by anything learned from the canons or creeds of all the Councils, from that of Nice to the last Methodistic Conference." [12]

The basis for this contention is that all non-Biblical phrases and words of the ecclesiastic system are rooted in unreliable and unimportant human speculations and traditions. "All of the abstract and metaphysical dogmas of the best creeds now extant are the most difficult of apprehension and comprehension," he concluded, and are composed of merely the inferences of human understanding based upon speculations about the revelation of God. These inferences partake of all the defects of that understanding—from prejudices in upbringing, education, various circumstances of thinking, passions, and interests of very human men of different intellectual capacity.[13]

Because of these prejudices, along with the natural change in meanings of certain words through the years, Campbell felt that the King James's translation of the Bible made for confusion. For example, he construed King James's instructions to his translators to mean that words like immersion should be omitted for "baptism," although they actually said to use " 'the *old* ecclesiastical words' " and to follow the church fathers when words had diverse meanings.[14]

Therefore, when councils are held in regard to a quest for unity in understanding various human opinions, their cause is hopeless.

11. *The Millennial Harbinger*, 1835, p. 352. He also included "the two seeds" in reference to Daniel Parker's "Two Seeds in the Spirit Baptists" fellowship. See also *The Christian Baptist*, VI, 283.

12. *The Christian System*, p. 126.

13. *The Christian Baptist*, II, 177–179.

14. *Idem*, II, 85 ff. See also *The Living Oracles*, 3d ed., pp. 8–16. Consequently, Alexander Campbell substituted "immersion" for "baptism" and added his own notes and prefaces to his various editions of this vernacular English version of the New Testament.

Opinions are "private property." It would be as difficult to get unanimity and adoption in human creeds as in features of color, height, and weight.[15]

All the divisions, "partyism, vain jangling, and heresies which have disgraced the Christian profession" have come from human philosophy and tradition. "Let human philosophy and human tradition, as any part of the Christian institution, be thrown overboard into the sea," declared the reformer, "and then the ship of the church will make a prosperous, safe, and happy voyage across the ocean of time." [16] This means that all creeds must be thrown overboard, too.

At their best, creeds, ancient and modern, are only guesses about divine truth but they do not speak divine things. Being of human language, origin and authority, they cannot rise above their source, as the entire system of innate ideas has been exploded. If divine truths are spoken or taught, it must be through divine language. Creeds are human attempts to speak divine things in human language with an authority which is paramount to the word of God; and, therefore, they are of a presumptuous and vain nature. It is one thing to *speak about divine truth* and an entirely different thing to "speak divine truth!"

Furthermore, creeds do not produce formal church union, much less good will. God could not be the author of such confusion.

Being speculative, they have always proved themselves to be "apples of discord" or "roots of bitterness" amongst the Christian profession. They have . . . erected pillories, founded prisons, provoked wars, kindled fires, consecrated *autos da fe,* instituted star-chambers, courts of high commission, and horrible tribunals of papal inquisition. Exile, banishment, confiscation of goods, lands, and tenements, and martyrdoms, have been their convincing logic, their persuasive rhetoric, and their tender mercies. . . .[17]

No earthly princes or ecclesiastics have the power to bind the consciences of the subjects of Christ. Part of the duty of members of Christ's kingdom is to tolerate differences of opinion and sentiment in some matters of religion without forming creeds and confessions of faith which produce such strife and bitterness. But the very existence of creeds is "an abomination." [18]

15. *The Christian Baptist,* III, 179–180.
16. *The Christian System,* pp. 124–127.
17. *Christian Baptism,* p. 16; *The Christian Baptist,* III, 4, 6.
18. *Idem,* III, 4.

Yet creeds are made and enforced by parties which seek to maintain their particular speculations as orthodox for all. Good men who cannot subscribe to all their tenets are excluded from the church by the orthodox; whereas evil men who do not believe in the same tenets will be admitted for the sake of church office or reputation in so long as they agree to the formal words of the creeds.[19] Their champions place creeds over and above the New Testament as a bond of union and condition of church membership. In every way, creeds are "wicked," "presumptuous," and "divisive."

This is not all theory to Campbell. He used illustrations from the bitter nineteenth-century scene of sectarian rivalry which added a thrust of realism to his assertions. Typical of his efforts to prove that creeds produce hypocrisy was the data he presented from his three months' tour in 1825:

William Pedibus, the shoemaker, lost the custom of all the Presbyterians in town, because he said that Parson Trim denied free agency. And *Thomas Vulcanus,* the blacksmith, never shod a Methodist's horse since the time he censored Elder Vox's sermon on the possibility of falling from grace. John Paidogogus, the free-thinker, though an excellent teacher, lost the school of the village of Romance, because his competitor, though of limited acquisitions and less talents, could say shiboleth. . . . In many of our towns and neighbourhoods, when a young man gets himself a wife, he must join some sect, or, at least, support one if he intends to have bread and butter. Thus inducements are presented to hypocrisy, and men are forced into a profession which neither their judgment nor their inclination prompts them to, but which become necessary to the success of their calling.[20]

Thus, he concluded, "the only chance of success in most places for

19. *Idem,* II, 48. Rice pointed out that Campbell had the same trouble with the words of the Bible in that, on his principles, he will receive a Universalist or Unitarian as a member of the church if only they will consent to use Biblical phrases *verbally at the time of admission* to membership. *Campbell-Rice Debate,* p. 804. Campbell said that he would not receive them *as such,* nor Trinitarians, Arians, Baptists, Papists, or Calvinists as such but as *men,* if they profess Jesus as the Messiah, the Son of God. That reminded Rice of a man who would not buy a sheep *as a sheep* but *as a horse;* or the dignitary who was both a bishop and a duke but, when caught swearing, he explained that he *swore as a duke.* But the dignitary was asked, "When the devil comes for the duke, what will become of the bishop?" Rice asked Campbell, "When the devil comes for the Universalist, what will happen to the reformer?" *Idem,* p. 805.

20. *The Christian Baptist,* II, 142.

a non-professor of a creed . . . is, to pay a tribute of respect, or a tribute of money to the more powerful or more popular creed of his vicinity." [21]

Besides the fact of creeds' denying the rights of men to their own conscience and opinions, their speculative jargon usually results in controversies that become "a mere logamachy, or war of words." This, said he, is the course of most theoretic, scholastic, metaphysical, and speculative theology. As one of his choice illustrations, he frequently referred to the "*homoussos* and *homoousios* of the ever-memorable Council of Nice" as "a fair sample" of the quarrels of the church "about words and phrases coined in the mint of speculative theology." He declared that little reflection is needed to discover that the fiercest disputes about religion "are about what the Bible does *not* say rather than what it *does* say." [22]

One of his most persistent arguments against confessions of faith and creeds is that their dogmas are "farther from the comprehension of nine-tenths of mankind" than the language of the Bible. This led him to attack, especially, the orthodox usage of the Trinity, as he put it, "because of the metaphysical technicalities, the unintelligible jargon, and the unmeaning language of orthodox creeds." [23] In these doctrines and creeds men are asked to believe and subscribe to words which they cannot understand. On the other hand, he would have the New Testament as the only bond of union.

To those who hold that creeds are expedient as summaries of faith in order to keep others from error, let it be said that this is impossible, for they originate from the fallible human mind. Errors only produce more errors, therefore, more heretics. In fact, creeds are necessarily heretical, for " 'they strain out the gnats and swallow the camels'; nay, worse, they rack off the pure wine of the church and retain the lees . . . driving out the good and retaining the bad." They have been unappreciated by the majority of professed Christians ever since Nicaea; consequently, the world's greatest benefactors have been called heretics, schismatics, apostles, prophets, and reformers.[24]

21. *Idem*, II, 142–143.
22. *Idem*, III, 217; *The Christian System*, p. 126.
23. *The Christian Baptist*, II, 177.
24. *Campbell-Rice Debate*, pp. 764–765. In his debate with Purcell, Campbell pointed out that the Apostles' Creed was not written by the Apostles. But

Ecclesiastics, to Campbell, swallowed more camels and retained more lees progressively in the history of the church. The Apostles', Nicene, and Athanasian creeds are the choice productions of the creed "manufactories" of the ancients, for they are more in keeping with the Scriptures of truth. They are superior to the "modern affairs" such as those fashioned at Trent, Augsburg, Dort, Westminster, the Thirty-Nine Articles, the Baptist Confession of Faith, or the Methodistic Discipline, for they had some compounds of Christian truth. But the later creeds are as much records of modern opinions and inferences concerning them as portraitures of ancient times. The ancient ones had "some use for a heart as well as a head, on the part of those who approved the symbols, but the moderns have no use for the heart, having imposed all the labor on the brains, in acknowledging their tests of orthodoxy." Yet the Greek symbols would not be in any better keeping with our day than "a continental almanac, published by Ben Franklin in the days of Peter Porcupine." [25]

The most vicious thing about creeds is the circle in which they are hopelessly enmeshed in being mutual causes of sects and orthodoxies. Sects and orthodoxies create creeds and creeds create sects and orthodoxies.[26]

Campbell never changed his views about orthodoxies. In 1840 he was still saying that orthodoxy is not Christianity: "The dregs of her most bitter cup are only the wormwood and gall of ecclesiastic curses." In 1855 he reiterated: "Christ's Church is not founded on theology, polity, or on any speculative dogmata whatever." [27]

To him the Pedobaptist sects particularly were zealous to make their creeds national in scope by an alliance of the church with the

---

he admitted that it was "apostolic" and affirmed that he would agree to every article of the creed, except for changing one expression, "'I believe in *a* Catholic church.'" But creeds were not to be made a bond of union among Christians. *A Debate on the Roman Catholic Religion, Held in the Sycamore-Meeting House, Cincinnati, from the 13th to the 21st of January, 1837, between Alexander Campbell of Bethany, Va., and the Rt. Rev. John B. Purcell, Bishop of Cincinnati* (Cincinnati, J. A. James & Co., 1837), p. 77. Hereafter this will be referred to as the *Campbell-Purcell Debate*. However, when asked what he would propose as a basis for agreement among Christians for the proposed Evangelical Alliance, he pointed to the truths of the Apostles' Creed to which he thought all could agree.

25. *Campbell-Rice Debate*, pp. 759–762.
26. *Ibid.*
27. *The Millennial Harbinger*, 1840, pp. 529–533; 1855, pp. 361, 448.

state; these orthodoxies, therefore, were all the more dangerous. With their theories of incorporating the whole community within the church, disregarding the voluntary decisions on the part of believers, their form of church government and organization were especially susceptible to inducing tyranny over ecclesiastical opinions. Also, he held that a Pedobaptist, in general, was less intelligent in his knowledge of Christian scriptures and less spiritually minded than the Baptist or immersed person.

In the context of sectarian opinions, Campbell reduced the modern missionary enterprise to one of competition between sects to win individuals from pagan systems of philosophy and theology to their own speculative ideas. In spite of their zeal, privations, and sufferings for the missionary cause, he claimed that he would not hesitate to say that they have "left the heathen no better than when they found them, nay, in some cases they have left them much worse; and, that there is as much need for their conversion from the religion of those missionaries, as there was from the religion of idols." [28]

The paradox of Campbell's bitter cry against the tyranny of eccleciastical opinions and traditions in the forms of orthodoxies, creeds, and sects is that he himself was accused by those of his own day of creating the very things which he was fighting. One of the most sympathetic warnings came during his *Christian Baptist* period when Spencer Clack, an editor of the *Baptist Recorder,* pointed out the divisive nature of Campbell's own program. He expressed the doubt that Christians could love one another more by devouring one another. And he criticized Campbell for only adding

to the confusion of tongues. . . . To be plain, you have, in part formed a new creed; not a lifeless or inefficient one . . . ; but one which effectually influences the conduct of your abettors as any confession of faith. Your creed, I mean your writings, is not the Bible . . . and yet it is manifest that those who embrace your *views* of divine truth and conduct, are governed by them.[29]

Clack reminded Campbell that he and the rest of the Baptists acknowledge the same authority but the difference between them is this: "We cannot agree to what the Bible *teaches*. The Baptists think the Bible *teaches* the doctrines contained in their creeds;

28. *Idem,* 1855, pp. 47–51.
29. *The Christian Baptist,* V, 12–13.

you think it teaches what you have written and published, and what you will hereafter write and publish." [30]

Clack suggested that they all bow before God and ask forgiveness for all evils which they had done and seek future divine guidance. But Campbell, as sure of himself as ever, replied that the "gospel of Jesus Christ" never produced schisms but that its opponents did; and he would persevere "until the Lord says, Stop." [31]

Sixteen years later, Rice effectively used the same types of charges against Campbell in their debate. He asked if Campbell were not in the same predicament in which he was placing Presbyterians and others in accusing them of making the Bible "the subterranean foundation of the church" and basing the rest of it upon creeds. "His Christian Baptist, Christianity Restored, Christian System, and other writings, contain his creed—the foundation above ground. Unfortunately, I think, the Bible is not quite under him." [32]

Rice observed that the only difference between Campbell's "church" and "the sects" is that the notions and opinions of each individual form their foundation and, therefore, if there be ground of boasting over his church, it lies in the fact that it has a greater number of foundations than any other.

One of his arguments to prove human creeds necessarily heretical and schismatical, is—that there is in the Bible no command to make a creed. But there is no command to make a "Christian System," as he has done, and to write and publish anything on religious subjects. Are we to conclude, that everything is unlawful, that is not in the Scriptures directly commanded? If so, the gentleman has seriously erred in making his various publications. But I contend, that "where there is no law, there is no transgression." Let him prove then that we are forbidden to make a creed. . . . Another argument is—that creeds are *fallible*. But his writings are also fallible . . . an influence on multitudes. . . .[33]

Rice quoted Fishback and Barton W. Stone from the *Millennial Harbinger* as objecting to the divisive and sectarian tendencies of Campbell's particular opinions on immersion. This ref-

30. *Idem*, V, 13.
31. *Idem*, V, 16.
32. *Campbell-Rice Debate*, pp. 770–771.
33. *Ibid*.

erence hurt, for Fishback and Stone were allied with the Reformers or Disciples of Christ.

Stone's statement held that if the Reformers insist upon their peculiar views of immersion they will never be able to

repel successfully, the imputation of being sectarians, and of having an authoritative creed (though not written) of one article, at least, which is formed of their opinions of truth, and this short creed would exclude more christians from union, than any creed with which I am acquainted.[34]

Fishback's protest was similar to Stone's. Consequently, Rice declared:

Thus it is evident, that whilst the gentleman declaims so eloquently against the schismatical tendence of creeds, and in favor of christian union, he is himself denouncing and excommunicating the whole of Christendom, as being in Babylon, as using the language of Ashdod, because they will not adopt his opinion on some one or two points. It is true, his own brethren being witnesses, that he has a creed, though not written, more exclusive and sectarian than any sect in Christendom! ! [35]

Campbell defended himself on the grounds of the distinction between writing a book and making a creed but it is interesting to note that he never really came to grips with the charge of producing *an unwritten creed*. Also, his Scriptural proof-texts from Timothy, Jude, and Thessalonians, to support his position that creeds are prohibited by the Bible, paradoxically called for more inference than his theory, at that time, allowed: "Hold fast to the form of sound words, which you have heard from me"; "Contend earnestly for the faith formerly delivered to the saints"; "Hold fast the traditions which you have heard from us, whether by word or by our epistle"; and "This is my beloved Son, hear him. . . !" [36]

Roman Catholicism as the Mother of Sects

Where did Protestantism get its corruptions in theory, practice, creed-making, and sect-forming? From Roman Catholicism, is the cry and lifelong assumption of Campbell.

34. *Idem*, pp. 771–773.
35. *Idem*, p. 773.
36. *Idem*, pp. 782, 794, 901.

The errors of Protestantism were borrowed from the Catholic Church and they have been perpetuated especially through the Pedobaptist creeds. He traced "this sacred gloom, this holy melancholy, this pious indolence" in seminary graduates to the Catholic monastery.[37]

Illustrative of his attitude toward Roman Catholicism is his play upon words in 1843: "Oh! for a second Luther to whip out of Protestant temples the speculators and dealers in Italian wares and merchandize!" In this context, even the American Protestant Association was too much entwined with Roman Catholic ecclesiasticism to suit Campbell but he resolved to work with it on the principle that

Half a loaf is better than no bread at all. . . . I am no friend to Protestant Popery any more than to Papal Popery; but the Protestant Popes are pigmies compared with his Roman Holiness. . . . And, therefore, I say, let all the Protestant Popes unite and bear their united testimony against the Grand Papa, and then they will be the more able and willing to recede from their unequal assumptions.[38]

A statement like this needs to be compared with those in which Campbell attacked the whole Protestant structure for, as we have shown, in dealing with them alone he said that Protestant clergy are as pretentious as Catholic popes and he accused them of ridiculing Catholic papal claims only when it suited their interests. Obviously, Campbell was moved by expediency according to the prospective victim of his blows. However, it was only when he was speaking as a Protestant against Catholic ecclesiasticism that he softened his striking power and intensity against Protestantism.

The first proposition of his debate with the Catholic Bishop Purcell of Cincinnati was his affirmation that the sometimes called "Holy, Apostolic, Catholic Church" was never catholic, apostolic, or holy but is only *a sect*, older than any other sect now existing and an apostasy from the only true, apostolic, and catholic church of Christ.

He affirmed that the term "A Roman Catholic Church is a contradiction"; for it is sectional, unscriptural, and even dishonora-

---

37. *The Christian Baptist*, I, 22 ff.; IV, 110.
38. *The Millennial Harbinger*, 1843, pp. 352–353. We shall discuss Campbell's position in regard to the American Protestant Association in the third section of this book.

ble, in that it is as opprobrious as ever were the names Lutheran and Protestant, since it was named by its enemies. He also argued that Roman Catholicism came out of the bosom of the Greek Church because all leading ecclesiastic words, as well as ancient ecclesiastic historians, are Greek.[39]

The Roman diocese, he said, "degenerated" from its true faith in 250 A. D., in the controversy between Cornelius and Novatian concerning the bishopric of Rome, "before a church of nations with a political head ever existed." The Roman Church was contaminated with error and immorality; and the quarrel at that time was about church purity, communion, and discipline rather than doctrine. "The *orthodox*" were the "*strong* party" and "the *heterodox*" were the "*weak* party," as is always the case with orthodoxies and heterodoxies, he declared. Throughout Catholic Church history, "heretics" are those parties which Catholics have branded as such. "The spirit of true religion seems to have fled from Rome from the first appearance of the Novatians." [40]

The first quarrel over speculative ideas of doctrine and creed-making, "*a Catholic quarrel*," occurred at the Council of Nicaea in which the emperor made the final decision—a political one at that. Had Constantine and his views not interfered and had the orthodox Alexander and the rest of his bishops left Arius "*ecclesiastically alone*" and treated the "incomprehensible nothing" with indifference, Arianism and its "opinionism" would have died out like all other early feuds. It was then that the "CHRISTIAN SWORD of proscription" was first manufactured and the "vagaries of these moon-struck theologians were now embodied in permanent form." From that day until this creeds, which are really misnomers as they are merely "collects of speculations and tests of orthodoxies," have reigned. The great source of "all ecclesiastical divisions were the dogmatical opinions of churches and synods." Campbell concluded, "before creeds were, unity was."

Roman sects or orders, as they call them, declared Campbell, are no more united in worship and orthodox points of doctrine than Protestant sects. The Augustinians, Dominicans, Franciscans, Jansenists, Jesuits, and others are as pugnacious amongst themselves as Protestant parties of Lutherans, Calvinists, Arminian, and others.

39. *Campbell-Purcell Debate*, pp. 10, 146 ff.
40. *Idem*, pp. 65, 68.

Roman Catholicism gave birth to sectarianism which resulted in numerous parties seeking to make their opinions orthodox in the rise of ecclesiasticism. For ages, Christendom has been turned from "the pure, peaceable, and holy temper of Christianity" to the weak and beggarly elements of speculative, scholastic, and polemic theology." [41]

The dogma that the church is as necessary to salvation as the gospel itself and the resulting practice of man-made salvation by merit is derived from Catholicism. This is the root of the whole papal system of superstition which includes "priests, penances, confessions, masses, remissions, purgatories, intercessions of the saints, angels, and almost all of their ceremonies," for it makes the death of Christ as little more than the death of a martyr and as insufficient for the cleansing of man's sins. In that sense Roman Catholicism strikes at the root of the doctrine of salvation by faith, claimed the Reformer.

According to the Roman Catholic conception of the church, salvation and the Bible itself must be accepted only by the authority of Roman Catholic tradition. Yet, in fact, it has "no infallible expositor" of its "one hundred and thirty-five folios" of tradition. Worse than that, it gives infallible authority to a human head, the pope, who often is corrupt and immoral; and it gives unlimited power and authority to the priesthood to forgive sins (and thus encourages men to sin), whose right or wrong *intentions* really determine the efficacy of the ordinances of the church.

Its ridiculous Noah's Ark conception of the church "with clean and unclean *beasts*," and the sprinkling that accompanies it, still survives in Pedobaptist Protestant churches. The Roman Catholic rule of faith can be summarized as uninspired, unauthoritative, unintelligible, and immoral.[42]

When Luther sought to reform Popery and when he emerged "from the great city of mystical Babylon, he saw as clearly . . . as any person could see in such a hazy atmosphere." [43] But all errors were not detected, discussed, and repudiated. When Luther died there was no Joshua to take his place. Calvin renewed Augus-

---

41. *Campbell-Rice Debate*, pp. 784, 786, 809, 837; *Campbell-Purcell Debate*, p. 177; *The Millennial Harbinger*, 1838, p. 7.

42. *Campbell-Purcell Debate*, pp. 113–275; *Campbell-Rice Debate*, pp. 183, 199.

43. *The Christian System*, p. 179.

tinian speculation and soon made Geneva the Alexandria of modern Europe.

While Protestant hatred to the Roman Pontiff and the Papacy continued to increase, a secret lust in the bosoms of Protestant power and patronage worked in the members of the Protestant Popes, who gradually assimilated the new church to the old. Creeds and manuals, synods and councils, soon shackled the minds of men, and the spirit of reformation gradually forsook the Protestant church, or was supplanted by the spirit of the world.[44]

The reformation of Popery ended in Protestant hierarchy and swarms of dissenters. Successive reforms resulted in Protestantism taking the form of Presbyterianism, Congregationalism, and Wesleyanism in many varieties. "All of them retain in their bosom, in the ecclesiastical organizations, worship, doctrines, and observances, various relics of Popery. . . ." [45]

44. *Campbell-Rice Debate*, p. 50; *The Christian System*, pp. 3–4. Campbell's views of Luther vary. Sometimes he sees him as a genuine religious reformer of Catholicism. At other times he described his reforms as "ninety per cent political" and therefore weak. In the Rice debate, p. 305, he said Luther was prevented from freeing his church from all errors by the "Catholic Echius." Another time he blamed the failure upon Luther's friends who favored "papistical doctors." *The Millennial Harbinger*, 1831, p. 52.

45. *Christian Baptism*, pp. 15–17.

CHAPTER IV

CONCURRENCE WITH OPPONENTS OF REVEALED RELIGION

EFENDERS of orthodox Christianity did not take Campbell's attack upon ecclesiasticism sitting down. Soon he was accused of 'sweeping away the vitals of religion." [1] He was given such choice heretical titles as: an Arian,[2] Socinian,[3] Arminian, Pelagian, Antinomian,[4] and Sebellian.[5] Some called him a Sandemanian, Haldanian, and Calvinist.[6] A college president said that he was the Devil. An editor of the *Christian Herald* was sure that he was one of "the deceivers" who was to precede the millennium.[7]

Others called "Campbellism" an "invention of Mr. Campbell's" and an attempt to create a "new religion." [8]

It is not surprising that bitter and hasty critics of Campbell branded him as an infidel,[9] a deist,[10] as well as a Universalist [11] or Unitarian.[12] There is a certain meeting of minds and temper between Campbell and the opponents of revealed religion in their onslaught against traditional Christianity and ecclesiasticism

1. *The Millennial Harbinger*, 1831, p. 250.
2. *Idem*, 1831, p. 105; *The Christian Baptist*, III, 158.
3. *Ibid.; Idem*, III, 159; IV, 91; *The Millennial Harbinger*, 1831, p. 531.
4. *The Christian Baptist*, III, 159.
5. *Ibid.; The Millennial Harbinger*, 1831, pp. 84, 105.
6. *The Christian Baptist*, III, 159, 226.
7. *The Millennial Harbinger*, 1832, p. 189.
8. *Idem*, 1831, pp. 216, 221. See also Joseph C. Stiles, *A Letter to Alexander Campbell in Reply to an Article in the Millennial Harbinger*, (Lexington, Ky., Intelligencer Printers, 1838), pp. 12–13.
9. *The Millennial Harbinger*, 1830, pp. 541, 544.
10. *Idem*, 1831, pp. 43, 84, 531, 1833, p. 186; *The Christian Baptist*, III, 159. See also Alexander Campbell, *Lawrence Greatrakes Calumnies Repell'd* (Buffaloe, Va., Alexander Campbell, 1825), p. 5.
11. *The Christian Baptist*, III, 159; *The Millennial Harbinger*, 1831, pp. 84, 105, 249, 251.
12. *Idem*, 1831, pp. 105, 249, 251, 1830, pp. 541, 544, 1833, p. 8, 1836, p. 290; *The Christian Baptist*, III, 158, 159, IV, 90, 188.

which cannot be disregarded, if his relation to natural religion is to be seen in its proper perspective.

Even "Robert Cautious," as one of the most patient and sympathetic friends of his *Christian Baptist* reform signed his name, warned the fiery iconoclast of his tendency. In the context of his attack upon all Bible and missionary societies, he opined that Campbell was in danger of defeating his "own good efforts" by outstepping the "fixed boundaries of truth" and, in his *haste to get out of Babylon, he was running past Jerusalem!* [13]

That is no wonder. Indeed, Campbell was well read and familiar with the works of Voltaire, Volney, the Earl of Shaftesbury, Gibbon, Godwin, Paine, Rousseau, Hobbes, Hume, and Bishop Herbert. He referred to and quoted from them frequently [14] in his own writings and public addresses. In spite of his opposition to them in regard to their disapprobation of revelation, there is no indication that he did not share, in part, their spirit and continue their program relating to the orthodox and traditional institutions of revealed religion.

As will be seen later, he was saturated with the works of John Locke. But that was no guarantee against an attack upon the established church, clergy, and theology, for the thought of Locke cuts both ways. It became the base from whence deism radiated, as well as a defense for Christian revelation within the atmosphere of the Enlightenment.

On the surface, his opponents could not overlook certain phrases and statements, such as: "No man of good sense can imagine that the god of the Calvinists and the god of the Arminians are the same god"; [15] "Christendom in its dotage"; [16] and the "reign of Sanhedrims over the understanding, conscience, and estates of men, is now in its dotage." [17] Nor could they forget that he de-

---

13. *Idem*, I, 127.

14. The specific extent of his familiarity with these men will be discussed in greater detail later. Also it will be seen how paradoxically Campbell tended to inculcate certain characteristics of those ideas and personalities whom he most violently opposed; for example, he became theological in his attempt to abolish theology and orthodox in his efforts to get rid of orthodoxies. We have already seen how his own colleagues, as well as opponents, judged that, in his efforts to abandon creeds, he had set up one of the most rigidly enforced unwritten creeds in church history.

15. *The Millennial Harbinger*, 1830, p. 6.

16. *Idem*, 1834, p. 371.

17. *Idem*, 1832, p. 33.

fended John Paidogogus, "the free-thinker, who, in spite of his beliefs, is a good school teacher"; [18] or that he praised Stephen Girard of Philadelphia, "whom the clergy call a Deist," and his will for an orphanage institution which excluded ecclesiastics of every type from its premises.[19]

His advocacy of a new translation of the Bible, the publication of Campbell editions of the New Testament, and his attack upon the King James version drew the suspicion of many. For this, he was readily charged with impiety.

Another factor which cannot be ignored is that Campbell was a habitual reader in French. This gave his French iconoclasts a psychological advantage in infusing their temper and spirit into the mind of the American iconoclast. This is especially true in regard to the French Revolution. Campbell read, lived, and viewed it with a focus which brought it close to him.[20]

His sympathy was with the people and particularly with the anticlerical and antiecclesiastical leaders. Their blows were aimed at what he also regarded as a corrupt Christianity. Their attack was an attempt to undermine Roman Catholicism and the whole of organized Christianity as they knew it, from established institutions to the systems of thought. So was his.

Their strategy was to expose and depose an immoral, presumptuous, and tyrannical priesthood. So was his. As we have seen, he regarded the clergy as the greatest tyrants in history. He never

18. *The Christian Baptist*, II, 142.

19. *The Millennial Harbinger*, 1832, p. 127.

20. This is not an effort to interpret *all* of his antiecclesiasticism in terms of simple and single causation. W. E. Garrison, in *The Sources of Alexander Campbell's Theology* (St. Louis, Christian Publishing Co., 1900) and *Religion Follows the Frontier* (New York, London, Harper & Brothers, 1931); Errett Gates, in *The Early Relation and Separation of Baptists and Disciples* (Chicago, The Christian Century Co., 1904) and *The Disciples of Christ* (New York, The Baker & Taylor Co., 1905); B. L. Smith, in *Alexander Campbell;* C. A. Athearn, in *The Religious Education of Alexander Campbell* (St. Louis, The Bethany Press, 1828); and others have well supported the influence of other factors, from the Haldanes, Sandemanians, and other sectarians to the common-sense emphasis of Scotch thought in which Campbell was schooled. Certainly his Calvinistic background was there, too, in giving force to his analysis of the *pride, selfishness, vanity,* and *worldliness* of the clergy. Also it will become apparent later that his conception of the *sovereignty of God* and the *impotence of man* added drive to his scornful attack. And the *"word* of God," as conceived by Campbell is much like Luther's conception of it.

failed to remind patriotic American laymen that leaders who ought to have been in "the van of the preachers of righteousness," at home and abroad, "opposed the American Revolution." [21] Moreover, to him, the American Revolution had gone a long way toward the freedom of man but not far enough. His revolution would bring complete religious freedom. Priestcraft must go the way of kingcraft in this country.

French revolutionists bitterly sought to disentangle and disestablish the church from its alliance with the state. So did he. In fact, by 1829, Campbell was almost convinced that the "unhallowed alliance between kings and priests of church and state, is destined to be finally destroyed by a momentary triumph of infidelity." [22]

Furthermore, enthusiasts and popular philosophers of the French Revolution derived public support and power through their ability to generalize in undermining the basis of authority in established religion. So did he. They had a genius for forming striking slogans out of words and phrases, such as: "the rights of man," "conscience," "human liberty," "mankind," "kingcraft," "priestcraft," "common sense," "reason," and analogies to "nature." Campbell was not far behind in this skill. Their wit, satire, and irony lingered upon their pronounced statements of ridicule concerning the superstitions, rites, beliefs, and other institutions of organized religion. His delight was in that law of his mind.

There are further striking similarities between Campbell and these theoretical and practical philosophers. Among other things, a Voltaire-type of caustic cynicism penetrated Campbell's antiecclesiasticism. Even though he made his pleas for the liberty of "the people," "the masses," and "the laity," at least in theory, he had other theories which made the former difficult to practice in fact or always to contend. He could declare his faith in the common opinion of the laity, believing that they would listen to reason; yet, paradoxically, he held a certain contempt for the

21. *The Millennial Harbinger*, 1831, p. 4.
22. Alexander Campbell and Robert Owen, *A Debate on the Evidences of Christianity, Containing an Examination of the "Social System" and of All the Systems of Scepticism of Ancient and Modern Times, Between Robert Owen of New Lanark, Scotland, and Alexander Campbell, of Bethany, Virginia, With an Appendix Written by the Parties* (Bethany, Alexander Campbell, 1829, 2 vols.), I, 14. Hereafter this will be referred to as the *Campbell-Owen Debate*.

"uncharactered ignoramuses which constitute the majority." [23] He knew them well, as did Voltaire, but was not one of them. At heart he was an intellectual who preferred and favored the court of the learned while he championed the rights of the deprived multitude.

Campbell could deride the vanity and ambition of "the master-spirit of the master-spirits of the French Revolution," [24] as he termed Voltaire, but he was never free from that charge himself. In fact, one of the reasons a critic accused him of being "unregenerated" was his "insatiate vanity." [25]

Campbell did not like the expediency of "the fickle-minded, wavering and inconstant Voltaire, who, as some one has justly said, was a free-thinker in London, a courtesan at Versailles, a Christian at Nantz and an infidel at Berlin." [26] Yet Campbell, as a Protestant, spoke against Roman Catholicism. When he debated Robert Owen, the secularist, he spoke as a Christian. When he attacked Protestantism he spoke as a Baptist. When he derided the Baptists he spoke as an individualistic sectarian at times and at other times as a sort of Campbellized freethinker who opposed all authority and all tradition in organized religion.

Campbell had a way of sensing changing needs and circumstances. After all, his most rigorous antiecclesiasticism corresponds roughly with the most robust period of Jacksonian democracy and with its lay spirit on the American frontier. The "spoils system" may have been heretical to traditionally seasoned political leaders but it was well received by certain elements of laymen. "An Independent Baptist," as we have seen, in 1826 analyzed Campbell's connection with the Regular Baptists as only a "time-serving expedient," although he did not doubt his conviction. Rice, in 1843, noted that his iconoclasm was not out of harmony with the trends of the time.

I will not charge my friend with courting popularity; but I will say, that he has, by some means, happened to adopt a course of conduct by which he secured much greater popularity, than he could have gained, had he remained in the Presbyterian church.[27]

23. *The Christian Baptist*, IV, 10; see also *idem*, I, 160, II, 72; *Campbell-Rice Debate*, p. 765; *Campbell-Purcell Debate*, p. 294, as mere samples.

24. *Popular Lectures and Addresses*, pp. 82–87.

25. *The Christian Baptist*, II, 39.

26. *Popular Lectures and Addresses*, p. 84.

27. *Campbell-Rice Debate*, p. 511. The Disciples of Christ developed and spread along the frontier of nineteenth-century America. This is indicated by

It was no accident that his thought was described by some as "religious infidelity." [28]

In 1830 a critic, who assumed that Whitefield was a humble man, asserted that there is the same difference between Campbell and Whitefield as between Lord Byron and Milton, or as between Paul of Tarsus and Paul the Apostle. Campbell, he declared, had "no grace or disposition" but plently of "vanity." [29]

His method of attack, especially through his *Christian Baptist* reform until 1840, is reminiscent of the Voltaire-Paine type of reckless abandonment, ridicule, and scorn. Coupled with the influence of lay-spirited and individualistic-minded sects, this was a potent weapon against the church on the American frontier of Jacksonian democracy.

As they had done, he consciously set out to undermine the whole structure of authority and organization of the established churches and theology. The main battle was "to raze the foundation of the Paidobaptist system," as he called the process from 1813 to 1830; but after 1830 it was against even the Baptist structure. The rights of men and the analogies of kingcraft and priestcraft and divine right were his streamlined weapons for the frontier. But for hand to hand fighting he chose the Bible as his bow and he used as many quivers of proof-texts as were expedient to employ. Antiecclesiasticism was his chief emphasis during that period and not primitive Christianity, although the latter was constantly marshaled to combat. At that time, he conceived his task to be so simple as merely to undermine all established religion; after that, primitive Christianity would automatically take care of itself and the situation. Paine and Voltaire did not have primitive Christianity to fall back upon but they used it to mock modern Christians, as did Campbell.

The "Philomathesean Society" of the Literary and Theological Seminary [30] of New York wrote Campbell on August 24, 1826, that they, too, agreed there is much that is reprehensible in the church but inquired if sarcasm and ridicule were the way to affect the needed change. This is significant in that these pious young gentlemen were more discriminate than many of his hasty

---

the suggestive title, already noted, to W. E. Garrison's modern history of the Disciples of Christ, *Religion Follows the Frontier*.

28. *The Millennial Harbinger*, 1830, pp. 541, 544.

29. *Idem*, 1830, pp. 98–99.

30. Hamilton Seminary, Hamilton Village, New York.

critics of the pulpit and press; and they were hoping to mend his approach. They suggested a "dignified, argumentative, and candid exposition of error, and a mild and persuasive invitation to amendment." Also they reminded him that the "cold hand of death" might suddenly be laid upon him and that he would have to answer for his work of "continual warfare with our fellow creatures." [31] They asked for a discontinuance of his monthly.

Not all of the society were united in asking a discontinuance of his magazine, which he sent them free of charge. Consequently those that favored the publication wrote him another letter to make the situation clear. But even that group cautioned him to use "plain persuasive and christian-like argument" and wished him to have the "peaceful satisfaction of reflecting upon a life spent in the service of God" after he is called "to pass the Jordan of death." [32]

Not only does Campbell remind one of the Paine-Voltaire type of antiecclesiasticism' but also his attitude is remarkably like that of William Godwin in certain conclusions. He well knew the works of this first systematic anarchist. He, like Godwin, thought that all reforms were worthless in the long run.[33] This meant, when applied to Christianity, as the *Millennial Harbinger, Christian System,* and *Christian Baptism* reveal, that even a reformation of Protestantism is worthless, for all others have failed. "The stream of Christianity has become polluted, and it is useless to temporize and try experiments. All the reformations that have occurred and all the religious chymistry of the schools have failed to purify it." [34]

He could say, with Godwin, as we have already seen, the more government the more tyranny. In his atomistic period he concluded that church government is hopeless as far as human effort is concerned, for it only results in the exploitation of the

31. *The Christian Baptist,* IV, 85. This is not unusual for him to be warned of the hand of death. Elder John Taylor referred to the death of Paine to warn Campbell of the fate of those "at war with religion and morality." *The Millennial Harbinger,* 1831, p. 43.

32. *The Christian Baptist,* IV, 88.

33. This is particularly characteristic of him in the 1830's. As we have already pointed out, until 1830 he considered the Baptists capable of being reformed. He finally decided by then that it was easier to restore primitive Christianity than to reform any part of modern Christianity: "We turn from the stream, therefore, and seek the fountain." *The Millennial Harbinger,* 1832, p. 13.

34. *Ibid.*

people. He further resembles Godwin in his economic determinism, although he does not reject his rapidly accumulating private property as an evil. He describes the clergy and church organizations as hopelessly enmeshed in the greed for money and wealth and declares again and again that " 'the love of money is the root of all evil.' " [35]

Like the deists, Campbell was concerned with religion and he retained many of the choice words and ideas of conventional Christianity but he sought to disconnect them from orthodox and popular contexts within the ecclesiastical atmosphere.

His reliance upon reason in appealing to the people and uprooting the authority of theology and the traditional church is much like the cry of reason which the opponents of revealed religion generally made. It is no accident that he was accused of leading his movement into "Rationalism." [36]

In short Campbell was willing to go, and actually did go, far with all opponents of revealed religion. He shared with them in a common skepticism of all traditional religious absolutism and claims to infallibility in theory or practice. He went as far as any of them, with the possible exception of the advocates of total political anarchy, in pleading for the separation of the church from the state. He agreed that conventional religion, in its present state, should be abolished for the good of mankind. His mind met with theirs in the following general principles:

1. Denying the authority and good intentions of the clergy as a system. 2. Denying the grounds for the speculative theology, philosophy, and creeds of the established church. 3. Ridiculing the traditions and customs of organized Christianity as superstitious and unwarranted. 4. Assuming and defending the natural and acquired rights of man, such as, liberty of conscience, speech, and press in all religious and political thought and belief; freedom of action and body; freedom to form character; and private property. 5. Upholding individualism. 6. Relying upon reason and appealing to common sense. 7. Assuming the validity of the social contract of the Enlightenment.

He explored with them the heights and depths of techniques and strategies in undermining the accepted religious order and absolutism of his day. He admired reason and its powers in contrast with what he called the brute force of dogmatic orthodoxies

35. *The Christian Baptist,* VII, 6; see also *idem,* I, 140, 158.
36. *The Millennial Harbinger,* 1831, p. 249.

which employed the eloquence of highwaymen. He detested emotionalism and sentimentality in religion. But regardless of his extremes in this exploration, he never went into complete rationalism.

As early as 1832, when reviewing his life and thought from that close range and in the midst of gradual change from his *Christian Baptist* type of antiecclesiasticism, he rightly said; "We became sceptics in everything sectarian—in everything in religion—but the Bible." [37]

This was his point of departure from the opponents of revealed religion. The reason for this difference, as we shall see immediately, is his conception of revelation which was inseparably connected with the Bible. Although he journeyed with the natural religionists for many a mile, he did not finish the trip with them, for he did not begin with them. He had met them along the way at points in which their minds and spirits concurred.

He became a skeptic of all established religious absolutism but also he was a skeptic of all established secular absolutism. He was skeptical of what he conceived to be the claims to religious and secular infallibility; but he was equally skeptical of what he regarded as similar claims of infallibility upon the part of the conventional church of nature.

37. *Idem*, 1832, p. 313. In his debate with Robert Owen, Campbell said, "I am not as sceptical in scepticism as Mr. Owen is in Christianity." It is "lawful to learn from the enemy." *Campbell-Owen Debate*, II, 133.

PART TWO

DEFENSE OF REVEALED RELIGION

The voice of nature will never contradict the voice of revelation. . . . We fear nothing from true science.

Alexander Campbell

CHAPTER V

CLASSICAL SKEPTICISM

ALTHOUGH many casual observers thought that Alexander Campbell was in the ranks of natural religionists, he departed sharply from their course. In 1829 he defended Christianity in a public debate with Robert Owen which attracted attention in America, England, Ireland, and Scotland. A turning point in Campbell's career was reached.

He was willing to wage a common assault against what he regarded as a corrupt ecclesiastical Christianity, but to him that did not mean all Christianity. Just because the stream was polluted he was unwilling to assume that the source was. Inevitably he was led to a defense of revelation.

From 1828 until his death in 1866 a new emphasis was stressed. His friendly combination of terms, "reason, common sense, and the Bible," was retained. But an unfriendly trio, "atheism, deism, and skepticism," became more prominent in his writings. His disapproval of natural religion had been expressed here and there in earlier writings; but, as we have seen, the attack upon ecclesiasticism had been his chief burden.

Within a decade of the Owen debate, Campbell was working inside the framework of the organized institutions of society and religion which he had once bitterly fought. A major reason was that he sought more effective means of combating deism, atheism, and infidelity in both their classical forms and their more recent nineteenth-century appearances under new names.

This does not mean that his negative view of ecclesiasticism entirely disappeared, but the objects of his attacks were singled out with greater discrimination. Not all of the clergy were under fire as a system but only certain types. Instead of all seminaries, colleges, and religious societies being attacked, certain aspects of some of them were criticized. Instead of all organized Christianity being razed from its foundations, specific sectarian types of organized Christianity, especially the Roman Catholics, were razed. The *Christian Baptist* Alexander Campbell did not die a quick and easy death. Nothing describes this better than Camp-

bell's words in 1849 when he complained that "the spirit of the
Christian Baptist has been groaning within me" and "cannot be
suppressed much longer, unless there appear a spirit of reformation."

The general course of his defense of revealed religion was
begun spasmodically in the *Christian Baptist,* developed more
systematically in the *Millennial Harbinger,* and carried on most
extensively in his public discourses. The most outstanding occasion was his debate with Robert Owen which he published in
1829 in two volumes.[1] Other specific publications were *Christian Preachers Companion* in 1836, and *Letters to a Skeptic* in
1859.

His spirit in the battle is characterized by his review of a
book by Elder Jonas Hartzell in 1854:

Elder Jonas Hartzell, of Ohio, not long since, had a debate of days
with an apostate Christian, named Joseph Barker. He put his foot
on the infidel's head, drew his own sword and most surely cut off
his head. He has given us, in one volume, his own speeches, leav-
ing the rights of sepulture to Mr. Barker's friends.[2]

In combating natural religion and the classical expressions of
skepticism, Campbell used three major types of strategy. First, he
placed deists, skeptics, and infidels within an objectionable context in the history of the Enlightenment. Second, he criticized
the specific presuppositions on which they based their attack
upon revelation with the focal points being the plight of man and
the problem of knowledge. Third, he presented his conception
of the nature, evidences, and tendencies of Christianity in the
course of human history and destiny.

However, these strategies were intermingled unsystematically,
although the consistency of his total position is apparent. To
discover where his theory of knowledge ends and his conception of the nature and evidences of Christianity in history begins
would be as difficult to detect as the end and beginning of a well-
linked circular chain. Perhaps a more fitting analogy would compare the interrelation of his strands of thought with the strands
of hay in a haystack. It would be hard to distinguish which ones
hold up the stack but they all contribute to its total unity. Yet, at
times, Alexander Campbell's haystack could be lopsided.

1. See p. 48, n. 22, for full title.
2. *The Millennial Harbinger,* 1854, p. 472.

To illustrate this and the energy which Campbell devoted to "unmask the Infidels," observe the reaction of a youthful editor of the New York *Christian Palladium* of February 12, 1834. The writer claimed that Campbell had delivered ten addresses in ten days in New York City but with only two topics engrossing his attention: "the 'divine original of Christianity' " and "the 'doctrine of baptism for the remission of sins.' " He reported that Campbell's discourses against infidelity were "delivered at Concert and Tammany Halls" which "are occupied by the Infidels on the Sabbath day." His reasoning in behalf of Christianity "was unanswerable" and his "exposure of the sophistry and inconsistency of *Infidelity* was highly amusing." [3]

Campbell was displeased with this condensation of his discourses, for he could see no praise in spending "ten discourses on but two topics." His notes revealed that he had spoken on many more subjects.[4] But he was unaware of his tendency toward lengthy tangents. Frequently he was sidetracked from his main course in the defense of revelation to expound his doctrine of immersion. Immersion was an evidence of revelation to him but also a tempting detour from announced topics.

The nature and rise of nineteenth-century attackers of revealed religion were no mysteries to Alexander Campbell. Back of them were their ancestors—the deists, the skeptics, and the infidels of the Enlightenment. Back of them was a corrupt Christianity, springing from the false pretensions and practices of its leaders against which the French Revolution was a reaction. If "Christianity was persecuted by its enemies, it was corrupted by its friends."

This corruption was threefold in origin. It came from the Roman Catholicism of pre-Revolutionary France as a logical outcome of an unhallowed alliance of church and state which can be traced to the "dark ages" and to the origin of the theory of "popery" itself. It was the result of a creed-making ecclesiasticism which produced religious sectarianism. It was the invasion of the spirit of the world in the church.

A lifelong position of Campbell is that France was converted

3. *Idem*, 1834, p. 138.

4. *Idem*, 1834, pp. 138–139. The Philadelphia *Liberalist* of December 28, 1833, gave the same type of reaction to Campbell's "irresistible" defense of "Divine Revelation" and "the divine origin of Christianity." But it also disapproved of Campbell's tangent on immersion. *Idem*, 1834, p. 139.

into a nation of infidels by the Roman Catholic Church. France and Italy became the centers of European infidelity and atheism. French liberalists had the Bible "dragged through the streets of Paris by the common hangman" before burning it because they thought that it "countenanced the pretensions of Kings and Priests." Skeptics mistook anti-Christ for Christ when they thought they were opposing Christ. He felt that Robert Owen conceived of Christianity as being ill-adapted to the needs of man because he identified the Christian religion "with papal enormities." [5]

In his debate with the Roman Catholic Bishop Purcell, Campbell blamed the real opposition to Christianity not on infidelity as such but on the spiritual and temporal despotism of the Jesuit connection with the State of France. He argued that the theory of spiritual despotism always precedes the practical display of it by "papal Rome." Also, he asserted that belief in the doctrine of transubstantiation "destroys the credibility of all testimony, human and divine, and necessarily tends to atheism." [6]

If people wish to see what Roman Catholicism is like, they should view it at home in countries where it is dominant and, therefore, the most corrupt. They must judge it in Rome and Paris rather than in places where it is the visiting minority and on its best behavior.[7]

In his debate with Robert Owen, Campbell deduced Owen's distrust of Christianity as the result of his distrust of the "creed-system" which originated from Roman Catholicism. If it had not been for that, "Deism, Atheism, and Skepticism would have found no resting place among us." [8]

However, he did not confine all his remarks to Roman Catholicism in tracing the origin of skepticism from the creedal systems. For example, in 1835 he denounced the "Regular Baptist" doctrine of "what they call 'regeneration (religious experience)' " with the complaint that its irrationality affords "no small amusement to the Skeptics." [9]

In his debate with Rice, Campbell warned that the land, schools, and colleges are "full of skepticism" with the "great majority"

5. *Idem*, 1840, p. 234; *Campbell-Owen Debate*, I, 96.
6. *Campbell-Purcell Debate*, pp. 291, 294.
7. *The Millennial Harbinger*, 1852, p. 256.
8. *Campbell-Owen Debate*, I, 96.
9. *The Millennial Harbinger*, 1835, p. 336.

of educated men being "infidels." The reason for this is the discords, hatred, and strife engendered by sectarianism.[10]

Another reason Campbell gave for the current increase in skepticism is the obvious mistranslations of the Scriptures.[11]

One of his most vivid articles, "Christendom in Its Dotage (A Hint to Reformers)," portrayed the morals of Christendom as "the best evidence of the influence of corrupted Christianity." Popular justice, mercy, and piety were pictured as far from that of Christ, for the "love of the world triumphs over the love of God" with the spirit of the world invading the church. As a result "new frauds and fictions" are taking advantage of the ignorance and credulity of the age.

Pyrrhus down to Fanny Wright—from the pure idealist to the gross materialist—is taught with the zeal of the crusaders and the perseverance of Saint Xavier, under the pretence of superior wisdom and a more elevated philosophy. Striplings in their teens, with Thomas Paine in their pocket, and a cigar in their cheek, who have read the Life of Franklin, and the Declaration of Independence by Thomas Jefferson; together with Ovid's Metamorphoses, and the Seven Wonders of the World, pity the weakness of Newton and Bacon, and Locke and ten thousand others, *and only wish, as duteous sons, their fathers had been more wise!* [12]

Skeptics are indiscriminate reasoners, Campbell held, for they fail to distinguish between true Christianity and its many corruptions. If there were no true coins, there would be no counterfeit coins. If there were no true Christianity, there would not be so many counterfeits of it. Corruptions of it are *"no argument against its Divine Origin."* [13]

Campbell maintained that the priesthood of Catholic France were not the only ones whose personal interest and ambition colored their theories and practices in regard to the church and state. The opportunists among the opponents of revealed religion savored of the same lack of objective concern for truth's sake. They were as interested and biased in their theories of the separation of church and state as the ecclesiastics were in proposing the alliance. Furthermore, the violent excesses of the

10. *Campbell-Rice Debate*, p. 905. See also *The Millennial Harbinger*, 1854, p. 4.
11. *Idem*, 1835, p. 49.
12. *Idem*, 1834, p. 374.
13. *Idem*, 1832, pp. 11–13, 310.

Revolutionaries cannot be traced to *"Christian influences"* in spite of all the corruptions of Christianity.

Extremes led to extremes. The height of corruption of Christianity was in the Roman Catholicism of France. But the height of the corruption of reason and humanity was in the extremes which reacted against Catholic corruptions. To this Catholicism of France can be traced.

all the covert deism, atheism, and skepticism which the vices of popery had generated like worms in a putrid carcass. . . . Kingcraft and priest craft became odious all at once, and infidelity . . . shook itself clean of both crafts, and ignorantly and impiously attempted to deify matter, and dethrone the legitimate Sovereign of the Universe. . . .[14]

It was vengeance and free booting, not benevolence and freedom that erected bastiles and guillotines during the Reign of Terror.[15]

The motivations of the rebellious spirits of the Reign of Terror were different from those of true Christian reformers who oppose the alliance of the church and state. Campbell would credit Hobbes with one truism:

If men found their interest in it, they would doubt the truths of Euclid's elements. . . .[16] State religions are deprecated by Christians as much as by infidels, but from very different motives. The infidel opposes them, because they are in the way to his political aspirations; while the Christian repudiates them because they are in alliance with the corrupt genius of human nature, and tend not only to corrupt religion, but to acts of tyranny and persecution.[17]

Another thing which impressed Campbell was the skeptics' ignorance of the Christian Bible. He contended that the Bible should be well known by skeptics if they are to attack it successfully. But he had found all of them unfamiliar with the Bible of which Owen confessed only a "school-boy-reading." [18] "Thomas Paine wrote against the Bible from recollections and acknowledged that he had not read much of it. David Hume acknowledged, not long before his death, that he had never seriously read the New Testament through." [19]

14. *Campbell-Owen Debate*, II, 131.
15. *The Millennial Harbinger*, 1852, p. 496.
16. *Campbell-Owen Debate*, I, 69.
17. *The Millennial Harbinger*, 1840, p. 536.
18. *Campbell-Owen Debate*, II, 163.
19. *The Christian Baptist*, IV, 258.

Thomas Paine, declared Campbell, opposed the Bible only because he thought it opposed him. He would never have written his *Age of Reason* if he had not thought that the Bible was in the way of his politics and attempt to oppose the doctrine of the divine right of kings. Had he understood the Old Testament, the *"unreasonable author of the Age of Reason,"* would have been obliged to appeal to its authority. He would have known that God merely permitted monarchy for punishment and that a commonwealth was the only government set up by divine authority for the nation which he took under his care for special purposes.

However, typical of skepticism is its inherently negative character. It seeks to do away with Christianity and the Bible but offers no substitutes. Infidelity is chiefly "a negative state of mind." From ancient Pyrrho to modern Hume they have all been doubters with nothing positive to offer civilization. The infidel "is but the incarnation of a negative idea." [20]

Since the French Revolution, it has been popular for men to style themselves as skeptics in anything true or false in an "indiscriminate crusade" against Christianity as well as Judaism. Under the influence of the alliance of kingcraft and priestcraft, "free-thinking" became popular with the downtrodden masses and "was sped and assumed as a characteristic of at least a clever fellow, if not a philosopher." Especially was this seen in the works of Paine and Volney, who merely watered the seeds of irreligion, anarchy, and libertinism which Voltaire had sown. [21]

Campbell described the main figures connected with the French Revolution as men of perverted genius. They were clever but not as scholarly as their idolizers have fancied them. " 'Smart men' " of this class, like Voltaire, Volney, Rousseau, and Paine, are "the worst guides of the public mind." Like the moon, "they give but little light, less heat, and are subject to many changes." [22]

In an address before the Union Literary Society of Miami University of Ohio in 1844, he classified the real men of genius and "master-spirits" of the French Revolution as men like Voltaire, Volney, Diderot, and Gabriel Mirabeau, among whom Vol-

20. *Campbell-Owen Debate*, I, 87 ff., 66–665; II, 167. See Campbell's Introduction to the 1852 edition of the *Campbell-Owen Debate; The Millennial Harbinger*, 1835, p. 317, 1852, p. 663, 1863, pp. 226–227.

21. *Idem*, 1852, pp. 661–665.

22. *Idem*, 1839, pp. 13–14.

taire was the chief. The "Dantons, the Marats, the Robespierres" of the "age of despotism" and "anarchy" merely followed them and practiced their principles. The cup of the Revolution was "poisoned by the brilliant display of perverted genius" administered by such men as "the speculative Hume, the eloquent Gibbon or the accomplished Rousseau."

Thomas Paine was "less-gifted" but as "morally distempered and licentious" as Voltaire, Volney, and Diderot. He had just enough intelligence and wit to please and beguile "the multitudes" into "ruin and disgrace." [23]

Campbell charged that the skeptics of revealed region are even more divided among themselves than the sects in Christendom. At least, professed Christians have certain standards and general principles upon which they can agree. They have the Bible, an ancient and honorable tradition, and the spirit and mind of Jesus Christ which condemn them when their greed and personal interest seduce them from the paths of things for their own sake. But skeptics have nothing that they can agree upon, except to oppose revealed religion.[24]

They are as orthodox-minded, as speculative, and "to say the least, quite as dogmatic, controversial, and sectarian as Pagans, Jews, or Christians." This has been true from Pyrrho's *"free-thinkers,"* called *"The School of Skeptics,"* through the French Revolution to Robert Owen and modern times. From the French Revolution until now, skeptics have subjected "everything ancient and venerated" to "the same arbitrary inquisition." [25]

In an article on "The Liberals," Campbell distinguished between earlier and later natural religionists in terms of present and past power:

But who can persecute when they are in the minority of one to a hundred or a thousand? We do not expect a serpent to sting us in winter . . . countless myriads of christians were sacrificed by the sword of Pagan infidelity, of Roman atheism, deism, and polytheism.

And when had Sceptics power to persecute and did not suffer to sleep? Was it when France became infidel, philosophic, and

23. *Popular Lectures and Addresses*, pp. 73–94.

24. *Campbell-Owen Debate*, I, 61–67.

25. *Idem*, I, 60–61. See also Campbell's Introduction to the *Campbell-Owen Debate* (1852 ed.).

atheistical? Let the bloody scenes of the French Revolution speak out.[26]

In short, according to Campbell, the schools of skepticism have always been filled with men of perverted genius. Ignorance of things religious, the inability to see things whole, the ability to fracture society into negative-minded parts, and intolerant absolutism characterize the graduates of the classical schools of skeptical thought. After identifying his opponents in terms of their past and frequently hidden character, he was ready to fight them on the basis of their own assumptions. If they were willing to reason, he was!

26. *The Millennial Harbinger,* 1831, pp. 434–435.

CHAPTER VI

THE OWEN DEBATE AND THE PLIGHT OF MAN

ALEXANDER CAMPBELL'S debate with Robert Owen in 1829 is an important base from which to explore his criticism of the basic assumptions of the opponents of revealed religion. This is not because Owen was a genuine philosopher or logician but because he inculcated so many popular notions of natural religionists of the Enlightenment era and its subsequent influences.

Moreover, as he continued to use the same refutations of natural religion for the rest of his career, Campbell himself frequently referred to the issues of his debate with Owen. An example of this is his reply in 1840 to "an occasional reader" of his "debates and periodicals." He observed that the reader must have been only an *"occasional"* one, or his skeptical doubts would not have occurred. He recommended "not an *occasional*, but a *thorough* perusal of the 'Owen and Campbell Debate' on the evidences of Christianity, Butler's Analogy, Leslie's Short Method, and Keith's Demonstration." [1]

The similarities between Campbell and Owen are striking. Both were nineteenth-century utopians, each with his proposed system to free mankind from prejudices, classes, and sects. Neither could conscientiously identify himself with any established party. Both wanted an entirely new order of things. Both believed in education and development according to fixed or divine laws of man's nature and capacity. Both wished to reason as calmly and objectively as possible for truth's sake. Each highly respected the other's sincere desire to ascertain truth through public discussions. Both assumed that truth is always of one piece, consistent within itself, and without paradoxes. Both distrusted any alliance of church and state and both hoped that their debate would decide the issue over Christian revelation for all time.

1. *The Millennial Harbinger*, 1840, pp. 428–429. See also *idem*, 1852, p. 350.

The origin of the debate reveals the spirit and approach of Campbell, the debater and defender of the faith, when his anti-ecclesiasticism was at its apex. It has been alleged that the debate evolved from Owen's challenge to the clergy of New Orleans, on January 28, 1826, for a friendly discussion. He proposed to prove that "all the religions of the world have been founded on the ignorance of mankind"; that they are opposed to fixed laws of human nature; that they are "the real source of vice, disunion, and misery"; that they are "now the only real bar to the formation of a society of virtue," intelligence, charity, sincerity, and kindness among mankind; and "that they can no longer be maintained except through the ignorance of the mass of people, and the tyranny of the few over the mass." [2]

The challenge was not accepted. The *New Harmony Gazette,* the official news organ of Owen's experimental City of Mental Independence at New Harmony, Missouri, advertised the fact as evidence of the American clergy's unwillingness to face the issues of truth publicly. Finally Alexander Campbell, rising out of the dust of the tumbling ecclesiastical structure which he had attacked, accepted the challenge in 1828.

However, evidence from the *Christian Baptist* shows that Campbell, whose taste for argument had already been sweetened by two victorious public debates over sectarian clergymen,[3] craved

2. *Campbell-Owen Debate,* I, 30–31; *The Christian Baptist,* V, 237.

3. Campbell's debate with the Reverend John Walker, a Seceder Presbyterian, was held June 19–20, 1820, at Mount Pleasant, Ohio, over the proper subject and mode of baptism. Alexander Campbell championed the Baptist cause. It was a turning point in his career, for until then he was as opposed to religous debates as his father. The significance of this first debate is that it made him a recognized ally of the Baptists on the frontier, won about five thousand subscribers to the *Christian Baptist,* and encouraged him to conceive of the possibility of religious reformation beyond the confines of a local congregation. The ironical note is that it was held in a Quaker community.

Campbell's success in the Walker debate led him to challenge any Pedobaptist minister to debate on baptism. The Reverend William Maccalla of Augusta, Kentucky, another Seceder Presbyterian, accepted; and consequently Campbell's second debate was held with him in Washington, Mason County, Kentucky, October 15–22, 1823. After that Campbell's controversial life was fully decided, for, as Richardson and Gates point out, he concluded, "A week's debating is worth a year's preaching." See Robert Richardson, *Memoirs of Alexander Campbell* (Cincinnati, Standard Publishing Co., 1913, 2 vols.), II, chaps. i, ii, iii; E. Gates, *The Early Relation and Separation of Baptists and Disciples,* chap. iv; and J. J. Haley, *Debates That Made History* (St. Louis, Christian Board of Publication, 1920), chaps. i, ii, iii, iv.

the opportunity. Unaware of Owen's challenge, he had been running a series of articles since April, 1827, on "Deism and the Social System" to combat the views of "the Liberals of New Harmony of Mental Independence."

He welcomed a series of essays against the Bible, for he wanted the *New Harmony Gazette* to offer what light it had, in its first year, "in favor of no religion." If no "abler hand" would defend the Bible, Campbell would be "compelled to volunteer." He proposed to defend revelation in his *Christian Baptist* and offered space for his prospective opponents to reciprocate. He submitted several questions for the gentlemen of New Harmony to answer; two months later he chided "the *illuminati*" for not replying. He would "enter barefoot" into their "sacred edifice" and appeal to their "own goddess" of "Reason." [4] At this time his knowledge of Owen's specific religious views was scanty.

In February, 1828, he received a letter from a minister of Canton, Ohio, who requested him to come there and accept the challenges of a "Doctor Underhill" who, he reported, had been preaching Owen's philosophy at the cooperative society of Kendal. Campbell publicized his reply. If he lived in that community, it would be his duty to break his "lance over his cap" but it would not be compatible with his views of "propriety" to go out of his way to meet such an obscure person. But if "his great master, Mr. Robert Owen," would debate him, he would "gladly negate the whole system" of his "atheistical sentiments." He felt that such a discussion was needed and was prepared to meet "the sage philosopher of New Harmony at a proper time and place." But "I will not draw a bow, save against the king of sceptics of the city of Mental Independence." [5]

When Owen read Campbell's reply, he agreed, through the *New Harmony Gazette* of May 14, 1828, to meet Campbell in public discussion, although he admitted that he knew neither Underhill nor Campbell. In the meantime, a copy of Owen's original challenge to the clergy of New Orleans had reached Campbell; and in the same month he published it with his acceptance of its terms in the *Christian Baptist*. They finally agreed to debate in the exact terms of Owen's original challenge to the clergy of New Orleans. [6]

4. *The Christian Baptist*, IV, 209–212, 255–259; V, 7–10, 53, 236.
5. *Idem*, V, 207–308.
6. The debate was held in Cincinnati, Ohio, beginning April 13, 1829, and

As a logician and debater Owen was a failure. He was accustomed to proclaim his social system, not to defend it. He lacked the debating experience and training of his opponent. Furthermore, claiming to be the originator of all his ideas, he could appeal to no other authority.

Reading from a manuscript, he merely affirmed and reaffirmed twelve propositions which he defined as "the primary laws of human nature." Unfortunately, he assumed that if he could prove the validity of these "laws" his point would automatically be proved; namely, that all religions are false and are founded upon ignorance and are the source of all human unhappiness. A knowledge of these laws would unveil the three prejudices of society which ignorance has made almost universal: unnecessary private property, indissoluble marriages, and "district religions." [7]

The Board of Moderators agreed with Campbell and ruled that to establish his affirmative position Owen would first have to prove that all religions were false, including Christianity, before he could legitimately offer his alternative to those religions. This point Owen failed to grant and his procedure was unaltered.

Alexander Campbell detected the plight of man and the problem of knowledge in relation to natural religion as inherent difficulties in Robert Owen's position. Inevitably, the basic issues which gave rise to the problem of knowledge in the controversy came from their clashing interpretations of the plight of man. These issues may be isolated in order to get at the subsequent problem of knowledge: Is the will independent of the beliefs of man? Is man independent of society? What is the relation of the origin of spiritual ideas to the plight of man? What is the nature, the origin, and the solution to the problem of evil? One question recurred throughout these four problems: Is man entirely determined by the natural, social, and physical circumstances into which he is born, or is it possible for him to transcend them?

Campbell granted Owen's assertion, for the sake of argument, that all religions are founded upon man's "ignorance," providing the term were employed logically. Also all schools, colleges, books,

---

lasting for eight successive days. It consisted of twenty-five addresses each. *The Cincinnati Chronicle* reported that an audience of over twelve hundred people attended the discussion daily. Many reporters and members of the press who visited Cincinnati for the occasion were unable to obtain seats and had to leave. People came from New York, Pennsylvania, Virginia, Kentucky, Indiana, Tennessee, and Mississippi.

7. *Campbell-Owen Debate,* I, 9 ff.

human testimony, and instruction are founded upon man's ignorance and corresponding needs; yet that does not cast "disparagement" upon them. Consequently, this fact does not substantiate any prejudice against religion but, rather, proves the necessity of it, he declared.[8]

However, the word ignorance had another meaning to Owen. It meant a lack of the knowledge of his twelve "divine laws of human nature." According to his deductions, these so-called laws, taken as a whole, reveal that man is totally a creature of the natural and social circumstances under which he is born and over which he never has any control.

These twelve "all-important truths" are the "facts" which "determine by what unchanging laws man is produced and his character is formed." They are constant and universal revelations to the whole human race. They are a "divine standard of truth," the knowledge of which will give happiness and perfection to all mankind.[9]

Robert Owen's Twelve "Laws" or "Facts of Nature"

The facts which I am compelled to believe . . . are:

1. That man, at his birth, is ignorant of everything relative to his own organization, and that he has not been permitted to create the slightest part of his own natural propensities, faculties, or qualities, physical or mental.

2. That no two infants, at birth, have yet been known to possess precisely the same organization, while the physical, mental, and moral differences between infants, are formed without their knowledge or will.

3. That each individual is placed, at birth, without his knowledge or consent, within circumstances, which, acting upon his peculiar organization, impress the general character of those circumstances upon the infant, child, and man. Yet that the influence of those circumstances is to a certain degree modified by the peculiar natural organization of each individual.

4. That no infant has the power of deciding at what period of time or in what part of the world he shall come into existence; of whom he shall be born, or by what other circumstances he shall be surrounded from birth to death.

5. That each individual is so created, that when young, he may be made to receive impressions, to produce either true ideas or

8. *Idem*, I, 45.
9. *Idem*, I, 21–27.

false notions, and beneficial or injurious habits, and to retain them with great tenacity.

6. That each individual is so created that he must believe according to the strongest impressions that are made on his feelings and other faculties, while his belief in no case depends upon his will.

7. That each individual is so created that he must like that which is pleasant to him, or that which produces agreeable sensations on his individual organization, and he must dislike that which creates in him, unpleasant and disagreeable sensations; while he cannot discover, previous to experience, what those sensations should be.

8. That each individual is so created, that the sensations made upon his organization, although pleasant and delightful at their commencement and for some duration, generally become, when continued beyond a certain period, without change, disagreeable and painful; while, on the contrary, when a too rapid change of sensations is made on his organization, it dissipates, weakens, and otherwise injures his physical, intellectual, and moral powers and enjoyments.

9. That the highest health, the greatest progressive improvements, and the most permanent happiness of each individual depend, in a great degree, upon the proper cultivation of his physical, intellectual and moral faculties and powers from infancy to maturity, and upon all these parts of his nature being called into action, at their proper period, and temperately exercised according to the strength and capacity of the individual.

10. That the individual is made to possess and to acquire the *worst* character, when his organization at birth has been compounded of the most inferior propensities, faculties and qualities of our common nature, and when so organized, he has been placed, from birth to death, amid the most vicious or worst circumstances.

11. That the individual is made to possess and to acquire a *medium* character, when his original organization has been created *superior,* and when the circumstances which surround him from birth to death produce continued *vicious* or *unfavorable* impressions. Or when his organization has been formed of *inferior* materials, and the circumstances in which he has been placed from birth to death are of a character to produce *superior* impressions only. Or when there has been some mixture of *good* and *bad* qualities, in the original organization, and when it has been placed, through life, in various circumstances of *good* and *evil.* This last compound has been hitherto the common lot of mankind.

12. That the individual is made the most *superior* of his species

when his original organization has been compounded of the best proportions of the best ingredients of which human nature is formed. And when the circumstances which surround him from birth to death are of a character to produce only superior impressions; or, in other words, when the circumstances, or laws, institutions, and customs in which he is placed, are all in unison with his nature.[10]

Campbell first challenged the *"manner,"* rather than the *"matter,"* of Owen's illogical reasoning upon what he called *" 'facts'* and 'laws of nature.' " He objected to Owen's vague usage of terms such as *"divine, divinity, religion, virtue, moral law, created, Creator,"* without specifying their meanings. Owen should define his terms, whether he uses them in their logical import or gives them meanings of his own.[11]

Campbell was willing to concede many truths within what he called Owen's twelve "premises," but he could not see that they proved anything. He asked if he were expected to deny all of his opponent's philosophical, scientific, and mathematical facts in order to take logical exceptions to any of them. If Owen were going to attempt to prove a metaphysical position by arguments that can only "elucidate a truth in physics," he could not join issue with him. Owen should not expect to prove the "fallacy of *christianity* by *mathematical* demonstrations," for "the grand question at issue is a question of fact, chiefly dependent upon historic evidence." Historic evidences cannot be measured "as if they were so many mathematical lines." He affirmed that Christianity is founded upon facts "triable by all the historical criteria." Owen must "impugn them, or put me to the proof." [12]

However, disregarding the objections of his opponent and moderator, Owen reiterated that his twelve laws and their deductions are "self-evident truths." He insisted that all religions are ignorant of these laws and, therefore, are "untrue and founded upon ignorance."

Throughout the controversy Owen's definition of *"fact"* was "that which exists." [13] Campbell claimed that no philologist would assent to such a definition. "Stones, trees, and opinions exist" but could these alike "be considered as matters of fact? . . . *Fact*

10. *Idem*, I, 22–24.
11. *Idem*, I, 23, 29–32.
12. *Idem*, I, 30–34.
13. *Idem*, I, 195, 228, 235–236, 240.

is derived from *factum*. It means that which is done. Now it is not a fact that I have two eyes. This is not a *fact*, but a truth. It is a fact that I rose up or sat down." [14]

Nevertheless, Owen insisted that it is a fact that Campbell has two corporeal eyes. He contended that fact must be used in terms of its common acceptance and that his opponent is merely burdened by metaphysics.

This disagreement over the definition of a fact is important, for Campbell's lifelong defense of revealed religion in terms of the history and evidences of Christianity hinged partly upon his conception of the term. Also, it involved the debaters' crucial dispute over Owen's sixth law.

As noted, Owen's deductions from his laws resulted in a completely deterministic view of man. He maintained that man is a being so created that he can never "be made responsible for his nature." His character and conduct "proceed essentially" from "his organization and natural capacities." Although all human beings are different by birth and environment, individuals cannot be responsible for these differences "without great injustice." There is no basis for "praise or blame" of their conduct. All human beings are merely *"effects of causes irresistible in their influence."*

In illustration, Owen asked who in the audience can say that he determined "the period *when* he should be born, of *whom,* in *what* country," of what religion he should be taught to believe, or whether he should be born a prince or peasant. If we had been born "among a tribe of thorough-going cannibals" would we not "delight in killing and eating our enemies?" This proves that "all religions are untrue and founded on ignorance." [15]

The Relation of the Human Will to Belief

In challenging Owen's "matter," Campbell stressed Owen's sixth law which to him implied determinism. Campbell's correctness in concentrating upon "the fatal sixth" is well seen in the importance which Owen himself placed upon it. Owen was willing to rest "the whole controversy upon this single affirmative proposition," " 'That no human being ever had the power of belief or dis-

14. *Idem,* I, 195 ff., 221, 235.
15. *Idem,* I, 41–44.

belief at his will, and therefore cannot be merit or demerit in any belief. . . .' " [16]

Campbell refuted Owen's complete determinism as a basis for demolishing all religions of the world because of their alleged ignorance on two grounds: First, he argued that many religionists believe as firmly in man's being a creature of circumstance as Owen. Second, such drastic determinism is questionable in the light of actual human experience.

He acknowledged that the difficulties on the subject of human responsibility are of "no ordinary magnitude," for the most profound ancient and modern philosophers have differed upon the knotty problem. But for the sake of argument let us admit that we cannot trace just how far we are creatures of necessity. Would this failure discredit the evidence of the truth of Christianity? "How many necessarians are there who believe in supernatural revelation?" [17] Owen ignores a learned body of Christians who attribute as much to *"necessity"* as he does, only under other names. They think that every human action is "foreknown" and "predetermined from all eternity." Yet they are rational believers in the divine authority of Christian truth.[18]

Moreover, let us learn from our own experience of "liability to err" if we are to be governed by common sense and reason. In sense perception errors often elude us which are discoverable by sense evidence which we have before us. Although it is axiomatic in mathematics that two parallel lines extended ad infinitum never meet, who can decide at a glance whether any seeming parallels are perfectly mathematical parallels? Yet we all confess that there are inherent difficulties in ascertaining abstract metaphysical truths which are greater to overcome than those appertaining to sensible objects. In spite of this, Owen would establish "a whole system of skepticism upon a dogma of one metaphysical school."

Owen denied Campbell's contention that his sixth law involved metaphysics and asserted that it was "a question of *fact*" and any one "can ascertain the real merits of it for himself." [19] Campbell retorted that if so we need a new vocabulary but the public could decide whether it were a metaphysical question.

16. *Idem*, II, 161, I, 199.
17. *Idem*, I, 199.
18. *Idem*, II, 124–125.
19. *Idem*, I, 67, 81, 203, 206.

He was willing to make "ample concessions to the doctrine of circumstances," although "many honest minds have been deceived by its plausibility." We cannot choose our birth or control the "circumstance of our nature and education." But does it logically follow that all religions are founded upon ignorance because men did not create themselves?

Facts and arguments are available "to prove, to a very considerable extent, we are not the pure creatures of circumstances." Owen himself is a "living refutation of his own doctrine." He ascribes "everything to circumstances" but "talks of happiness." "Has he ever seen such a set of circumstances as would make a man perfectly happy? How did he come by his peculiar ideas? They are the creatures not of circumstances, but of a warm and over-heated imagination." [20]

Campbell pressed his effective illustration. He described Owen as "a striking contradiction of his law of necessity." He asserts that our faith is entirely

involuntary, and that our volitions have nothing to do with our belief; but he has just shown you that he disbelieves in his own sixth law. He has the most voluntary faith I ever knew. He wills to believe all history that reflects any stigma upon nominal christians—the cruelties and persecutions practiced by pretended disciples of his who prohibited all violence, cruelty, and revenge; he wills to believe certain matters of fact from Roman history. The rest he wills to disbelieve. . . . He was born in great Britain, consequently was bred in a state of society very different from that which he is so anxious to introduce. Now the question is, did his early circumstances originate those ideas . . . ? . . . What has distinguished Mr. Owen from his neighbours? [21]

Nevertheless, Owen was not baffled by those problems. He explained that his organization differed from others and that the circumstances under which he had been placed had produced all the "character and conduct" of his life. He had "escaped" the "religious circumstances" in which Campbell had always remained; and thus he had "freely examined and experienced the influences of almost all the other circumstances to be found in civilized society." He had been able to study men by a close observation of the facts of human nature.[22]

20. *Idem,* I, 46, 48.
21. *Idem,* I, 46, 235–236.
22. *Idem,* I, 67–68, 79–80, 165–166, 236, 239.

To Campbell it was not "strange that Mr. Owen should diverge so far from the beaten track of common sense," for many philosophers have done the same thing. Some have gone further. Hobbes "reasoned himself into a perfect conviction that there is no such thing as right or wrong." Hume "convinced himself that there was nothing else in the world but ideas and impressions." Bishop Berkeley "persuaded himself that matter did not exist." Descartes doubted his own existence until he could prove it by affirming *"Cognito, ego sum,"* which was about as logical as saying, "I have an eye or ear, and therefore I am." Pyrrho was so incredulous of the testimony of his sense that his friends had to protect him from danger, for he "would not turn away from the brink of a precipice." Such "philosophical reveries" have "no stopping place." [23]

Campbell stated that Godwin, "a highly gifted writer," ran at random much like Owen but stopped "some miles on this side of materialism." He met an insuperable difficulty in the doctrine of causation. After exploring materialism and determinism, Godwin found that it was "most philosophic" to make concessions which saved him from materialism and which would afford "wholesome admonitions to our modern wise men who are dressing up anew the long-exploded doctrines of fate and materialism." Campbell cited Godwin's conclusion that we are universally unable to discover the ground of necessary connection between thought and matter or motion; that although *"materialists make thought the effect of matter or motion impressing upon us,"* yet these effects are again causes of matter and *"there may be no thoughts altogether unattended with motion."* [24]

Owen approached his final proof that the will can in no way affect belief in this manner: He invited anyone in the audience to demonstrate that he possessed such power of will by believing that he was not standing before them, or by believing in "the divinity of Mahomet's mission." This impossibility proves that we cannot "disbelieve according to the evidence of our senses" or according to "the strongest impression which the circumstances of birth, nature, and education have forced upon them." Yet he claimed that the "main pillar of all religions" is the teaching that "our will has power over our belief." [25]

23. *Idem,* I, 47.
24. *Idem,* I, 47–48.
25. *Idem,* I, 55; see also pp. 199, 206.

Campbell had little patience with this maneuver. He declared that Owen falsely "supposes the capital error of all religions to be that they teach belief is under the control of the will—whereas he supposes the contrary." Furthermore, his difficulty lies in his indefinite usage of the word "belief" [26] and his erroneous views of faith, or in supposing that one has "uncontrolled power" over his belief. Such an appeal could not be made rationally unless a Christian were to affirm that one could "believe without *evidence*." Yet he contended that "testimony is essential to faith" and whether we "have testimony sufficient to constrain belief generally depends upon our determination or volition.

Campbell felt that Owen confused or used interchangeably such terms as belief, knowledge, and opinion.

> *Belief* always depends upon the testimony of others; *knowledge,* upon the evidence of our senses; *opinion,* upon our own reasonings. . . . In a word, I *know* this desk is before me; I believe that Thomas Jefferson is dead; and I am of the opinion that Symmes' theory is all a mere fancy.[27]

He maintained that Owen's sixth law was not "anything more than an assertion that our belief is independent of our volitions." On the contrary, "our volitions have as much control over our mental as our corporeal eye." Granting that frequently our physical and mental eyesights are involuntarily exercised, it is not fair to argue from "these particular premises" to the general conclusion that "in no case whatever is my belief, or my vision, under the control of my volition." [28]

In an attempt to prove that volitions do, "in many instances, determine our beliefs," Campbell offered the example of one's

26. *Idem,* I, 66, 199. Throughout the debate Campbell protested at Owen's vague usage of terms like *"heaven, divine law, religion, virtue, and morality"* (p. 234), *"feeling"* (p. 238), and *"belief."* He claimed that from "such confusion of terms we may infer that there is a corresponding confusion of ideas; for confusion of terms is the offspring either of confusion of ideas, or a mistake of the meaning of terms. Whatever a person conceives, he can clearly express. *Verba sequantum res;* or in English—words follow ideas, is a true and instructive maxim. Whole systems of error, when analyzed, have been found to proceed from a misapprehension and misapplication of terms. And, indeed, I am not without very considerable misgivings that this may be one radical cause of the illusion which has captivated my friend and opponent, Mr. Owen." *Idem,* I, 239.

27. *Idem,* I, 66–67.

28. *Idem,* I, 203–204.

having been informed that a certain event occurred which was very important to him. Assuming that his informant were a man of "suspected veracity," because of his interest involved, he sought to collect enough evidence to convince him of the truth of the first report. His belief was withheld until he attained a full report. Now the question is, was not my belief of this fact in some way dependent on my volition? [29]

Owen agreed with Campbell's discriminations between knowledge, belief, and opinion but maintained that "in the case to which he has referred, it was his interest that generated his will, and therefore compelled him to investigate." [30]

But the relation of interest to volition was precisely the problem which Campbell had in mind in terms of the reasoning powers of the human mind, for he held that we can make certain conclusions in regard to certain objectives which we have in mind. Suppose Owen is correct in stating that it is interest that excited the investigation? Am I not at liberty to act according to my true interest? And if I so act, do I not act rationally and voluntarily?

For example, in exercising the faculty of imagination, I can, at will, transfer the external peculiarities of one animal to the body of another, and thereby create an imaginative monster. . . . But this license of imagination is entirely under the control of my volition. I can recollect only by making an effort, and consequently must determine that effort. I can reason only when I decide to reason; and my placing myself in the attitude of a judge, is as much in obedience to a previous determination, as the eating of my supper, or my going to bed. . . .[31]

We can form judgments which may or may not call for activity on our part when objects that excite our reasoning powers are thrown in our way or when we seek them. We act not because of "the mere presentation of the object" but because of our reasoning powers, he avowed. The mind can determine to examine and re-examine the object before making the decision to act. For example, the Mexican Government wanted to dispose of some territory. When Owen heard of it he investigated the possibilities of obtaining the territory to test his social theories. By his own

29. *Idem*, I, 67, 72.
30. *Idem*, I, 67.
31. *Idem*, I, 72, 142–143.

determination and examinations he finally made his ultimate decision.[32]

The Relation of Man to Society

Campbell claimed that his opponent's "no praise, no blame system" of irresponsibility not only presupposes that belief is independent of volitions but presupposes that men are independent of society. It saps the foundations of morality and society. However, it breaks down, for Owen cannot show that we are irresponsible without proving that we are independent.[33]

Campbell had in mind Owen's conception of society both as it is and as it is to come. As mentioned, Owen held that his twelve laws form a perfect foundation for a "divine moral code" sufficient to produce the practice of all virtue in the individual and society; to enable man, through a correct knowledge of himself, to "work out his own salvation from sin or ignorance and misery"; and to secure the happiness of the whole race. They will

enable us to open the road for the removal of all the poverty, ignorance, disunion, vice, and crime which everywhere abounds . . . to act upon the rising generation in such a manner that there shall not be one individual trained to remain inferior in society. We shall discover a mathematical mode of training the rising generation, by which they shall be prevented from receiving one error, one bad habit, or acquiring one injurious passion. . . . And whenever we become only slightly rational, there will no longer be either anger, or irritation, or disunion, among the human family.[34]

Campbell contended that Owen might as "rationally inveigh against benevolent as malevolent feelings." He lays as much basis for the latter as he does the former. His plan of "cultivating kind feelings would extirpate all feeling," and "we should stand toward each other like trees in a forest." "Like the rash and unskillful physician, he kills the patient while he kills the fever. All the kind feelings, complacency, affection, and social delights are murdered by the same sword which is unsheathed to stab religion to the heart." [35]

32. *Idem*, II, 125–126.
33. *Idem*, II, 57–59, 66.
34. *Idem*, I, 41–44.
35. *Idem*, I, 57–58.

Furthermore, Campbell challenged Owen's static conception of society. He granted that "the infant man" could not help being surrounded with his circumstances but must man forever remain an infant? If man were to remain in a state of "infantile imbecility, then he might be likened to the tree or to the stone located in the soil, subject only to the laws of mere organic nature." Campbell argued that we change our circumstances and our circumstances change us. While in a sense man is dependent upon his circumstances, he can change them with "as much ease as Mr. Owen changes his coat, his climate, his food, or his country."

But the logical conclusion of Owen's conception of man and the doctrine of irresponsibility is that all men are "reduced to the state of *non compos mentis.*" In real society, "infants, idiots, lunatics, and the *non compos mentis*" are irresponsible and we place guardians over them. Rationality is presupposed in the very concept of responsibility; we never think of rewarding or punishing an infant until it develops its rational faculties. Owen "renders men as incapable of society and of moral and civil government as if they were trees, stones, or machines."

Owen's system reaches further. It saps the foundation of "all obligations to any being in the universe." It leaves us "in impenetrable darkness with respect to our origin" or to "any relation which, as creatures, we stand to our Creator." [36]

Campbell did not wish to waste time by proving a point "which is itself as plain as the proof could be, viz.: that mankind are dependent, and therefore responsible." Every human being's experience concurs with the fact that he is placed in circumstances which suggest his "dependence and consequent responsibility" as soon as his "reason dawns." This is true of the child who is born in "a palace or wigwam," for either set of circumstances suggests to him a "sense of dependence upon his protectors." This sense of dependence and consequent responsibility is

the foundation of all moral obligation of every social compact, of all civil and political security. . . . [37] A being, independent of any other, has no rule to obey but that which his own reason or will prescribes. But a state of dependence will inevitably oblige the inferior to take the will of him on whom he depends as the rule of his conduct, at least, in all those points wherein his dependence consists; consequently, as man depends absolutely upon his Crea-

36. *Idem*, I, 58 ff., 182.
37. *Idem*, I, 182.

tor for everything, it is necessary that he should, in all points submit to his will. This I do hold to be the true and immovable basic of natural, social and religious obligation and responsibility.[38]

Owen's system "proscribes all dependence upon any unknown, unseen cause whatsoever." Before Owen can prove his first proposition, he must account for the relation in which we stand to a supreme or superior being, or discard it altogether. If he discards it, he must explain our origin before he can ascertain our relations.

Toward the end of the debate Campbell confessed that he still was "at loss to know what Mr. Owen means by *society.*" To him "a society without a social compact" is "unintelligible." Owen's system is contrary to all the experience of society. No society can exist without "some sense of responsibility and obligation," declared Campbell. When we speak of *"a lawless banditti"* it is understood as a *"sub modo."* A banditti of highwaymen could not exist without laws among themselves. Yet Owen persists in ignoring this universal societal experience.[39]

Campbell stated that Owen's twelve laws do not go far enough in presenting "the whole man." The "admission of these facts does not involve an admission of all the reasons and deductions superinduced upon them." They reveal only the "animal man" and do not take into account man's moral, spiritual, and intellectual nature. They deal only with the "external case," the "irrational part of the animal creation that is in man." They could as logically be affirmed about a goat.[40] In fact, Campbell substituted the word "goat" for "man" and "kids" for "infants" and read the twelve propositions. He entitled them "The Twelve Fundamental Laws of Brutal Nature, *on which Robert Owen Bases a Change of Society That Will Form an Entire New State of Existence.*"

He charged that Owen's conception of man is based upon this hypothesis: that man is purely an animal and, therefore, cannot believe in a spiritual system. He offered to add four laws to them, which are "as palpable as the first one" but will "exclude the goat and every other animal," stating that man has fundamental aspirations after knowledge, society, happiness, and the ultimate

38. *Idem,* I, 66.
39. *Idem,* II, 129–131.
40. *Idem,* I, 48–89.

meaning of his origin and destiny which this life on earth cannot satisfy. He would prefix two more laws to the original twelve of Owen's animal code, namely, that the first man was not born but was the child of somebody upon whom he is ultimately dependent for his existence and nature.[41]

The Importance of an Analysis of the Origin of Spiritual Ideas

Throughout the debate Campbell contended that Owen must present "an analysis of our mental powers," and account for the origin of the spiritual ideas which already exist in the world, before he could try to destroy them and affirm logically that all religions are based upon ignorance. He must show that ignorant men, in the rudest ages of the world, were capable of inventing and establishing religion. This is the problem that always confounds "the materialists of all schools." [42]

Owen had addressed the audience at one occasion as follows: "You have been taught some fanciful notions of what you have heard termed God, Deity, or *First Cause;* and you have been taught some other fanciful notions of a being who has been introduced to you by the name of *the Devil. . . .*" [43]

Campbell was "glad to hear the assertion." For the sake of argument, he would "rest the whole merits of the discussion" upon the assertion "that the idea of God is fanciful," although he acknowledged that the real merits of the controversy did not rest upon that assertion.[44]

Campbell submitted five questions about the problem of knowledge to Owen in order that he might proceed more philosophically in supporting his affirmation that all religion is founded upon ignorance.

Owen protested at the metaphysical character of the questions. He had "totally avoided metaphysical reading, because I discovered it was not calculated to relieve society from its errors and difficulties." Metaphysics "has too many words and too few facts." He accused Campbell of endeavoring to "embark with him into the ocean of metaphysical disquisitions, where we might be tossed

41. *Idem,* II, 182–184.
42. *Idem,* I, 50, 59, 65–66, 95 ff.
43. *Idem,* I, 69.
44. *Idem,* I, 74.

about for ten thousand years, and then be no nearer the port than we are now." Owen wanted to stick to "plain and practical facts." In his travels he had presented his principals to "minds of the first caliber in the world" but had never met one which could detect "error or inconsistency" in any of them. If Campbell could, he would admit that he had been deceived and would amend his ways by promulgating the truth.[45]

Campbell replied that if Owen will not admit the legitimacy of any authority, "we cannot admit the experience of Mr. Owen as an authority." At that, he wanted to "hear the *names* of some of these *'intelligent men.'* "[46]

He did not propose the questions to puzzle Owen but to elicit logical reasoning and conclusions. He had not tried to lead him into the mazes of metaphysics "any further than the nature of the argument itself requires." But Owen himself had introduced the first metaphysical proposition of the debate in his sixth law. Now it is up to Owen to prove that "all our ideas of Deity, and all other spiritual existences" are entirely at variance with the beneficent objects which he contemplates to consummate. If he thinks that "our religious (superstitious) ideas, and his social ideas can never exist together in the same mind," he ought to give some sort of argument, proof, or illustration "calculated to eradicate such ideas from our minds."[47]

The Problem of Evil

Another issue raised early in the debate involved the nature, origin, and solution to the problem of evil. Owen had asserted that any religion "which presupposes man bad by nature must surely be founded in utter ignorance of human nature." Yet he had said that "the whole system of the world" is "bad from its foundation." He had also declared that no "intelligence infinitely wise, good, and powerful, ever did make (knowing what he was about) a devil, to torment us" and that he could not believe "any absurdity so monstrous as this."[48]

Perhaps nothing could have pleased Campbell more. He replied:

45. *Idem*, I, 51–52, 67, 94–95.
46. *Idem*, I, 95, 169, 432.
47. *Idem*, I, 75, 85–86, 95.
48. *Idem*, I, 41, 69–70, 80.

Mr. Owen told us he could never believe that a good and wise being created a Devil; yet he could believe that the Devil created himself, or that a wise and kind Nature created evil. Natural evils do exist from some cause; there are poisons, pains, and death. Yet, with Mr. Owen, there is neither a God nor a Devil! Everything made itself, or all things together made each separate agent! ! . . . Now the question which he has not answered, and which we know he cannot answer, is *How came the social circumstances to be irrational and antinatural, seeing necessity, or what he called nature, has introduced them?* [49]

He felt that Owen's theory is saturated with a "morbid sympathy" which keeps him from acknowledging the real world of pain, misery, sin, and the consequences of sin. Owen's difficulty is his unwillingness to reconcile his sympathies with these facts, for he supposes that it is "impossible for rational beings to be virtuously happy under a government which involves partial pain and misery." He destroys the "inseparable connection between virtue and happiness" by making "virtuous happiness" depend upon "such circumstances as to preclude all possible pain in any sentient being whatever." The sight of a "broken finger or a dislocated joint" would make one miserable.[50] At this point, Campbell was reminded of the same type of tendency within the ranks of theism and deism.

He cited the materialist, M. Mirabaud, who censored "the Theist" for humanizing his God too much and for giving him the character and too many of the attributes "which are supposed to be essential to a good governor." Mirabaud described their continual embarrassment in having to reconcile the conduct of God with the evils in the world without the supposition of those absurd fables which "recur to the sin of *Adam,* or to the *fall of the rebel angels,* or to the crime of Prometheus and the box of Pandora to find in what manner evil has crept into the world, subjected to a benevolent intelligence." [51]

Campbell declared that the deists have little curiosity at the point of contemplating the justice of God. He quoted the creed of Thomas Paine, in his *Age of Reason,* as an example: "I believe in one God, and no more, and I hope for happiness beyond this life." And, again, his creed of morality runs, "I believe the

49. *Idem,* I, 73, 130.
50. *Idem,* I, 130–131.
51. *Idem,* I, 62.

equality of man, and I believe that religious duties consist in doing justice, loving mercy, and endeavouring to make our fellow-creatures happy." [52] He wanted to see God's justice and mercy in "the *book of creation*" as a "revelation." But "Mr. Paine did not want to see his justice; and therefore, failed in telling us what to contemplate in order to discover this." [53]

Campbell regretted that men have founded theories of religion upon "imperfect, and, perhaps, inaccurate ideas of the character of God." Some have founded systems of religion "upon the idea that the mercy of God is not reconcilable with the idea of punishment, present or future," in their conception of Christian happiness. Campbell contended that "however correct their views of divine justice or mercy, contemplated apart from all other perfections, yet the compound attributes of divine character" are "beyond human comprehension." If the Creator tolerates "the scene of animal sufferings perpetually before him," how can we infer "that the future punishment of man would mar the felicity of his creator, or be incompatible with his character?" [54]

Campbell contended that the Scriptures explain to us the origin of evil in the world and man's original state. They adapt men "to these preternatural circumstances, and bring them out of them." Owen does not explain them and cannot. Materialists, in order "to make out a system contrary to all *experience and history,* . . . have been constrained to suppose . . . that man was originally a being very different from what he is now. But whether he has degenerated, or improved, they do not testify." Campbell had in mind the doctrine of the fall of man and original sin. He felt that man's inferiority "to all other animals in instinctive powers" and his "helplessness at birth support the account of the fall." [55]

He wanted to know how Owen's amelioration of man would take place. If the origin of natural evil is found within the elements of the human constitution, he declared, Owen must present some plan of remaking man.

He cautioned Owen that Mirabaud, "though one of the oldest advocates of atheism, declares 'that atheism will not make a wicked man good.' " In contrast to materialistic systems, including Owen's, he proposed to show that the Christian religion is

52. *Idem*, I, 62–63.
53. *Idem*, I, 63.
54. *Idem*, I, 130–131.
55. *Idem*, I, 115.

adapted to the needs and condition of man so as to exalt him higher and to render him "incomparably more happy than Mr. Owen has ever conceived." He would thus defend the Christian religion by discussing its "purifying influences" and its "tendencies upon the hearts and lives of men." [56]

Owen replied that Campbell misunderstood him in regard to *"natural* evil," for he intended to speak only of human nature. Surely "we cannot derive the natural evil of human nature from any other source than defective organization." As soon as men attain the true knowledge of the twelve fundamental laws of their nature, they will know what manner of beings they are. Then they will discover that a combination of the best organization and circumstances produce the most favorable character. Already "there is a science by which any animal, whether human or irrational, is capable of receiving great improvements at *birth.*" As soon as we fully acquire this science of "the animal man" it will provide "the unerring method of obtaining the best raw material for the manufacture of man." Now we possess the power to withdraw the "most unfavorable circumstances from around all humans at birth." [57]

From this context, Owen expounded his philosophy of history of "three distinct states of society" to "show how directly opposed the twelve fundamental laws" are to the principles "inculcated and always implied by all the religions of the world."

The first state is universal. In it man is forced to believe or to profess a belief in some respective "district religion" which forms the individual's character. The second state, the painful transitional stage of society which we are now undergoing, is a step toward real knowledge. In it we are moved to renounce our belief in district religions and to withdraw from the "former character formed for us by religious belief." If society is to be improved, we must pass through this gulf like "vessels on the ocean without a helm, chart, or compass." The third and "superior state of existence," "the Millennium," will come when the individual is taught to know these twelve fundamental principles of human nature. With the former errors of religion disabused, he shall know what manner of being he is and his relation to his fellow creatures.

56. *Idem,* I, 64, 96; II, 124.
57. *Idem,* I, 100.

The first two stages are characterized by irrationality. But in the final stage there cannot be anyone who is irrational in "thoughts, feelings and conduct." This "change in your minds will produce vice instead of virtue." In the new society even "the infant schools" will be so qualified that they "will make Angels of any children, except their wings." The change should come gradually by the union of "some of the leading governments" and "hands of the chief sects of religion" so as not to shock the "interests or feelings of any portion of society." [58]

Most of Owen's time in the debate was used to describe the conditions of the third and final stage of society and the things necessary for human happiness under a natural government. No restraints or punishments will be needed to blame individuals falsely for their actions. With all the religions of the world abolished, "true religion, or truth, pure, and undefiled, without useless and senseless rites, forms, or ceremonies, will alone remain." All human laws and governments are now artificial, for they presuppose that man has the power to think and feel as he pleases. They shall be abandoned. The "rising generation, will obey the laws of human nature." Private property will cease. Wars will be no more. "The artificial bonds of indissoluble marriages and the family arrangements" are to be abolished. Only rational proceedings will come from all who are not insane. It will be a classless society. No fears or superstitions will exist. "When we remove the priests, lawyers, warriors, merchants, etc. what a happy state of society shall we enjoy! None of us shall have occasion to be employed more than two hours a day; yet we shall have an abundance of everything!" [59]

This was too much for Alexander Campbell! He avowed that in undertaking to encounter Mr. Owen with controversial weapons, he did not know that he "was to combat with a *divinity*." He had expected to encounter "the much boasted reason of the skeptics." But on the foundation of a few facts Owen has placed "mankind under a modern Theocracy" with a new revelation. Although one might suppose Owen to be a prophet, unfortunately his former predictions will not sustain this. Three years ago he prophesied that Cincinnati would "become a deserted or evacu-

58. *Idem*, I, 81–82, 103, 158, 217. We shall contrast Owen's view of history with Campbell's in the third major section of this book.

59. *Idem*, I, 112–115, 120, 159, 181.

ated city before two years; that the citizens would all migrate to New Harmony." That time has passed, yet a "few people are still living there and the sound of the workman's hammer is yet heard in the streets." [60]

Ironically, Campbell appraised Owen's social system as "the most Utopian project in the annals of society." Children are to be "reared without a lesson upon obligation or duty," yet "they are to be most orderly." Owen's "romantic genius" gives them all "angelic charms, excepting wings." With a total destitution of all evil disposition they are to be perfect giants in literature, virtue, and benevolent enterprise—able in two hours, per diem, to provide for all their own happiness! If Owen could cover the earth with his "parallelogram communities," man, "at *his* zenith, is a stall-fed ox." In "its best possible state" it is "founded upon the half of man, and only promises to make him a happy animal." He mistakes the capacity of man like the vintner who strove to fill a vessel with two gallons when it held four; nothing but experience could convince him of his error.[61]

In short, when Owen and Campbell clashed over their conceptions of the nature and plight of man, the latter maintained that man is not a creature totally "riveted to his physical and social circumstances." [62] As sinful and responsible as he might be, man has elements within his nature which enable him to transcend the time, space, and natural environment into which he is born. Yet, in spite of his capacities of mind and spirit for self-transcendence, man is in a situation in which he cannot entirely extricate himself without dependence upon a being greater than himself.

To Campbell, the issues arising over the plight of man raised the problem of the origin and destiny of man in terms of his relation to this being and to the universe in which he lives. This called for an analysis of the powers of the human mind and an investigation of the origin of the spiritual ideas in the world.

60. *Idem*, I, 104, 159, 243. Owen denied that he was a false prophet for "years cannot mean the same thing in the language of prophecy, that they do in common language." He asserted that instead of Cincinnati "only being depopulated in a few years, the fact is, that all large cities will cease to be such." Inhabitants will find out that cities afford combinations of circumstances which are "extremely injurious to every individual." *Idem*, I, 249.

61. *Idem*, II, 127, 130.

62. *Idem*, I, 59.

Whenever Owen or other opponents of revealed religion based their assumptions of the nature of man and of divine truth upon a secular basis, Campbell raised the problem of knowledge. No skeptic could deny the validity of revealed religion without coming to terms with his theory of knowledge.

CHAPTER VII

CAMPBELL'S THEORY OF KNOWLEDGE

A T no point was Campbell more consistent throughout his career than in his theory of knowledge.

For him, as we shall see, the normal person in modern society is not only an animal but also a spiritual creature. He has both material and religious knowledge. Two worlds constantly impinge upon him and he can never escape the impact of either. His original ideas of the material world are derived through sense perception and natural reason, once he has acquired the use of speech and language through societal experience and tutoring. But his original ideas of the spiritual world are derived through direct revelation and are otherwise unattainable except through social traditions which already have been influenced by previous experience of revelation.

Campbell would have no commerce with natural religionists. To him they were traders in borrowed or stolen wares offered under the deceptive trademark of their own manufacture. All their basic spiritual ideas were derived from mines of revealed religion but they claim to have collected them from the free fields of nature as the common property of natural men.

This is the message that Campbell wanted to convey. But how? He could not employ solely the "pure speech" of the "saints" who are confined to Jerusalem, for they had no speculative vocabulary or opinions.

As a paradox of his *Christian Baptist* type of attack upon ecclesiasticism, he was challenged for using nonscriptural terms. Campbell's answer was that it is necessary to use Biblical language in controversial subjects when dealing with Christians. Yet, in dealing with nonbelievers in Christian revelation, we must go out of Jerusalem into Babylon and fight the enemies of pure speech and corrupt spiritual ideas with their own weapons. They hardly know what we mean when we use weapons with which only the saints battle. Moreover, they must be defeated on their own premises of reason and with their own instruments of vocabulary or they will never be convinced of error.

Christians are commanded to be always ready to give a reason "for the faith once delivered to the saints" but in meekness and firmness. "God is reason" and His communications are "rational." Man is a "reasonable being" and, therefore, must offer "good reasons" for "believing the Christian religion." It is proper for Christians to use reason in religion as long as it is not "perverted." [1]

Surveying his arguments in the Owen debate, Campbell claimed that he had shown that "no man philosophically or rationally can object to the christian religion; and that upon the principles of reason he is compelled to assent to the divine truths" of Christianity. He had welcomed the debate "because Mr. Owen was all for reason and philosophy, which no intelligent christian ever feared. . . ." [2]

Campbell frequently appealed to Lord Bacon in laying "the foundation for correct reasonings" upon "the subject of human experience and knowledge." Skepticism, he said, is founded upon "Assumption" and Christian faith upon "Experience." Campbell would "make the principles of the inductive philosophy . . . my rule and guide in this investigation." [3]

During the Owen debate, Campbell summarized his basic disagreement with the theory of knowledge in the whole realm of natural religion. He declared that "the system of *natural religion*" is founded upon the hypothesis that man, by exercise of his natural reason, "is capable of arriving at the knowledge of God and the relations to him and one another." He proposed three affirmations in order "to establish the true line of demarcation in this matter" and as a basis to disprove this theory:

All nature proves the existence of God, once the idea of God is originated. All nations have derived their ideas of deity from tradition and not from "the *light of nature*." Man, in possession of but five senses "and with no other guide but the light of nature," could never have "originated the idea of Deity." [4]

However, he logically began with his third affirmation. This

1. *Campbell-Owen Debate*, I, 13 ff.; *Campbell-Purcell Debate*, p. 256. *The Millennial Harbinger*, 1844, pp. 145 ff.
2. *Campbell-Owen Debate*, II, 161, 170–171.
3. *Idem*, II, 248–249.
4. *Idem*, I, 133–134.

called for an analysis of the mental powers of man before accounting for the spiritual ideas which the human race possesses.

The Origin of Ideas

Campbell accepted the premises upon which the theory of knowledge of his day was often posited, namely, that all our original ideas are the result of sense perception and reflection. He would examine the relation of sensation, reflection, and imagination by appealing to the acknowledged principles of "the most reputable in the christian and infidel schools," Locke and Hume, for his authorities.[5]

He named and described the functions of the five senses of "the animal man"—seeing, hearing, tasting, smelling, and feeling—to show that "the Author of Nature" has wisely and benevolently ordered their formation and location; that each different sense organ is the only means of our receiving our material ideas in those respective areas of life; and located elsewhere they would be of little value. "Sensation" is what we call the "impression made upon the sensorium" by "the impulse of each particle upon the sense."

Our five senses are "the only avenues through which ideas of material objects can be derived to us." For example, it is evident "that a blind-born man can never acquire any ideas of colors" and "a deaf-born man" of sounds. Destitute of all five senses, a man would not only be "idiotic" but a "lump of insensible matter." Since these are the only media through which our ideas of sensible matter are derived, there "must be a model or archetype of each of these ideas presented to the appropriate sense."

Man's rational or intellectual powers are "necessarily circumscribed by the simple ideas" acquired through the exercise of our senses upon the material objects around us." The intellect must have simple ideas to work upon, just as a manufacturer must possess "raw material" before manufacturing it for the various usages of life.

The human mind begins such operations as soon as the raw material is presented to the senses. A superficial observer overlooks the "important acquisitions of knowledge made by the infant in the first few months after its birth." But the infant is busy

5. *Idem*, I, 49, 116.

learning to use its hands, move various parts of the body, and adjust its "different senses to their proper objects." [6]

The primary faculties of the mind are perception, memory or imagination, and consciousness. Perception is that intellectual power which enables us to discriminate between different sensations and become acquainted with things external. These ideas "become the objects of memory" or imagination which has exclusive reference to recalling things past. Consciousness has exclusive reference to things present, "like the internal eye, enabling me to take cognizance of my recollections, reasonings, and all the operations of my intellect such as reflecting, comparing, discriminating, and judging." These primary intellectual operations are all necessary in order to arrive at certain conclusions about the material things of the "five worlds" of sense.

This is the way we obtain our ideas of material things, Campbell contended. But we have "ideas of spiritual and eternal things." The question is, how did we get them?

On the basis of his premises, Campbell maintained that "the human intellect has no *creative* power." Man is as unable to create a basic original idea as he is to create a particle of material substance. He is utterly *"dependent upon the given"* in life for all the primary materials with which he works. Campbell based his argument upon an analogy from "a law of physics," namely, we can neither create nor destroy "one particle of matter."

Imagination to the intellectual world is "what mechanical ingenuity is to the natural world." Neither can have results "without a stock to begin upon." Man can change and modify the given stock by converting a "fluid into a solid" and a "shapeless piece of wood into a polished piece of furniture." Imagination has unbounded power, as Locke and Hume admit, but it can only abstract, compound, and combine qualities from basic ideas of objects already known.

Borrowing original ideas from known physical objects, imagination can abstract from one and add to another until it creates images "unlike anything existing in nature." The Sphinx is an example, or a picture of a tree with iron roots, silver leaves, and gold apples. But imagination would have to travel out of its province to originate the first idea of God, a First Cause, or spiritual ideas.

6. *Idem,* I, 138 ff.

But we have the idea of God as a "creative power." Historic evidences show that all nations originally had some "ideas of the existence of a Great First Cause." Yet these ideas "can have no archetype." Therefore, man must rely upon a creative power which is not his to account for the origin of basic spiritual ideas. Consequently, divine revelation is the proper source for all basic religious knowledge of a spiritual world and spiritual realities.

Without the light of revelation to afford these ideas not derivable through his senses, it would be as absurd as to expect a man without the organs of vision to have the ideas of color which are possessed by those who enjoy clear vision.[7]

Speech and Language

Another rational necessity of divine revelation, essential to Campbell's theory of knowledge, is the endowment and origin of human speech and language. He used this as a "practical application" of his argument that the human intellect is devoid of real creative power.

The faculty of speech, he said, is not only the power to give utterance to feelings but also to give names to things. He argued that speech is not "natural" to man but "purely imitative." It is socially acquired. Infants do not learn to speak naturally as they learn to see or smell. They can sigh, groan, cry, laugh, and give inarticulate expressions for passion or feeling which are natural, as to most animals. The difference between man and animal, in the realm of audible vocal expressions, is speech. Speech gives systematic expression and names to ideas or sentiments as the result of educational training and the "imitative faculty of man."

The problem of the origin of language and the fact that "all nations have concurred in declaring that speech was the gift of the gods" have baffled all philosophers without "referring it to God." Yet, Campbell claimed, it has been experimentally demonstrated that a person "who has never *heard* the articulations of the human voice can never speak," even though he may have the most perfect organs of speech.[8] If language were natural to man, all men would speak the same language. But experience shows that a child born in France or Italy will acquire the language of that respective country.

7. *Idem,* I, 48–50, 138–142, 149–150.
8. *Idem,* I, 150–152.

Campbell concluded that there can be no logical objection to Newton's observation that God has given us both reason and religion in the gift of speech.[9]

"Credulity"

Campbell described "credulity" as another power which is as inherent in the human mind as any other faculty. This power marks the proper line between "mere animal instinct and the intellectual progressiveness of man." Upon this innate principle the whole system of human education is built. It is the power of "receiving instruction upon the testimony of teachers." It is the greatest moral power of man.

Campbell argued that man is born a creature of faith. He is dependent upon society for all language and basic ideas. In this light, modern knowledge depends upon the experience of the human race. "Experience" is only "another name for memory." [10]

In short, Campbell contended that true philosophy or pure reason, at its best, could not explain the origin of either religious knowledge or human speech without allowing for the logical necessity of revelation. At its worst, it could not disprove the possibility of revelation.

Revelation

Campbell rejected the term *"revelation"* in the "vulgar sense." Revelation does not mean the Bible as such, for "there are a thousand historic facts narrated in the Bible, which it would be absurd to regard as immediate and direct *revelation* from the Almighty." To him, revelation is just what Thomas Paine says it is:

"A communication of something which the person to whom the thing revealed did not know before," and I add, could not otherwise know. . . . The term revelation, in its strict acceptation among intelligent christians, means nothing more or less than a Divine communication concerning spiritual and eternal things, a knowledge of which man could never have attained by the exercise of his reason upon material and sensible objects, for as Paul says, "Things which eye has not seen nor ear heard, neither

9. *Idem*, I, 152.
10. *Idem*, I, 108, 152, 162–163.

has it entered into the heart of man to conceive, has God revealed to us apostles, and we declare unto you. . . ." [11]

Not only do many religionists indiscriminately regard "the whole Bible" as a "revelation from God" but "some ignorant skeptics" have ridiculed it under the same illusion.[12] The discriminate appraisal is this: although the Bible is a record of divine revelations, all of its contents are not revelations. Thus, man with his natural reason can understand some things in the Scriptures, for much of the Bible is "addressed to intelligent, rational, moral beings."

"Ordinary information" discernible by natural reason is distinguished from "divine communications" in the Old Testament by such intimations as: *"The word of the Lord,"* or *"A message from the Lord came,"* or *"The Lord said."* However, in the New Testament, *"The Word,"* or *"The word of the Lord,"* or *"The Truth"* is "almost exclusively appropriated to *the testimony which God gave concerning the person and the mission of Christ."* It teaches the nature of man, develops that nature, and *reveals* the character and purpose of the Maker of the universe.[13]

In this sense, the Bible became both the vehicle and the symbol of modern man's reception of revelation. It was a proper symbol for the battle between the defenders and the opponents of revealed religion in the eighteenth and nineteenth centuries. However, Campbell resented either group's taking the literal position that every statement in the Bible is a revelation from God. After 1860 he still cautioned his followers against traveling that beaten path. "It is not true that 'all Scripture is given by inspiration of God'— It is palpably false. But 'all Scripture given by inspiration of God' is profitable. . . ." [14]

Divine revelation is received by human faith through the power of credulity possessed by all normal people. If we could find a deaf man perfectly in the state of nature who had never learned of an "invisible Creator" from human tradition, he would be a fit subject for experiment after being taught "the usage of speech." Several European and American societies have conducted the only experiments on people who were born deaf and whose hearing was restored. After being taught speech, they all

11. *Idem*, I, 141–142.
12. *Idem*, I, 142.
13. *The Millennial Harbinger*, 1832, p. 110.
14. *Idem*, 1864, pp. 79–81.

testified that they had not possessed any spiritual ideas previous to their acquisitions of hearing and speech.[15]

Although faith, reason, and experience concur for many a mile, faith must travel on where reason and experience cannot tread in receiving the divine truths of revelation. Campbell placed "a very important point of the argument here"—that we may conclude that "Paul's was an axiomatic truth: 'By *faith* we understand that the universe was made by the word of God.' " But he did not say "by *reason*, observe, but by *faith*." [16]

Upon this argument he posited the crux of the problem of man's arriving at a sure knowledge of divine things. Since it has been questioned as to whether he held such a position, we must examine this in more detail.

Faith and Reason

Even in his most extreme *Christian Baptist* days of appealing to reason and common sense, Campbell maintained that revelation and faith are prior to pure reason or philosophy in receiving spiritual knowledge. He insisted that, in spite of "all the improvements in philosophy for 18 centuries the world is no wiser with respect to God" than "when Paul lived." Neither Greece, Rome, nor Egypt, with all their philosophy, knew God. And, now, "the God that was *unknown in Athens* is unknown in New Harmony, and to all who have no other lights than what philosophy affords." A "striking proof" of this is shown by the people of the city of " 'Mental Independence' " who "are said to have the best *library* on this continent." Having "voluntarily extinguished the lights of supernatural revelation," they now frankly and honestly avow that there is no God, immortality, heaven, or hell. These are *"unknown* and unknowable" to them.

He admired the logic of their conclusion, for, as he had "often" said, "there is no stopping place between Deism and Atheism." [17]

In the Campbell-Rice debate in 1843, Campbell declared that it is conceded that our "religion is built upon faith." However, he did affirm that faith must be rational and that it is impossible without intelligible language. On account of that, an infant cannot have faith, regeneration, or baptism, for it does not need

15. *Campbell-Owen Debate*, I, 160–161.
16. *Idem*, I, 161.
17. *The Christian Baptist*, V, 47 ff. See also *idem*, II, 11 ff. and V, 52 ff.

faith. The assumption that an infant needs faith is "a figment of St. Augustine, adopted by Calvin, propogated in his Institutes, and adopted by his children."

But such statements should not be isolated from their contexts. Campbell was refuting what he conceived to be the irrationality of "regeneration" as "a mystic mystery." [18] He never identified faith with irrationalism or naturalism as such. Also it must be recalled that Campbell considered the source of "intelligible language" as a gift of God which man cannot create by the sole aid of his natural powers. Campbell, in this context, declared that "supernatural knowledge or knowledge of God" comes through faith as a consequence of hearing. That is to say, the word of God must be proclaimed before the ear of man can hear it.

In 1846 he wrote that "the Book of God is addressed to the human understanding." He said that frequently speculative philosophy creates doubts as to whether there is such a faculty as faith marking the "intellectual faculties" of man. But

Christian philosophers say that man has just as much power to believe testimony as he has to reason, to hear or to speak. . . . Well did Paul, therefore, reason when he said "Faith comes by hearing; and hearing from the (speech or) word of God." . . . Revelation, though originally in the form of oral testimony, is now altogether in the form of the written record! . . . Faith, indeed, is always but the conviction of the truth of testimony, whether that testimony be human or divine.[19]

Nevertheless, he declared that the human infant is born more helpless than other animals and, therefore, must walk by faith, for he "cannot walk by reason." He is born dependent, destitute of reason, observation, and experience.[20]

18. *Campbell-Rice Debate*, pp. 90 ff., 618–619; also *Campbell-Owen Debate*, I, 195 ff.

19. *The Millennial Harbinger*, 1846, pp. 73–75. Note that Campbell uses "intellectual faculties" as synonymous with "powers of man," meaning in this context the power of man as a rational being to have faith and not meaning that man's reason alone can attain a knowledge of God apart from revelation, which is prior to that reason.

20. *Idem*, 1846, pp. 76 ff. Note the apparent inconsistency between this position and the one which Campbell maintains on pp. 97–98, n. 18. When thinking in terms of the doctrine of infant damnation, which he rejects, and immersion, which he upholds, Campbell is willing to conclude that an infant cannot have faith. But, when thinking in terms of general faith which is com-

The power of faith is in the truth believed. The power of faith is the power of truth. It is not eating that sustains or destroys human life. *It is what is eaten.* Some eat and live—others eat and die. Some believe and are saved—others believe and are damned. . . . *Salvation is not in the act of the believing, but in the object or proposition that is believed.*

That truth, object, or proposition to be believed by faith is the Gospel which is "ministered now by the Holy Spirit" from heaven —"Grace." [21]

Campbell had another conviction in placing faith and revelation above the natural reason of man. Some of the essential spiritual ideas which revelation and faith alone afford are *utterly* beyond human comprehension, especially regarding the compound of attributes of God, the explanation of "the *why* or the *how*" of "this natural machinery" which God operates, and the relation of the Creator to creature.[22] Campbell confessed that there are "many seeming incongruities" to man in "our beau ideals of perfection in nature, providence, and redemption" which we cannot comprehend. We have "surmounted some;" others we may not. Although the finite "can never comprehend nor apprehend the infinite," it is "the only fixture" on which "cultivated reason and educated imagination can find a moment's repose." Yet the Bible assumes this "as its first and fundamental article," whereas "human science and philosophy beg the question when they begin." [23]

In 1844 Campbell attacked rationalism as the most dangerous feature in the church.

---

mon to all of mankind, he is willing to assert that the infant can and must have faith. The distinction which Campbell so frequently makes between saving faith, as spiritual, and general faith, as natural, does not help him at this point: how can the infant have even general faith, if he cannot have saving faith? In fact, his distinction increases the difficulty of the problem which he does not face squarely. Similarly, he does not really come to terms with the question as to when the infant becomes rational and mature enough for saving faith.

21. *Idem*, 1846, p. 80. The proposition to be believed does not mean a cold rationalism in Campbell, although it often carries those words. Conviction, confidence, and trust are as important as understanding in receiving revelation.

22. *Campbell-Owen Debate*, I, 131; see also *The Christian Baptist*, II, 11–16, IV, 50–51; *Campbell-Rice Debate*, p. 797; *The Millennial Harbinger*, 1843, pp. 11 ff., 1844, p. 547.

23. *Idem* 1856, pp. 307, 481 ff. See also *idem*, 1864, pp. 146, 480 ff.

Reason is exalted a judge over revelation, and its power to *comprehend* made a test of the sound in doctrine, and the pure in faith. We have no objection to reason in religion when its use is not perverted. . . . But why should we reject anything in God's revelation because we cannot comprehend it? [24]

Upon surveying Campbell's lifetime view of the relation of faith and reason, we can only conclude that he made reason a necessary servant of faith and of revelation in the quest for religious knowledge. Faith is rational in so far as it can comprehend divine truth. But faith goes beyond reason, although never contrary to it.

Reason has a humble place in Campbell's epistemology, as it does in John Locke's. Reasonableness, to both, allows for mystery. Cold rationalism is not implied in their writings when taken as a whole.

Experience and Revelation

One of the most systematic efforts which Campbell made concerning the relation of reason and experience to faith is in a dialogue entitled "Reason Examined by Interrogatories." "Reason" affirms that everything that "God has spoken is true: for '*God is truth.*'" The province of "Reason" is "simply to decide all pretensions to truth; but a 'thus says the Lord' settles all debates and is absolutely authoritative in every question concerning the spiritual and eternal world."

The "Querist" asked "Reason" the climaxing question of the dialogue: "Is it not alleged by thee that God has always spoken in accordance with thee—that revelation and reason perfectly harmonize?"

"Reason" replies:

When men speak of revelation and reason according and harmonizing, they cannot mean a faculty of the human soul: for what sense is there in affirming that natural light and the eye harmonize and accord? . . . Reason is the eye of the soul to which the light of revelation is addressed. But the babbling world, perhaps, mean that revelation and experience agree; which is true just as far as we have experience; but as revelation immeasurably transcends our experience, it can only be affirmed that so far as human ex-

24. *Idem* 1844, pp. 145–147. As samples of other accounts of faith over reason, see *Campbell-Owen Debate*, I, 85 ff., 141; *The Millennial Harbinger*, 1856, pp. 214 ff., 1857, pp. 349 ff., 1860, pp. 481 ff., 1852, p. 139, 1855, pp. 42–45.

perience reaches, it accords with revelation; and hence it is fairly to be presumed that experience will continue to agree or correspond with revelation until the terms "revelation" and "experience" will be terms of equal value, and cover the same area of thought.

The improper use of terms, the confounding of words and phrases, is an error as common among sceptics as among christians, and it is equally pernicious to them as to any other class of reasoners. The phrases, *"above reason," "contrary to reason," "accordant to reason,"* when fairly tested, mean no more among those who think, than *above or beyond my experience, contrary to my experience, or accordant to my experience.* He, therefore, who says he believes nothing above his reason, nor contrary to his reason, simply says he believes nothing above his experience or contrary to it; and therefore revelation to him is wholly incredible.[25]

The relation of experience to faith was hotly contested in the Campbell-Owen debate. Campbell argued that Owen and anyone else must see Christianity in terms of the light of the total work of the God of nature exhibited in the intrinsic evidences displayed in both the material volume of nature and the sacred volume of the Scriptures. Owen's objections to Christianity, he said, were similar to the objections of the uninformed and illiterate who deny the mobility of the sun.

They reply, "We see the sun move; we see it rise in one place and set in another; and if the earth moved round the sun, the position of our plantations and houses must necessarily be shifted; your theory about the earth and sun, then is contrary to our experience and observation." [26]

Later, he quoted David Hume at length to show that Owen's objection to revelation is the same as the former's, namely, "that every man's personal experience is to be made the measure and standard of his faith." Without having seen a whole, he cannot believe there is one. We cannot have any experience of the future; how, then, do we learn that "the future will resemble the past?" Only the Christian can speak of the future with any certain knowledge; for here "the infidels' candle goes out" unless he obtains "some oil from the lamp of revelation."

Thus he charged, "Hume and other Free Thinkers preach *im-*

25. *Idem*, 1832, pp. 97–100.
26. *Campbell-Owen Debate*, I, 183.

plicit faith, and warn their followers of the danger of consulting reason." [27]

In brief, Campbell believed that reason, faith, and experience concur for many a mile in the quest for possible spiritual knowledge. Then faith must travel alone for a certain knowledge of spiritual things. Faith depends upon the initiative of God to afford man divine truths which cannot be attained and comprehended by natural reason and human experience apart from such revelation. Revelation is a communication or message from the Deity to man above and yet within the possibility of man's certain knowledge, once he has made the venture of faith.

Revelation and "Bible Facts"

Even if "the Bible facts did not support our reasoning" for the necessity of revelation, it would be as "logical and demonstrative" as any reasoning "upon an abstract speculation." However, the Bible does support our reason through its evidence of facts and we are "not compelled to rest the truth of this reasoning upon metaphysical deductions." [28]

At this point in his argument, Campbell sought to establish a foolproof conception of revelation. This effort was to explain the exact manner in which the truths of revelation appeared historically in terms of the origin of human speech and spiritual ideas on the basis of the Old Testament.

As a whole, this might appear to be a departure from his own principle against trying to explain the how of divine operations. He constantly objected to ecclesiastical speculations to account for the manner in which divine operations take place. In theory, he maintained that the "matter" or truth of revelation is more important than "the manner" in which it occurs and some Christian truth is beyond human reason and comprehension. However, he avoided a break in theory, in his own mind at least, by declaring that he was appealing to "the Bible facts" and records of events written by religious historians instead of human speculations about facts and events. [29]

His argument was twofold: first, the actual needs of man in terms of his dependent nature from birth through maturity.

27. *Idem,* I, 246–248.
28. *Idem,* I, 152.
29. *Idem,* I, 128 ff., 150 ff.; *The Christian Baptist,* II, 15–16.

Frequently he asked Owen if the "first man" were created an "infant" or an "adult." Campbell claimed that more is "couched" in this philosophical "speculation" than the "superficial thinker might realize." If the first pair came into the world as adolescents, they must have had knowledge of their origin when they first saw light; but if infants "they could never have reached maturity," for they would have "perished for the lack of nurture." Consequently, they must have been adults.[30]

Second, plain facts in the Bible support our personal experience of these needs and relations in society without speculation. The Bible describes the first man as an adult. He could remember his origin and conversations with his Creator. It is natural that the origins of things would rank first in society's traditions before writing and reflective thought appeared; for, as soon as infants become rational, they want to know what happened before they got into the world. These stories were handed down through the aid of man's "native bias," *credulity*.

Any one can tell that the first religious historians did not try to explain *"how"* revelations took place philosophically. They merely told what their ancestors had *"heard"* and *"seen."* These accounts are in *"narrative"* form, not in the form of "theory." The "first philosophers" who theorized upon this subject demonstrated that "their conclusions were wiser than their premises." That is, they possessed "previous information on the subject which they did not learn from reason." [31]

As neat as his method was, Campbell could not avoid interpreting the Bible by inference.

The Bible tells us most emphatically that the first colloquies ever held upon this earth were between the great Creator and our first ancestors, *viva voce*. The book of Genesis tells us that the first pair *talked* with God; hence the inference from the fact, that God first *taught* man to speak, is, that the art of speaking is not native and inherent in the family of man. . . .[32]

God tested "Adam's skill in speech" by requiring him to name the animals in Paradise; "and we are told that Adam's nomenclature was correct." Whether Hebrew was the first language spoken or not "is more of a matter of philosophic curiosity than of

30. *Campbell-Owen Debate*, I, 106–107, also 87.
31. *Idem*, I, 88, 98 ff., 142.
32. *Idem*, I, 152.

importance to our argument," for all languages can be traced to the same source.[33]

After man had learned the usage of speech as a gift from God, he needed revelation in order to learn a religious vocabulary. God had to teach man the elementary spiritual ideas. He taught this "new language" in terms of "symbols" or "pictures" such as the altar, the lamb, and the priest.[34]

However, Campbell could not rely upon this particular explanation of the manner in which revelation took place as the crux of his defense of revealed religion, for natural religionists did not grant those premises.[35] Thus, as a whole, he sought to show how they had borrowed and corrupted religious knowledge from revelation through the Bible directly or through the Christian tradition indirectly. He met them on their own premises to show that their own volume of nature, natural reason, intuition, or pretenses to "innate ideas" were inadequate to explain the origin of the basic religious ideas which they possessed.

Moreover, his burden was to prove that man is by nature a creature of faith—dependent upon a supreme being for his origin, his true moral and social obligations, his elementary religious knowledge, and his tendency to transcend the material world. Therefore the universe and man are creations, not creators.

33. *Ibid.*
34. *Idem,* I, 153–154, 196–197.
35. There is little indication, outside of the Owen debate, that Campbell deals much with this *specific manner* in which the revelation originally took place in refuting natural religionists. The more rationalistic type of supernaturalists majored upon detailed attempts to prove the manner in which original revelation occurred.

CHAPTER VIII

OTHER THEORIES OF KNOWLEDGE

ALEXANDER CAMPBELL did not confine to glittering generalities his critique of pure reason and naturalistic assumptions in theories of knowledge. He dealt with specific types of sophisticated and unsophisticated naturalisms in their nineteenth-century settings.

He divided them into two groups. The first involved the traditional trio of "Skeptics, Deists and Atheists" who were the successors of movements from the Enlightenment. The second included their new guises in terms of secularized movements, emphases in religious denominations, and new "sciences" and "philosophies" which tended toward natural religion in claims of knowledge and devotion.

He was convinced that, in spite of the "improvements of modern science," no systems of thought can afford certain religious knowledge without divine revelation. From Socrates, Plato, and Cicero on they confess "their own ignorance" and need "for further instruction." They all deal with probabilities, beginning with "a perhaps," proceeding with "a *may be*," and ending with "*a perchance*." [1]

Surveying them as a whole, Campbell distinguished between sincere and insincere modern skeptics.[2] The sincere are honest seekers after truth by speculation. The insincere are the ignorant and "imprudent infidels" who are in moral rebellion against God and whose prejudices against Christianity are dishonest. He approached sincere skeptics with sympathy but insincere skeptics with disdain.

1. *Campbell-Owen Debate*, I, 59–60.
2. Campbell used the word "skeptic" in several ways. In the strict sense it meant the honest doubter of religious truth but neither a believer nor unbeliever in deism or atheism as such. Loosely used it meant any ancient or modern objector to Christian revelation. In another sense he confined the skeptic to the historic context of one who is associated with the deists and infidels of the Enlightenment but not identical with them.

A typical example of Campbell's approach to sincere skeptics occurred at Tammany Hall in 1833. He spoke where the Skeptics had their meetings because Robert Dale Owen and Miss Frances Wright had "made great inroads on the kingdom of the clergy" in New York. He congratulated them for choosing their name, for such a philosophy could not properly "affirm or deny the existence of God or the truth of revealed religion." No living person could say that he knows Christianity is a fraud or that he believes the Gospel is false, for no evidence from his senses or contradictory testimony supports such assumptions.

He acknowledged that many skeptics are "honest men and good citizens." But in the larger "sense of the word *honest,* comprehending our dues to God, to man, and to ourselves" he doubted whether there is "an honest Sceptic in the human race." [3]

Three main arguments were given in defense of revealed religion. He admitted that there are "incomprehensibilities" in arriving at the truth of the "divine authenticity" of Christianity but these are no objections to the truth of religion. The same principle would cause us to reject "Newtonian" and "all sciences of the universe," for they are based essentially upon "certain recondite and abstract principles" which are incomprehensible. Man cannot comprehend himself, "much less anything above himself, or anything out of himself." Both nature and religion are "comprehensible and incomprehensible."

His second point was that there can be no objection to Christianity's being founded upon miracles, "for so is every system of skepticism." When we affirm that nature existed before man, we cannot account for the origin of man without a miracle at some time, for nature does not continue to produce new men. The difference between Christians and skeptics is that the latter believe without testimony or evidence. His third point contended that Christianity is addressed to faith rather than reason, for faith is a "better guide than reason." [4]

Campbell was impatient with insincere skeptics. In 1831 he upbraided the "barefaced falsehoods" of the "atheistical doctor" Samuel Underhill of Ohio. Underhill had published an article

3. Campbell relates that a "number of Christians being present, we commenced by singing, '*I'm not asham'd to own my Lord, Nor to defend his cause, Maintain the honor of his word, The Glory of his cross.*'" *The Millennial Harbinger,* 1834, p. 38–39.

4. *Idem,* 1834, pp. 38–40.

accusing Campbell of "selling a blind Negro child in the night, and refusing to make restitution." Campbell felt that Underhill was "capable of any species of twistification" after reading the latter's statement that Campbell could believe in "the Holy Ghost begetting a child on a virgin, and of that child cursing a fig-tree for not bearing fruit in the winter, and sending six thousand devils into two thousand hogs." [5]

Deism

Alexander Campbell claimed that "there is not a *rational* Deist in the universe. Of this subject I am a master; if of no other." [6] He maintained that deists were the chief question-beggers among natural religionists who are pretenders to the throne of reason. In explaining the origin of religious knowledge on the basis of nature, they must assume that nature is an effect and not the first cause. It is as logical to find "penknives growing on apple-trees as Lord Herbert's doctrine in the mind of a savage." [7]

Particularly unreasonable, declared Campbell, are the boasts of Thomas Paine and others that the *"Word of God"* is easily intelligible from a reading of the volume of nature. In spite of their disclaiming any need for a prophet, an interpreter, or a *written* commentary to explain the volume of nature, there "are more versions of the volume of nature than of the volume of revelation." Ancient and modern nations have come to many different conclusions after following those premises. Rome and Athens not only believed in a "multiplication of gods" but affixed infamous crimes and characters to them. The Grecian states had so many gods that a wit once said, *"It is more easy to find a god than a man in Athens!"* [8]

Soon after the Reformation, Campbell related, some Italian and French skeptics "assumed the honorable title of *Deists*" and agreed upon three things: 1. To profess no system of religion but to oppose Christianity. 2. To contend for the existence of one God. 3. To follow "what they called 'the light of nature.'" Yet they could find no agreement on the last two principles. When Dr. Clarke classified "four grand classes of Deists or of deistical

5. *Idem,* 1831, pp. 434–435.
6. *The Christian Baptist,* IV, 40–41.
7. *Campbell-Owen Debate,* I, 118.
8. *Idem,* I, 61.

writers," they, too, agreed in acknowledging one Supreme God but disagreed upon everything else.

Campbell cited the five points of Lord Herbert's book, *De Veritate,* as an attempt to give system to skepticism in order to "form a universal religion for all mankind, predicated on what he calls 'reason and the light of nature.'" But the "head of the English fraternity" was led to publish it in the seventeenth century "by a miracle, as he represents it!" [9]

Campbell enjoyed contrasting the deists and atheists by quoting Paine and Mirabaud to "see how these skeptics of the two schools handle each other." A notable atheist asks if there is any miracle in any religion "more impossible to be believed, than that of the *creation,* or of the eduction from nothing? Is there a *mystery* more difficult to be comprehended than a God impossible to be conceived; and whom, however, it is necessary to admit!" A notable deist asserts that the only idea man can "affix to the name of God, is that of a *first cause,* the cause of all things. And incomprehensibly difficult as it is for man to conceive what a first cause is, he arrives at a belief of it, from the tenfold greater difficulty of disbelieving it."

Paine affirms that "*there is one true theology*—and one unadulterated revelation of God—viz.: the Universe,' whereas Mirabaud declares that 'All theology is false.'" But, said Campbell, the height of their contradictions is Paine's assertion that "'The belief of a God, so far from having anything of a mystery in it, is of all beliefs the most easy: because it arises to us out of necessity.'" And Mirabaud's inquiry, "'Can there be a mystery more difficult to be comprehended than a God?'" [10]

Another problem of knowledge which the deists cannot answer is how evil got into the world. Campbell asserted that "Deism makes God the author of moral evil as well as moral good."

Campbell published a series of articles in 1826 entitled "To Mr. D.—A Skeptic" in reply to a letter from a worried young man who had sought a change of heart within the Methodist Church because of "the death-bed injunctions of a beloved mother." Upon failing to receive "the Divine favor" from his Bible readings, prayers, and participation in church services, he was led to rethink the subject of revealed religion and "to doubt the divinity of the Bible."

9. *Idem,* I, 61–62.
10. *Idem,* I, 63 ff.

The young man reasoned that if the greatest degree of happiness were the design of the Almighty, he must have failed, for according to the Bible the majority of mankind must be forever damned. He thought, "as the Deity was the cause of all things, he was responsible for all things, especially for evil as he possessed a greater power to prevent it than the *immediate cause,* and if so, he could not punish any of his creatures with *external* misery." If man is as accountable for his actions as the Bible records, then free will would be a curse to man rather than a blessing. The troubled skeptic concluded that if there is a place for reward and punishment, he could do nothing about it for his destiny had been foreseen anyway.

Campbell replied that the young skeptic was "too *rational* to become a downright enthusiast" in the Methodist society and "not rational in the right place in examining the evidences of the christian religion." Although not all Methodists are enthusiasts, "there is more religion in the *blood* than in the heart or head of those who begin in the flesh and think to end in the spirit." [11]

However, Campbell observed that the young man admitted the main points of deism. Although it would be an "irrational conclusion for him to become one, he might easily become a Universalist. He demanded the evidence for his conclusions of the self-existence of an Eternal Creator," immortality, and a future state of rewards, "if not of punishments." All of these are truths of which deists boast but they are really borrowed from the Bible and not derived from their own reason. Theirs is circle-thinking. "They prove that there is a creator, because things are created; and they prove that things are created, because there is a creator. Sagacious doctors! . . ." [12]

Campbell declared that if the possibility of evil were excluded, God could not be the Governor but only the Creator of the universe. If man were infallible as a creature, he would not be a rational being capable of obedience or disobedience; he would act like a mill wheel with no virtue or vice. Sheer power that is not moral power in subduing evil would not be able to prevent the recurrence of the same thing; a display of more than physical energy is needed.

When you talk of the deity being *responsible,* you lose sight of the essential attribute of Deity. A Supreme can neither be re-

11. *The Christian Baptist,* IV, 38–40, 79.
12. *Idem,* IV, 40–41.

sponsible nor accountable; for responsibility and accountability imply dependence. . . . Moral evil exists as sure as we exist. From all that we can reason on its origin, nothing can be concluded against the divinity of the Bible. The Bible is the only book in the world which pretends to give us a history of the origin, progress and cure. . . .[13]

The Bible shows that moral evil is rooted in the act of man's disobedience to the law or will of God. But deism makes God as directly the author of moral evil as moral good.

Campbell illustrated his argument with "Inquisitas," who was told as a child that there is one God who creates and governs all things. Yet he observed that peach and apple trees blossomed and had fruit but were destroyed. The problems arose: How could God bother to send a favorable south wind for so long in bringing forth the blossoms and fruit and then destroy them all in one night with the north wind? How could the same God make his brothers, sisters, and others want apples and peaches all the year round? How could any but a *cruel* God allow his little birds to freeze to death in their cages? Why did not the whole earth have the same comfortable climate and fertility? Informed of the death of an idiot whose brothers and sisters were normal, Inquisitas asked why one member of the family was "punished" and others were "blessed." On the basis of the data which Inquisitas had, what could reason say about the character of God? Without the aid of revelation, how could he tell that God is the wisest, the most powerful, and the most impartial being? Finally, Inquisitas questioned *"whether there is any such thing as a reasonable being!"* In thus trying to reason about the character of God, he found that there is no character of man; "but that was the central point of the contradictions."

Campbell concluded, "Every system of scepticism founded upon the Divine attributes, and of religion at variance with the Bible facts, is a mere spider's web woven out of its own bowels, and designed only to catch flies." [14]

In his *Christian Baptist* attack upon Presbyterianism, Campbell charged that Calvinism is another form of deism or natural religion. He claimed that Calvinism is founded upon the "doctrine of innate ideas" which John Locke exploded.[15]

13. *Idem*, IV, 43, 76–78.
14. *Idem*, IV, 50–53.
15. *Idem*, III, 4.

In this light, in 1825, he described the "new crusade" of the Presbyterians concerning Transylvania University as an effort "to be in the president's chair or perish in the attempt."

The Presbyterian Luminary says that Deism, that is NATURAL RELIGION, is taught there. But is not natural religion, or Deism taught in every college under the control of the Presbyterians? . . . I am prepared to show that the *Calvinistic doctrine of natural religion* is pure Deism, and I would just as soon have a child taught Deism by Michael Servetus as by John Calvin. The Socinian hypothesis I have repeatedly declared to be a poor and wretched scheme. And as long as *natural religion* or Deism is taught in our colleges, I care not who teaches it; if any preference, let him teach it who teaches it with less injury, that is, less bigotry. . . .[16]

Attacking the Westminster Confession of Faith, Campbell charged that the whole defense of creeds is based upon the "Deism, or natural religion of John Calvin" when it is argued that the adoption of a creed is not only lawful and expedient but indispensably necessary. If any church professes to have authority from God to form creeds without divine revelation to support it, it is substituting its own speculations even of the Scriptures themselves "from nature."

He cited from Calvin's *Institutes* regarding the human mind as being "rationally endowed with the knowledge of God." In opposition to this Campbell declared that "the word of God says that 'the world by wisdom knew not God.'" And "so say the history of the world" and the conscious experience of every individual regarding the doctrine of innate ideas which Locke exploded. This doctrine roots in pagan philosophy incorporated in the Christian religion through "scholastic theology and mystic divinity." However, true philosophy and the Bible prove that revelation is essential to religion itself. Although men are "born with innate capacities or susceptibility for acquiring the idea or knowledge of God," "supernatural revelation is 'necessary' for so enlightening" that capacity.[17]

In 1827 Campbell received a letter from a reader of his letters addressed to "Mr. D., A Skeptic." He thought it was strange that Campbell should take the position that the possibility of the existence of God cannot be known apart from the Bible; and that

16. *Idem*, II, 164.
17. *Idem*, III, 2–4.

the infallible, all-wise Creator should make the most fallible kind of evidence, namely, testimony, the only possible vehicle through which he can be known to his creatures to the exclusion of the work of his own hand—the Book of Nature. He cited John Locke to show that man is capable of arriving at the knowledge of God by intuitive certainty. Human reason leads man to the knowledge that he himself exists as a rational creature, that something cannot be produced out of nothing, and that our eternal source of all power and the original of all being must exist.[18]

Campbell admitted the infallible certainty of intuition but denied that it is of greater importance than fallible or infallible evidence derived from our senses or from testimony. He declared:

Locke and other philosophers who have rejected the doctrine of innate ideas and who have traced all our simple ideas to sensation and reflection, have departed from their own reasonings when they have attempted to show that, independent of supernatural revelation, a man could know that there is an eternal first cause uncaused.[19]

The error of such reasoning is that they begin with the idea of God in their minds, then "fondly imagine" that they have acquired it. The first logical effort would be to show, without the idea of the First Cause or God in their own minds, how it could be attained.

Alexander Campbell did not set natural and revealed *theology* over against each other, except to establish the priority of the latter over the former. He held that once the idea of God is suggested to our minds through revelation, there is a legitimate place for *natural theology*—but not *natural* religion.[20] In natural theology, he explained, the textbook is nature or the universe; in revealed theology the textbook is the Bible. The Bible "puts a tongue into nature, and enables her to speak intelligibly." The Bible and nature "are God's two grand witnesses and preachers to the human race." [21]

18. *Idem*, V, 49–51.
19. *Idem*, V, 52–56.
20. We shall discuss his distinction between *natural theology* and *natural religion* later.
21. *The Millennial Harbinger*, 1853, p. 285–286.

Atheism or Materialism

Campbell felt that atheists or materialists, like deists, cannot agree upon any system of nature, human nature, or morality, for they have no fixed principles by which to go. Citing "Cudworth's *systems Intellectuale*," he found four distinct sects of ancient atheists: disciples of Anaximander, "who attributed the formation of everything to matter destitute of feeling"; atomists, or disciples of Democritus, "who attributed everything to the concurrence of atoms"; stoical atheists, who admitted blind nature but acted after certain laws; and disciples of Strato, who attributed life to matter. Arstippus, Theodorus, the atheist, Bion, Pyrrho, and Epicurus added their bits to the other diversities.

Campbell listed as "atheistic" such modern writers "as Spinoza, Hobbes, Vannini." He commented that Spinoza taught that there is but one *substance* in nature and that all souls are modifications of this one substance—that there is but one *being* and one nature producing "by an immanent act" all those called "creatures." He said that Spinoza's deity "is both agent and patient, creator and creature."

Campbell noted that one of the most ancient pantheists, Orpheus, called the world the body of God and made the whole universe one divine animal. He thought that Aristotle was much of that opinion, holding that God and matter are coeternal and conceiving between them a union similar to that which exists between the body and the soul. And polytheists went to such extremes as to deify dead men, animals, and vegetables, ascribing to them "attributes which belong to the Creator alone." Paul is still right by saying, "professing themselves to be philosophers they become *fools*." [22]

Campbell declared that atheism is full of mysteries, such as: the origin of matter; the principle of motion in matter; the specific origin of the earth; the origin of man; the elements of bodies; the nature of magnetism; the nature of attraction; the nature of repulsion; the nature of cohesion; the nature of elasticity; the nature of electricity; the destiny of any part or of the whole of the universe; and the relation of will, belief, knowledge, faith, and opinion to one another. Other inexplicable mysteries of atheism are: why man is interested in his origin; why he believes "himself a privileged being in nature"; whether the first parents of

22. *Campbell-Owen Debate*, I, 64–65, 75, 89 ff.

the human race had parents; whether man originally was like his present species; whether matter and motion originally had the same powers which they now possess; and accounting for the origin of the idea of God which is so universal among men.

But *"the great mystery of mysteries* of atheism"* is the problem of regularity in motion which is assumed as only a property of matter. Why should motion have acted so irregularly as to form man at one time and so regularly ever since?

The atheist, Campbell maintained, is actually the most credulous of all people, for he has to "confess as much ignorance and to believe more mysteries" than the Christian. He has to "teach, admit, and contend for a number of absurd mysteries" which are "much greater than any taught in the most corrupt schools of pagan priests." [23]

Of all professed atheists Campbell particularly stressed Mirabaud. He resented Mirabaud's explanation that "savages invented the idea and name of God and spiritual existences"; that savages invented all the religions of the world which make men labor incessantly for unknown objects to which they attach great importance and never dare "to examine cooly." [24]

In his objection Campbell declared that there are only two ways in which ideas can be communicated: either through the presentation of the archetype which those ideas represent, or "by *speech* describing the thing to be revealed or communicated by something already known." If understood, these premises would be as decisive proof that the name and idea of God first entered the human family by revelation as the discovery of a gold or silver coin among savages would prove that they are the finders rather than the makers of the respective coin. Mirabaud might as well assert that savages made the first gold coin without fire, mold, and metal.

Moreover, upon this theory, one would expect to find that the nearer man approached the savage state, the more exact would be his views of all religious relations, duties, and obligations. If this were true the converse must be true: the greater the philosopher, the less the saint; the more civilized, the less religious is man.

Campbell charged that Mirabaud requires faith, too, to believe and adore his system of nature. It is a hard faith to believe his assertions that we must not doubt the power of nature, the im-

23. *Idem,* I, 78–81, 90 ff.
24. *Idem,* I, 89, 154.

mutability of its laws, the self-existent cause of everything, and that we must listen to her voice "of which reason is the faithful interpreter."

The infatuated sage tells you that you must believe without evidence; that Nature never errs—even when mysteries impenetrable hide her operations. And you must worship and adore her goodness, just because she is blind and cannot see you—because she is deaf and cannot hear you! But to suppose that Nature is either rational, good, or kind, would be most abhorent to all his philosophy. *Blind Fate* and *inexorable Necessity* is all that is to be feared, loved, adored, hated, or what you please, you owe her nothing; and, after all, she is a "pure abstract being," who has no existence save in the brain of such crazed philosophers! *Sic transit gloria philosophiae!* [25]

The Hybrid: Owenism

Without unnecessary repetition, it is important to notice Campbell's analysis of the real origin of Owen's ideas to prove that the "human faculties" cannot originate "anything new."

He traced the basic principles of Owen's social system to the influence of Christianity in Scotland. The Christian benevolence of Mr. Dale, Owen's father-in-law, prompted him to invent his cooperative system of educating and caring for children. Owen saw Dale's system in operation over forty years ago in Scotland.

In his attempt to improve the animal man and his mental endowments upon "scientific principles," Owen had a forerunner in Dr. James Graham, a philanthropic physician who was born in Edinburgh. Graham administered relief in needy causes in travels over England and America. After realizing a fortune, he settled in London about 1775. There, said Campbell, he erected institutions for the gratification of "the votaries of pleasure" under the pretense of teaching both sexes "the art of preventing barrenness, and of propagating a much more strong, beautiful, active, healthy, wise, and virtuous race of human beings, than the present puny, insignificant, foolish, peevish, vicious, and nonsensical race of christians; who quarrel, fight, bite, devour, and cut one another's throats about they know not what." As advertised in the London papers, the names of the institutions were a Temple of Hymen and a Temple of Health.

25. *Idem,* I, 89–91, 154.

By 1781 Graham returned to Edinburgh and announced that he was a teacher sent from God

to announce the millennium, the second coming of Christ, and the final consumation [*sic.*] of all things. He styled himself the servant of the Lord, O.W.L., i.e. as he explained it, Oh Wonderful Love. He commenced a new era, dating his bills, "1st, 2nd, and 3d days of the first month of the New Jerusalem." But before the commencement of the second month he was constrained to confess "he felt the devil, the world, and flesh too strong for him, and therefore supposed the Lord must look out for another forerunner of his second coming." [26]

Campbell enjoyed relating that Graham fell in love with the "celebrated Mrs. Macauley, the historian" and proposed to her. If the lady had not accidentally discovered that the doctor already had one wife, she would have accepted his hand. Unruffled by the discovery, the good doctor claimed that the ardor of his passion for her had made him forget that *circumstance!* He died in 1794 after being placed in a lunatic asylum.

Besides these models in Scotland, Campbell reported, Moravian and other societies were practicing types of community enterprises which could have strengthened Owen's convictions. Also, we know from Owen's testimony that he attended church regularly in his youth.

Owen may not have borrowed directly the ideas on matrimony of Godwin's *Political Justice* but they were common topics of the day. Owen had the moral courage to take conclusions which Godwin feared from his premises. Owen's skepticism came from the popular ideas and impressions which carried over from the "skeptical philosophers" of the French Revolutionary infidel regime.[27]

New Forms of Theism or Deism

As a whole, Alexander Campbell classed both Universalism and Unitarianism as new forms of deism and theism in opposition to revealed religion.

In 1855, in an address at the "Hopkinsville Female Institution" in Nashville, Tennessee, he asserted that no "more can the deistical, theistical, or atheistical philosopher" know his origin,

26. *Idem,* I, 131, 162, 180, 188; *idem,* II, 136–137.
27. *Idem,* II, 132–133.

his relations to the universe, or his destiny in it, than the eye can see itself, without being educated in Biblical literature.

Society is of sublime origin. Deists, Theists and Unitarians, cannot comprehend it. The reason is, their God is a mere solitary personality, without anything kindred in him or beyond him. He is the mere *Great Spirit* of the North American savage. But the God of the Bible has society in his very nature, developed, too, in three distinct personalities. Society is not possible in absolute unity. Society is possible, but not perfect, in a mere duality. There must be I, Thou, and He, in the essential idea of society.[28]

Two years previously Campbell opined that "Elder Jesse B. Ferguson," in his *Christian Magazine* and church in Nashville, has presented views on the future state of those who die in sins that are "essentially Unitarian and Universalian—or, in other words, Deistical." Ferguson would find a more cordial brotherhood in Dr. Clapp of New Orleans "and in his view, a much more pious, enlightened, free and charitable paternity, in Boston or Cambridge, than amongst us." [29]

Campbell declared that Dr. Clapp is the only preacher in the United States with whom he would refuse to commune. He would as "cordially commune" with Thomas Paine, Lord Holingbroke, Volney, or Voltaire. We are not simply deists, or theists, but Christians. We have the same theology which the patriarchs and Jews had—but, under the government of Christ, we have a Christology, too.[30]

At this time, Campbell was having trouble with ministers in his own communion who had theological leanings similar to those of Universalists and Unitarians. He was anxious to repudiate orthodox charges that his followers and he were tending toward Universalism and Unitarianism.

In 1830 in an article, "Universalism and Atheism, as Expected," he observed that some prominent Universalists have announced "their attachments to the doctrines of *Frances Wright, R. D.*

---

28. *The Millennial Harbinger*, 1855, pp. 146 ff.

29. *Idem*, 1853, p. 515. In 1854 Campbell ironically remarked that he was willing to admit that there is much of the Bible that is human but Ferguson made the mistake of telling *how* much is of human agency, namely, that Universalism is more ancient than Christianity and was born of the Devil in the garden when the Devil tempted Adam and Eve to eat by saying, *"You shall not surely die." Idem*, 1854, p. 414.

30. *Idem*, 1854, pp. 162, 550.

Owen & Co." He cited the example of Mr. O. A. Brownson, "a Universalist preacher and editor of the Gospel Advocate," who had abandoned his editorship of the Universalist paper to become the corresponding editor of the *Free Inquirer*, published by Robert Dale Owen, the son of Campbell's former "sceptical antagonist," in New York.[31]

In 1831 Campbell charged the Universalist paper, the *Star of the West*, with going "beyond the Deists—beyond the Theists" to become "almost as *liberal* as *Robert Dale Owen* of the Free Inquirer." Its facetious attitude toward the fall of man and *"apple-sinners"* seemed more like Voltaire or Paine or the "Editor of the Free Inquirer than a believer in Jesus Christ." [32]

Later he quoted the editors' reply that were Campbell to convince them that their views would lead into atheism or deism, they would prefer their system to orthodoxy. Campbell responded, "No wonder, then that the spirit and efforts of Universalism are more directed against orthodoxy, than against Deism or Atheism!" [33]

The outstanding controversy of Campbell with the Universalists was a written debate with Mr. Dolphus Skinner of Utica, New York, an editor of the *Evangelical Magazine* and *Gospel Advocate*. It comprised a series of thirty-eight letters exchanged from April, 1837, until August, 1839.[34]

The controversy evolved from a letter written by a Universalist who signed his name "Spencer." He questioned the Biblical translations of words like the Greek "gehenna" which, on the authority of Dr. Adam Clarke, originally meant the valley of Hinnon southeast of Jerusalem instead of the translated word *"hell"*; and the Greek terms *"aion"* and *"aionios"* and their corresponding Hebrew and Latin words *"olem"* and *"avum"* which were used to express unknown limited time instead of the translated words "everlasting" and "eternal," and the Hebrew word *"olem"* signifying anything "old or ancient" pertaining to customs and institutions and not "everlasting."

He asked Campbell if this did not imply that the Scriptures

31. *Idem*, 1830, pp. 144–145.
32. *Idem*, 1831, p. 532.
33. *Idem*, 1832, p. 81.
34. The debate was published by Skinner in a volume of 436 pages entitled, *A Discussion of the Doctrines of Endless Misery and Universal Salvation in an Epistolary Correspondence between Alexander Campbell, of Bethany, Va., and Dolphus Skinner, of Utica, N. Y.* (Utica, N. Y., 1840).

really do not teach punishment beyond the present stage of human life. Does not the *"hell fire"* really mean the fire of Hinnon "where criminals were sometimes burned to death?" If future punishment could be proved, would it not merely mean that we have no reference to "the time of its duration?" He cited Parkhurst, Professor Stuart, Macknight, and Wakefield as agreeing with the definition of *aion* and *avum* as meaning limited time.[35]

Campbell replied that all educated people in religion conclude that "things figuratively represented are to be understood in accordance with such representation" and, similarly, in things not figurative. He cited references to the *"saved"* and the *"damned"* by "the Christian Lawgiver," which were not "figurative representations through the imagery, or costume of society." *"Saved"* and *"damned"* are opposites; if one is temporal and spiritual, so is the other. He, too, censored the abuses of *"gehenna"* by " 'hellfire preachers.' " He also conceded the interpretations of *olem* and *aion* but he would not grant his inference and generalizations, for they "destroy the eternity of God and the immortality of man." An oracle of reason and logic is "what proves too much proves nothing." The trouble with "Spencer's" reasonings is that there are no human words which can "express duration without an end"; and that all reasoning in terms of "minutes, hours," and "years after death" is fallacious. If "God be eternal, then are life and death, happiness and miseries eternal realities. . . ."[36]

Four months later, the Reverend G. W. Montgomery, a Universalist of Auburn, New York, responded to Campbell's reply to Spencer in behalf of Universalism. He added to Spencer's argument by defining the Greek word *"katakrino"* to mean what the English word *"condemned"* means and not the commonly translated *"damned."* The Biblical word *"condemned"* refers solely to the present stage of human existence. As an illustration he quoted Jesus as saying, "He that believeth not is *condemned* already." Campbell should prove that a person, once an unbeliever, must always remain an unbeliever if he were to establish his position. He further contended that mankind will be saved from sin and won to truth in the fullness of time.[37]

Campbell replied that he never held that "a person once an

35. *The Millennial Harbinger*, 1835, pp. 449–452.
36. *Idem*, 1835, pp. 452–455. Campbell parenthetically informed Spencer, "Your *avum* is not Latin." He never heard from Spencer again.
37. *Idem*, 1836, pp. 70–74.

unbeliever once condemned, must always remain an unbeliever" but a person who always rejects the Gospel upon hearing it would always be an unbeliever and forever condemned. He disallowed the Universalist teaching that an unbeliever in this life would inevitably be converted in some intermediate stage after physical death. But he would not choose spirits like Pharaoh, Nero, Caligula, Judas, and Voltaire for his eternal companions, unless they might repent in some *"unknown"* purgatory in another world beyond death.[38]

While in Auburn in June, 1836, Campbell was visited by Montgomery, who asked if he would continue to publish his letters in reply to Campbell. Campbell reported:

I looked upon the young gentleman, in the bloom of 25, or thereabout, as quite a promising Goliath, and upon the whole thought it safest to decline the combat; yet, as one does not like to be called a coward, I got off honorably, telling him that as I was going "down East" to the regions of light, I would, when nigher the sun-rising, in Boston, or somewhere thereabouts, rather encounter some of the older giants, the Anakims or Zamazummins of Universalism; for if I killed him, these sons of Hercules would say I only killed a mere stripling, which would be unmanly and dishonourable. I very gravely, indeed, inquired of my redoubtable friend the names of the mighty men in Boston, and he gave me a full statement of their respective merits . . . he represented Mr. Skinner, of Utica, to be as competent as the best of them; nay perhaps, *"a more ready writer than any of them! . . ."* [39]

In November, 1836, Skinner sent Campbell a letter from Montgomery in which the latter agreed to let him substitute in the controversy. He wished to find when Campbell could renew the discussion in view of his planned debate with the Catholic Bishop Purcell. However, he supposed that "two or three controversies in progress at the same time with different individuals of different denominations, is no uncommon, nor perhaps inconvenient thing for you." [40]

The controversy and big words were similar to those discussed. In addition, Campbell affirmed that with or without its adjuncts

38. *Idem*, 1836, pp. 74–78.

39. *Idem*, 1837, pp. 175–177.

40. *Idem*, 1836, pp. 70–74; *idem*, 1837, pp. 68–74. Campbell preferred an oral discussion but agreed to the proposal, providing Skinner would "suspend hostilities for three weeks at a time" in order that they might be on "equal footing," since the latter had a "weekly" paper and his was a *"monthly."*

"sheol" and *"hades,"* *"gehenna,"* as used by Jesus Christ, does denote *"the future interminable punishment of the wicked."* He proposed that the subject of a future state depends wholly upon the authority of divine revelation through the Bible, especially the New Testament; Biblical words are subject only to the same laws of language and interpretation which are applied to other words of the same antiquity; and the King James or the Campbell-Macknight-Doddridge versions of the Bible should be the only ultimate appeal to translations.

Campbell concluded that Universalist teachings upon the words *"everlasting"* and *"eternal"* have been interpreted "beyond these shores in their unfigurative and unrestricted signification." [41]

Campbell had no place for "Universalist teaching of retribution in this life or Universalist Destructionists" of souls and bodies. It is "hard to reason" with those who feel competent to "improve" the universe "already in being." In 1844 he declared:

. . . there is but a very narrow isthmus between absolute scepticism and the affirmation of those views of the new philosophy of man, and of the intermediate state—the denial of a universal resurrection, and the eternal punishment of the unbelieving and ungodly man—I cannot but observe with great solicitude every attempt made to weaken the sanctions of the gospel and to reduce man to a mere two-legged animal, whose soul is blood, whose spirit is breath, and whose destiny in sin is but the punishment of an insect—the decomposition of an organized atom.[42]

We have already seen the similarity between Campbell's appraisals of the theories of knowledge of Universalists and Unitarians. To avoid repetition, his separate survey of Unitarianism may be summarized from two sample statements made in 1836 and 1863, respectively. In the first he wrote:

They say we have gone over to *Unitarianism.* What is Unitarianism? Is it not the doctrine which denies that Jesus Christ is a divine person and an object of religious worship? Has this reformation such a feature as the above? Who of us have ever avowed any such notion? Is any thing like Unitarianism to be seen in our writings? *No.* Have we ever been heard to preach it? *Never.*[43]

41. *Idem,* 1836, pp. 77–78. Campbell was amused that Thomas Paine paid a "left-hand compliment to the Quakers by saying that the Quaker, of all christian sects 'make the nighest approach to the true Deism.'" Campbell would substitute the "word Universalist in the place of the word Quaker."

42. *Idem,* 1844, pp. 529–530, 545, 547.

43. *Idem,* 1836, p. 290.

In 1863 Campbell concluded that "Deism and Unitarianism are twin sisters." He held that there is no excuse for churches in England, Scotland, and the United States *"undeifying* our Lord Jesus Christ." Unitarianism "is not Christianity . . . not the gospel of the grace of God." [44]

Aged, tired, and frequently ill at this Civil War period, Alexander Campbell revived his fighting spirit enough to offer to maintain his claims against any Unitarian, Arian, or Socinian in "New England" or in "Old England" by "tongue or pen." [45]

44. *Idem,* 1863, p. 12.
45. *Ibid.*

CHAPTER IX

"NEW PHILOSOPHIES" AND "SCIENCES"

CAMPBELL placed the phenomena of "phrenology, mesmerism, clairvoyance, and the spiritual rappings" within the "purview of the new philosophies, theoretic and experimental, of the nineteenth century." [1] He regarded them as expressions of natural religion.

In a college address in 1852, he declared that to comprehend the "prolific genius of full-bred, Americanized, Protestant Anglo-Saxons" one needs only to spend "one leap-year in the Patent-Office and its correlated museums" in Washington, D.C. He finds everything from "the cranium of an Indian trapper to the trap of a spiritual-rapper of the Rochester school." [2]

Phrenology

He observed that "George Combe's Phrenology" is built upon the "fatal assumption" that "the constitution of this world appears to be arranged . . . on the principle of slow and progressive improvements." It is in direct antithesis with "Moses" at an irreconcilable point, namely, *"Man never fell, but rather grows better."*

There are four unanswerable arguments against Combe's position: Universal history does not prove that any barbarous tribe or nation, by its own innate constitution or unassisted efforts, made one step in intellectual and moral improvement. Most ancient nations were further advanced than their successors in such attainments. Combe's geological analogies to support his position actually prove the contrary. The present Anglo-American and Old World civilizations are not the products of unassisted barbarism but, rather, of "successive conquests and intermixtures with other nations; and especially of the early introduction of Christian principles and a Christian people."

1. *Popular Lectures and Addresses*, p. 191.
2. *Idem*, pp. 190–191.

Geological researches show that no "race of animals was ever derived from an antecedent or contemporary species or was gradually perfected." Combe's own "geological statistics" demonstrate that it required "various successive exertions of creative power 'before the jarring elements were reduced to order': that no less than *five successive races of plants and four successive races of animals appear* to have been *created* and swept away by the physical revolutions of the globe before the system became so permanent as to be fit for man." [3]

In his first of a series of articles on phrenology Campbell was cautious enough to be "a believer in phrenology, but a greater and a stronger believer in the Book of God and the Gospel of Christ." He was "inclined to correct phrenology by the Bible, rather than the Bible by phrenology." Regarding Edinburgh, New York, and German oracles of phrenology, he said, *"science is not equal to their art; nor their reasonings as strong as their conclusions. . . . But . . . an issue is drawing near between the Bible and phrenology, we must prepare for the battle."* [4]

In the second article, Campbell took issue with O. S. Fowler's *Religion, Natural and Revealed; or the Natural Theology and Moral Bearings of Phrenology and Physiology.* Fowler asserted that phrenology and the Bible, to be true, must coincide. He would make *"natural* theology the basis of all theology, and natural religion the basis of all religion." There would not be so much diversity over the same Bible if it were an all-sufficient guide. He would first teach children natural religion before teaching them the Bible for the same reason that he "would teach arithmetic before astronomy." They would "look through nature up to nature's God," for the human mind requires more *"proof* than it finds in the Bible." [5]

Campbell wrote that he had long cherished the desire to examine the pretensions of this "once latent, but now developed, scepticism." He ridiculed its "court" for deciding "by the bumps on a man's head *whether God has ever spoken to man on the subject of his origin and destiny."*

Campbell described three schools of phrenology: The "Phrenologists of the high school" generally conclude that the Bible is to be interpreted according to the laws of phrenology. The second

3. *Idem,* p. 192.
4. *The Millennial Harbinger,* 1852, p. 88.
5. *Idem,* 1852, pp. 136 ff.

school is more cautious and places the Bible and phrenology on the same throne in so long as they harmonize but goes no further. The third admits phrenology only so far as it harmonizes with the Bible on animal and material subjects but repudiates its authority on subjects purely moral, spiritual, divine, and everlasting. Campbell preferred the third group but without "full assurance of understanding or faith."

Regarding the assumption that phrenology reveals a "certain development of 'the moral character of God,'" Campbell asked where this knowledge is found. He defended religious diversity by pointing out that no truth, however self-evident, has compelled universal belief in moral or physical science or in religion. The science of phrenology is not needed to help the Bible interpret man's *natural* constitution. The best that phrenology can do is to make its own interpretation of man's natural constitution correct in moral and religious things. Voltaire, Paine, and "all the infidels" will "say to this *amen!* . . . Obey your natural constitution" which is *"right."* "Whatever differs from it is wrong." [6]

Campbell observed that phrenology was particularly popular "amongst an uneducated population." Walking "on stilts with rapid strides," it had "almost made the tour of Christendom within the memory of one generation. However, Christianity

fears nothing from any true science of body or soul, matter or spirit. But there is now, as well as in former ages, much that is called science, which is "science falsely so called." . . . No man that truly (that is, rationally) believes the gospel, fears any thing in the name of science, learning or wisdom, whether called phrenology, pneumatology, psychology or physico-theology. . . . None but a skeptic at heart could fear any thing from any alleged science, true or false, against the Bible facts, precepts and promises. . . . It has been laughed at, ridiculed, caricatured, anathematized, banished, inhibited, imprisoned, burned, dragged through the streets of Paris by a common hangman, as though it were an execrable felon; and yet it not only lives, but reigns and triumphs in the hearts and lives of the greatest, the wisest, and the best of mankind. It is being translated into all the dialects of earth. . . . [7]

This is true, Campbell declared, in spite of phrenologists who may doubt whether death be a punishment as a consequence of the

6. *Idem*, 1852, pp. 139–143.
7. *Popular Lectures and Addresses*, pp. 193–195.

sin of Adam or as the result of the wear of physical forces upon organic life. They can propose the physical improvement of man as the only means of improving his moral and spiritual health. They may disrespect prayers of thinksgiving for special providence and deliverance and the doctrine of the Fall as ancient "speculations of poets or fables of philosophers" for "the uneducated."

In "good old Scotland" Campbell had heard disquisitions upon the philosophy of man from learned men who could "show the exact difference between the south and the westside of a hair." But in speaking of man they always gave him "a *body,* a *soul,* and a *spirit,*" although they did give the Latin, Greek, and Hebrew words for "everything, sacred and divine." [8]

Mesmerism and Spiritualism

Mesmerism, Campbell contended, is literally the "German cousin" of phrenology. The new philosophy of animal magnetism was founded by Frederic Anthony Mesmer, a German physician. As early as 1766 he sojourned "among the planets" until he presented a thesis on planetary influence "endeavoring to show that these heavenly bodies diffused through this nether universe a subtle fluid, acting upon and impregnating the nervous system of all animate terraqueous beings." However, the philosopher "did not consult the souls of the dead, but only the souls of the living."

The science and art of mesmerism is simply the science and art of communicating a peculiar species of sleep, either by the eye or hand, so affecting the human body as to leave the mind active and intelligent—wide awake and watching; even more intuitive and penetrating under the conquest of the animal energies than when encumbered with the working of its own machinery and with the sights and sounds of earthly realities. [9]

Campbell judged that it could not be called a science, for it is a "new art and mystery." It adds a new meaning to the word *see.* We see by means of light with our eyes but its advocates claim to see "mesmerically without light and with their eyes closed and when asleep." Who could reason about such pretensions? No dic-

8. *Idem,* p. 196.
9. *Idem,* p. 197.

tionary expounds the terms and mysterious vocabulary of its premises; it is subject neither to reason nor revelation.

These "clairvoyants with a vengeance" are claiming a "new species of omnipresence and omniscience": selling medicines; examining pulses by looking through a man's skin, flesh, and bones; analyzing "every tissue from the centre of the brain to the centre of the heart"; differing among themselves as to whether they believe in spirits and miracles or not; and disagreeing as to the proper techniques. Their doctors and magicians deny spiritual inspiration but claim

an inspiration and a power above and beyond all the inspiration of prophets and apostles. . . . The true philosophy of mesmerism is to be found in the infirmities of human nature—its morbid sensibility, its credulity, its insatiate curiosity, its love of the marvelous, and the necessary absence of self-government. These render their subjects the easy prey of imagination, and of the faith or of the self-confidence of bold experimentalist, themselves too often as much deceived as deceivers.[10]

He agreed that all bodies, human, animal, mineral, and vegetable "are the subjects of an electric spirit." But it is beyond the province of science or the mind of man to penetrate and know its essence and mode of operating, although we can discover its laws. There is no basis for dogmatically affirming that the hand applied to the human body can abstract a "fluid-substance" which affects the brain and perfectly identifies the mind of the subject with that of the agent. To identify "the human understanding, spirit, reason, conscience or affection" with any type of matter is to war "with reason and revelation." [11]

Campbell said, regarding the more recent development of mesmerism and clairvoyance in the form of "spiritual rappings or knockings" as developed "in the recent conversations with the dead," it "would trench alike on our minds and patience" to trace the "links of this chain." To save time, he would grant their "questionable premises": the assumption of a "good medium," that "old Jeffrey's ghost" tormented the Wesley family, that the knocks were heard in Hydesville in 1847, and the prophecy of Swendenburg concerning the year 1852.

Necromancy is as true as history and the Bible and is "both a

10. *Idem*, pp. 197–200.
11. *Idem*, p. 202.

science and an art." There is a "spirit world as well as a material world." It was taught in Egypt before the time of Moses; laws concerning it were in the Jewish code. Spirits beset characters in the Bible in spite of "semi-infidels amongst modern Christians" who have "endeavored to ridicule the belief." Paul warned Christians concerning the sins of witchcraft.

True to

their prophetic character . . . these pretended spirit-rappers . . . are lying spirits, pretending to speak from heaven above, but they speak from the earth and below the earth. They are all genuine Universalians. They take away from sinners the fear of death and hell. Not one of them, so far as I have heard, give a single intimation of hell. All their communications allure to the belief that the friends of all inquirers are now in Abraham's bosom. . . . But in all that I have conceded, I have not yet conceded their reality. . . . We have read of demons of respectable character in former ages; but these New York demons . . . can speak neither a dead nor a living tongue. They peep, and mutter, and rap, and thump, as the most clownish, ill-bred demons in universal history. They are too exceedingly fond of the ladies, and associate quite too familiarly with them.[12]

He ended his discourse by defending divine revelation and *"communication from heaven"* as incomparable to "the proposing nonsense and folly of a mesmerized clairvoyant." Divine prophets and apostles did not resort to "fortune-telling" and private interpretations with no public importance attached to them.

Angels have been sent on special errands to special persons, for public interest; but the Divine Spirit never condescended to answer any man's petition concerning his own personal property, domicil [*sic.*], goods or chattels. These spiritual rappers and their spirits, in all their speculations, have stamped upon themselves the brand of their own frauds and imposition, and yet have not sense to read or see it. . . . There was always a Moses or a Joshua in the field—a Lawgiver or a Redeemer on the stage—when God "rapped" . . . . But that Spirit speaks in a style of lofty argument, of moral dignity and Divine grandeur, worthy of a Christian's heaven; of such a being as God, and of such a being as man, viewed in all the sublime and awful outlines of his moral nature, . . . and not in the grimace and silly buffoonery of those spirits

12. *Idem*, pp. 202–204.

that peep and mutter tales unworthy of man, and still more unworthy of woman.[13]

In 1853 Alexander Campbell delivered another address with similar ideas on "Spirit Rappings." For the sake of argument, he would admit them as true communications from the spirit world. He rejoiced that "in many instances" they are true indications of the "positive existence, intelligence, perspicacity and power of the ghosts" of other times.

He gave three reasons for this position: First, the "infidelity," the science, the learning, and the people of our age have "been tending or veering to a gross and palpable materialism." Second, the "genuine precedes the counterfeit: no true coins, no base coins; no honest men, no knaves." While materialists affirm that the human soul is material and mortal, Campbell would welcome any potential evidence of a "spiritual universe" to confirm the conviction "that death is no extinction" of either body or spirit as "preferable to a total apathy or indifference." Third, the Bible confirms the truth of such intercourse.[14]

Natural Religion and Natural Sciences

The Darwinian theory of evolution, with its implications in the realms of metaphysics and epistemology, did not appear on Campbell's lists of proscribed "sciences" before his death in 1866. However, we have seen how he rejected the doctrine of gradual evolution and inevitable moral, spiritual, and physical progress of George Combe. Campbell was ready to meet any scientific pretensions to knowledge which he regarded as presumptuous threats against a basis for revelation. He was convinced that there is no conflict between true science and true religion.

In 1842 a worried "believer" feared that geology, which now teaches that we live in death and sets "gradual growth" above "creation," was being "looked at as a God." He wanted "a believer in revelation" like Alexander Campbell to comment upon it.

Campbell replied that he disdained the "latent scepticism" of

13. *Idem*, pp. 209–212.
14. *The Millennial Harbinger*, 1853, pp. 253–255. Samples of similar discourses are: *idem*, 1844, pp. 529 ff.; *Popular Lectures and Addresses*, pp. 379 ff. on "Demonology"; *idem*, pp. 403 ff. on "Life and Death."

modern skeptics in science and preferred "Moses and revelation." He would rather choose the six-day creation account than that of gradual growth according to the scientists.

Cuvier, Buckland, Sullivan, and the other geologists of real merit, have accredited Moses without me, and I can fully believe in Moses without them. . . . The work spoke for itself, and the effects of the Creative voice that echoed through the universe, indubitably taught the "Cause Uncaused, sole Root of Nature, and Fountain of Universal Being." [15]

One of Campbell's most systematic efforts to relate natural sciences to natural theology was occasioned by an American edition of Henry Lord Brougham's *Discourse of Natural Theology* in 1835. He recommended it because so much "splendid talent" of "true science" was consecrated to "the cause of religion."

Campbell related that an endowment of "the late Earl of Bridgewater" had called forth several volumes from the "cream of all English and continental science." They contain "facts and documents from all the natural sciences in proof and illustration of the being and perfections of the Almighty Creator and Ruler of the Universe." He welcomed the undertaking, for the "Sceptics and Atheists of France, England, and America, to say nothing of the German, Spanish, and Italian schools" have been "arrogating to themselves much of the science and new discoveries of this wonderful age."

He welcomed among the authors of the *Bridgewater Treatises* such men as: "Sir Charles Bell, Peter Mark Roget, M.D. F.R.S.; William Buckland, Professor of Geology in the University of Oxford; and John Kidd, M.D. F.R.S." He would not "disparage" the names and accomplishments of men like Thomas Chalmers, William Kirby, and William Whewell of Edinburgh and Cambridge universities; but, as outstanding churchmen, they could not be regarded as impartial as the former from nonreligious professions.

Campbell welcomed Henry Lord Brougham's distinction between *natural theology* and *natural religion* in not making the two synonymous, "but alleging religion as the *subject*, and theology the science of religion." [16]

15. *The Millennial Harbinger*, 1842, pp. 193 ff., 271.
16. *Idem*, 1836, pp. 262–264. It is important to recall why Campbell favored this distinction. He held that once the idea of God is given to man through divine revelation, all nature testifies to the character of God which the Gospel

Brougham's object was not an "exposition of the doctrines" of natural theology but to "explain the nature of the evidence upon which it rests" by showing that it is an inductive science and its truths are discovered inductively "like the truths of natural and moral philosophy." Campbell agreed that there is no difference between the necessary method and evidence by which the truths of natural theology are to be discovered than the method and evidence of the sciences of astronomy, geology, or chemistry; and that there are two branches of knowledge which may be conveniently distinguished from each other in terms of "the Creator and creation." He was glad that Brougham showed that we cannot derive a "single idea without a process of reasoning, long or short," upon the objects of our sense perception of which we are conscious.

He was sorry to have to disagree with Brougham at the vital point—"the connection between natural and revealed religion" —after he had "taken the field from the Atheist and the Sceptic." That "connection" cut at the roots of Campbell's theory of knowledge. Brougham's analysis was this: Ordinarily, the arguments with which we have to contend against "Natural Theology" come from atheists and skeptics who deny or doubt the existence of a First Cause, respectively, because they think that reason is against the reality of a First Cause or is so evenly divided on the question that they cannot make up their minds. But another objection comes from an unexpected source—"the friends of Revela-

---

revealed—in that sense, natural theology is important; for "between *nature* and *theology, properly so called* there is not one discordant note in heaven, earth, or hades." But nature itself is merely "the course of things." Consequently, natural religion is a misnomer. The word "religio" means "*to tie hard, to bind fast*, indicative of an antecedent rupture or breach"; but there is no rupture or breach in "the course of things or *nature* indicative of what is properly called *religion*."

Religion, in its proper and logical sense, is supernatural; thus the term "*natural religion*" is an awkward expression, for there can be no "*natural supernatural*." Campbell disliked the expression "natural religion," although he used it in its popular sense in refuting its supporters, just as he often used "invent" and "create" in their popular senses. Without the aid of revelation, Dame Nature, to him, teaches nothing to establish religion.

Campbell taught natural theology at Bethany College but not natural religion. Natural theology and natural religion, when used as "verbal equivalents," he said, "have christianized many theists, deists, and atheists." *Idem*, 1844, pp. 145 ff., 1853, pp. 285–292, 1854, p. 75, 1857, pp. 439–451, 601–612, 1860, pp. 481–486.

tion" who fear that the "progress of Natural Religion" would endanger the "acceptance of the Revealed." He pictured them as those who, "without reflection," contend that "by the light of unassisted reason we can know absolutely nothing of God and a Future State." These "reasoners" are "neither the most famous advocates of revelation; nor the most enlightened."

Perhaps nothing could have had more sting in it for Campbell. He belonged to the second group but preferred to substitute the words *"without any supernatural aid."* Yet he feared no apparent rivalry between natural theology and revealed religion. Nevertheless,

the notion of natural theology as prerequisite to the revelation of God . . . robs the Bible of its supreme glory as making God known to us, impairs the evidence in favor of its divine origin, and weakens its claims upon society at large. Many are beguiled by such reasonings into the paths of Deism, and entirely misplace the proper effect which the works of creation possess in the argument for God and religion.

Campbell used the analogy that the material world of creation is but the picture which the *"eye"* of man sees but the Bible is the word of the Creator to the ear of man. He doubted that an untaught "Hottentot or savage" would be able to look at "a terrestrial globe one foot in diameter" or at a map of the United States and infer "that the former represented the whole earth, and the latter our own country." So would it be in learning anything about God and a future world "from the exercise of his mere senses on the objects around him." Such a person *"without faith"* could not attain this knowledge.[17]

Lord Brougham reasoned that names like Ray, Clarke, Derham, Keill, and Paley prove that "the greatest advocates of Natural Theology have always been sincere and zealous Christians." They used natural religion as essential to the support of revelation in combating non-Christians from atheists to theists and Mohammedans. Furthermore, "Natural Theology is most serviceable to the support of revelation."

Campbell conceded the statements but not the inferences. He argued that although believers of the Bible have "written and contended for natural religion" in their defense of revealed religion, many also have believed in the infallibility of the Roman

17. *Idem*, 1836, pp. 264–265, 510–511.

Catholic Church. Consequently, Brougham's argument is no logical ground for the inference that such evidence proves that "there is no rivalry between natural and revealed religion." He granted that "natural theology is most serviceable to the support of revealed religion"; Brougham's book is a good illustration of that until its final chapter. But this is no proof that natural reason can "see" divine truths without first having the light of revelation.[18]

Lord Brougham's final argument fired the timbers of Campbell's theory of knowledge. Brougham contended that "it is a vain and ignorant thing to suppose that Natural Theology is not necessary to the support of Revelation." Natural theology may be true. It might be proved or allowed that a God exists and yet "denied that he sent any message to man." "Revelation cannot be true if Natural Religion is false" and it cannot be proved without the support of natural religion.

In illustration, Brougham stated that the Epicureans believed in the existence of gods without believing in revelation. If a messenger from heaven appeared before us today and performed miracles to show "his divine title to have his message believed," this evidence would in no way prove the truth of his message or that it "was worthy of belief in any one particular except his supernatural powers." The capability of working miracles is also the capability of deceiving us; the "possession of power does not of necessity exclude either fraud or malice."

Campbell declared that the illustration regarding Epicureans is no logical proof that divine truths are not conceived without first having the light of revelation.

It is not usual for persons in possession of stolen goods to acknowledge that they have fraudulently come into the occupancy of them. Neither does it comport with the pride of philosophy, in any age, to own that she was debtor to the Bible for all her just conceptions of God and of the unseen and eternal world.[19]

Campbell claimed that Brougham makes no effort to sustain his position until this third step in arguing that miracles cannot be proved as bearing testimony from God unless they are supported by the discoveries of natural theology. He argued that Brougham makes the mistake of substituting "the *possession* of supernatural

18. *Idem*, 1836, pp. 511–512.
19. *Idem*, 1836, pp. 512–516.

power for the *exercise* of it." He granted that the possession of such power would not necessarily exclude the possibility of fraud and malice but the "miracle" is really the exercise of divine power rather than the possession of it. In the exercise of any power, supernatural or natural, we can well determine whether it is deceptive and evil. We know that the messengers from God in the Bible were sent from God because of their benevolent and God-like exercise of their supernatural power. Miraculous power must prove more than its own existence, for it must also

prove the possessor to be both a good and faithful witness. . . . If supernatural power can only prove its own existence, how will the universe prove any more than itself? For if supernatural power, wisdom, and goodness displayed in healing the sick or in raising the dead, cannot prove to us that the operator is as good and as wise as he is powerful, how can all the works of creation, all the displays of supernatural power in the universe convince us that there is one self-existent, good, and wise First Cause, the Creator of all things! Again, whatever power can suspend the laws of nature could establish them.[20]

Brougham asserted that natural religion relieves us of all ambiguities and difficulties in ascertaining "the existence of Deity and of his attributes." Campbell wanted to know what nations, including the Egyptians, Phoenicians, Greeks, Romans, and modern peoples ever learned from natural theology alone that "the Creator is one and the same" and any sure knowledge of his perfections.[21]

In short, Campbell was ready to challenge any metaphysics derived from reflection upon the discoveries and the analogies of natural sciences which appeared to elevate itself as an infallible authority beyond revelation through the Bible. Inductive sciences are subject only to inductive types of metaphysical reasoning and generalization. His attitude is summarized in an address "On the Importance of Uniting the Moral with the Intellectual Culture of the Mind":

The Bible offers no theories of astronomy, geology, chemistry, nor mental philosophy. It fears nothing, however, from the developments of the science of matter or of mind. Ignorance of nature, of the Bible, and of true science led the Pope and his ecclesiastics to denounce all the leading scientific innovations upon ancient opin-

20. *Idem*, 1836, pp. 513–514.
21. *Idem*, 1836, p. 514.

ions, on the ground, or under the pretence, that they were unfriendly to religion, and would finally destroy the credibility of the
Bible. But a better knowledge of nature and of the Bible has
shown that there is no discord or contradiction in their testi-
monies. . . .[22]

22. *Idem*, 1836, p. 599.

CHAPTER X

CHRISTIANITY AS A DIVINE INSTITUTION

IN describing the evidence of Christianity as a divinely established religion, Alexander Campbell sought a positive solution to the problems of the origin of religion which he thought natural religion could not explain. The evidences were miracles, prophecy, the Bible, the nature of prayer, and the genius and tendency of Christianity in history.

During his *Christian Baptist* years, he relied chiefly upon miracles and prophecy. Later his emphasis upon miracles was partly sublimated in behalf of the character and person of Jesus Christ. This trend is marked by his introduction to a new edition of the Owen debate in 1852, in which he asserted that the "simple character of Jesus Christ weighs more in the eyes of cultivated reason, than all the miracles he ever wrought." [1]

Miracles

Campbell affirmed that the truth of Christianity is supernatural in character. All basic religious knowledge is derived from the Spirit of God. One of the "plainest truths in Revelation" is that the Christian religion was "established and consummated by the ministration of this spirit." Universally admitted Christian principles are that faith "is necessary to salvation" and testimony "is necessary to faith." [2]

The Christian religion is "built upon faith" and "is universally represented to be a matter of belief" in the testimony concerning certain facts which are "things *done* by the divine power." These facts are that "Christ died for our sins, was buried and is risen from the dead."

The task of New Testament apostles was to deliver a "correct, intelligible, and consistent testimony of the facts of Christianity."

1. *The Millennial Harbinger,* 1863, p. 12.
2. *The Christian Baptist,* II, 11–12, 15–16, 33–34.

But miracles were "necessary appendages for their testimony" to be believed with certainty.

Campbell accepted the definition of a miracle as "the suspension of some known law of nature." The "connection" between revelation and miracle is that a power superior to the known law of knowledge which is suspended operates in conveying spiritual knowledge which is beyond the power of nature to afford. The term "miracle" applies not only to the power displayed in connection with this content of Christian faith but also to the "gifts" of imparting "light and wisdom" of the "new converts to our holy religion." [3]

Campbell held that the apostles, evangelists, pastors, and teachers of the New Testament period were "all supernatural characters" because of their supernatural gift of the Holy Spirit for imparting wisdom, healings, prophecy, and other manifestations of divine power. They were enabled to do this through *"faith"* which the Apostle calls a *"spiritual gift"* as distinguished from ordinary or "common faith of Christians." Spiritual gifts were only temporary to place the infant church upon its feet in order that it could have immediate and certain evidence of its faith and could defend itself until full manhood. Since its maturity, Christians have neither had nor needed those gifts which were to reveal and to confirm the whole of Christian "doctrine."

As a result, Campbell was accused by a Regular Baptist of denying the operations of the Holy Spirit "beyond the Apostolic Age." However, Campbell vigorously denied the accusation and maintained that the Holy Spirit continues to operate through the Scriptures to enlighten the man of faith who reads these recorded facts and the miracles and prophecy which confirm them. [4]

Citing Dr. George Campbell's "Essay on Miracles," Alexander Campbell maintained that Hume is wrong in classifying Christian miracles with those of "Pagan superstition" or "Popish" corruption. The difference is that the "false miracles" of paganism and Roman Catholicism are accomplished by *"natural* means" and are only *"incomplete"* and "temporary" in character, whereas Christian miracles are *"always instantaneous, always complete, and always permanent."* True miracles can be determined by

3. *Campbell-Owen Debate,* I, 194–243.
4. *The Christian Baptist,* II, 34, 56–63, 73–80, 97–104, 121–125, 145–151, 169–175, 193–198.

their *"numerous, public, beneficent"* effects which were wrought by the Holy Spirit through Jesus and the Apostles. Divine interpositions can be discerned by the spiritual and moral character of the power displayed.[5]

In the Owen debate Campbell promised to prove that Christianity is based upon facts which can be verified by all the criteria which determine the validity of any historical event. Although he did not fear all the lights that science could radiate upon Christianity, he contended "this is no scientific question for scientific men to differ and speculate upon." The facts to be examined in the Bible must be treated by the same *"criteria* which we would apply in an analysis of the writings of Cicero, of Demosthenes, of Sallust, or of Xenophon."

He required the concession of only one postulate to prove the validity of Christianity; namely, that both the Jewish and Christian religions are founded upon "matters of fact." However, the criteria for ascertaining the validity of present and ancient facts necessarily differ. We can rely upon our experience and knowledge of the character of the reporters of certain present alleged facts to establish confidence or distrust in his testimony. But other criteria must be used concerning the facts of antiquity.

To prove the validity of ancient facts we must use four criteria to show that they are: 1. sensible facts which eye witnesses could see; 2. facts of "remarkable notoriety" which the public could scrutinize; 3. facts which are memorialized by certain "monumental and commemorative institutions"; 4. facts which are memorialized by institutions which exist today. Campbell borrowed these fourfold criteria from Charles Leslie' s *"A Short and Easy Method with the Deists; Wherein the Certainty of the Christian Religion Is Demonstrated by Infallible Proof,"* etc.[6]

---

5. *Idem*, II, 33–37. George Campbell (1719–1796) of Aberdeen published his *Dissertation on Miracles* in 1762 from sermons which he had preached in replying to Hume in 1760.

6. *Campbell-Owen Debate*, I, 169–170, 183–194. Charles Leslie (1650–1722), a well-known English political and theological controversialist, wrote particularly against Roman Catholics, Deists, and Quakers. He had a gift for stating things which had popular appeal in religious strife; for example, *The Snake in the Grass and Satan Disrobed from His Disguise of Light,* which he wrote against the Quakers whose "sense," he said, "is harder to find out than confute."

His *Theological Works* were reprinted in 1832 from the original 1721 edi-

Campbell discussed the outstanding facts on which both Leslie and he thought that the Jewish religion was predicated. He particularly stressed the Old Testament account of "six hundred thousand men" walking "through the Red Sea as over dry land" and the subsequent drowning of the Egyptian army as the waters retracted to their normal position. He appealed to the account of the slaying of the Egyptian first-born to soften the hard heart of Pharaoh to let the children of Israel go. These facts meet the tests of the four criteria. They were sensible facts publicly exhibited in the most notorious manner. The Jewish nation exists today "in attestation of these facts." The anniversary feast of the Paschal Lamb, the segregation of the first-born of Israel, and the selection and support of the tribe of Levi "in the service of the Lord" are monumental and commemorative facts which "preclude" the possibility of deception and imposition upon us.

Campbell was impressed with these monumental and commemorative institutions, for the "avarice, the gratitude, and every other passion of the Jewish nation were made to cooperate in attestation" of the segregation of the first-born and the support of the tribe of Levi. No parent would give up his claims upon his first-born without "the most cogent reasons." No nation would celebrate a solemn annual festival in commemoration of a fact which never occurred. Nothing could compel the United States to celebrate the Declaration of Independence on the first of January when the whole nation knows the proper date is the fourth of July.[7]

Furthermore, "these mighty miracles of Moses" occurred among a rude, unlettered Jewish nation before a highly cultured Egyptian civilization. One must not regard the intellectual and scientific attainments of "the ancients" too lightly, or forget that the facts of Judaism and Christianity first occurred before skeptical minds of the best informed among the ancients. This helps to show the wisdom of the "Most High" to remove "forever all

---

tion. His most lasting work is *A Short and Easy Method with the Deists; Wherein the Certainty of the Christian Religion Is Demonstrated by Infallible Proof from Four Rules, Which Are Incompatible to Any Imposture That Ever Yet Has Been or Can Possibly Be. In a Letter to a Friend.* Campbell not only employed Leslie's four criteria of facts but also used his Biblical illustrations and familiar assertion that all religions are corruptions of Christianity.

7. *Idem*, I, 168–178.

rational ground of doubt or scepticism." Monuments stand today in attestation of the science and attainments of refinement among the Egyptions and monumental institutions in behalf of the miracles wrought amongst the Jews.

If the citizens of Cincinnati were to erect twelve stones to commemorate the fact that the city's founders had passed over the "refluent waters of the Ohio, as over dry land" before taking possession of the city, the stones would not be allowed to stand for a year or even for one day. Monuments like those would "shock the common sense of little boys" and would "prostrate them." [8]

Campbell was impressed with the phenomenon that "one monumental nation of antiquity yet remains" which verifies its record of historic facts. Its "circumcision" and "passover" have been kept. Yet the other mighty nations of antiquity have tumbled into dust. The Jewish nation is derived from a more ancient antiquity than "the Chaldean, the Medo-Persian, the Grecian, Roman, or any other empire."

For the Jews to learn the purposes and spiritual ideas of God, it became necessary for God to teach them a vocabulary in revealing religion to them. This he did through symbols in the "gradual development of those oracles of which the Jewish nation was designed to be the repository." Consequently God presented symbols to them: the altar, the lamb, and the priest. These symbols meant the progressive revelation of the central place of sacrifice in religion: the altar, the priest, and the mediator.[9] But the Jews did not understand the meaning of the symbols which they revered; and this proves the absence of fraud and collusion.

Campbell's purpose in these details was to prove that the Jewish religion was divine in its origin and that it became the means by which other nations of the world could be given supernatural vocabulary and prophetic conceptions of religion to arouse a universal expectation of the Messiah and to prepare the way for the Christian religion.

The Jewish records of miracles and revelations were scrupulously preserved and protected against interpolations. Because the Jews migrated and became a traveling people, translations of their scriptures were made into Greek "about 300 years before

8. *Idem*, I, 171, 178–179, 186, 195.
9. *Idem*, I, 195–197.

the birth of Christ" for the "benefit of foreign-born Jews" and "proselytes from other nations." [10]

Campbell gave two other arguments for the validity of these records of Jewish history: No contemporary testimony contradicted these accounts of the "Jewish institution"; documents from other nations of antiquity corroborated the Jewish history.

To establish the first point, Campbell used Warburton's *Divine Legation of Moses* as his guide to show that Greek writers confirm the accounts of Moses in describing Egypt *"as the most ancient and best policed empire in the world"* and in depicting the religious, civil, and funeral rites of the Egyptians.[11] He cited Shuckford's *Connections* to show that "the most ancient traditions confirm the Mosaic account of the creation, deluge, etc." This account traced the Chaldean, Phoenician, Chinese, and Indian traditions only as far as the time of Noah. He quoted Dr. George Campbell to show that traditions of India, Greece, and northern Europe "corroborate the facts recorded by Moses . . . and prove the common origin of mankind." [12]

He also read extensively from Haldane's *Evidence* to show similar concurrences between other ancient writers and the Hebrews and to show that Sir William Jones had satisfactorily traced "the origin of all the people of the earth to the three roots, Shem, Ham, and Japeth; according to the account given in the 10th chapter of Genesis." [13]

Robert Owen was mistaken in speaking of "the endless varieties of religion," for Campbell declared that there have never been "but three divine religious dispensations": the primitive or

10. *Idem*, I, 197–198, 203–206, 211 ff., 244.

11. *Idem*, I, 212–215. William Warburton, a prolific English writer, was born in 1698. His best known work is the *Divine Legation of Moses*, published in 1738–41.

12. *Idem*, I, 222–227. Samuel Shuckford's date and place of birth are unknown. He died in 1754. He was an English historian who is best known for *The Sacred and Profane History of the World, Connected from the Creation of the World to the Dissolution of the Assyrian Empire at the Death of Sardanapalus*, etc. This work was originally intended as an introduction to Humphrey Prideaux's *The Connection of the Old and New Testament* which appeared in 1715–1718. Shuckford's *Connections* appeared in two volumes in 1728, in three volumes in 1731–40, and were edited and published again in the middle of the nineteenth century by Adam Clarke.

13. *Idem*, I, 232–234. Robert Haldane (1764–1842), the brother of James Alexander Haldane, wrote *The Evidence and Authority of Divine Revelation*.

patriarchal, the prophetic, and the Christian. All "the world has grown out of these three developments of divine authority in matters of religion." As all of the divine truths of the Koran are borrowed from the Old and New Testaments, so are all the divine truths of the most ancient nations borrowed from the Mosaic accounts.[14]

Similarly, Campbell approached the three fundamental facts of the Christian religion: that Jesus Christ was crucified, was buried, and rose from the dead. These were sensible facts recorded by Apostles and religious historians who were selected because they were "obscure," "illiterate," and "humble" men. The "Founder" of Christianity wanted *"eyewitnesses* and *ear witnesses"* with good memories for the original Apostles. Fishermen were well qualified for the task.

Furthermore, Campbell argued that the Apostles of Jesus did not understand His mission until after the resurrection, although they saw the crucifixion and burial. Thomas would not believe until he saw the prints and marks of His crucified body after the resurrection.

Also we have the testimony of Paul who was not one of the original twelve Apostles. He did not believe these facts until he *"saw Jesus."* Then he preached "the old *Gospel"* that Jesus died for our sins, was buried, and rose from the dead on the third day. Paul did not soften his message to the Sadducees at Corinth who were materialists "like my friend Mr. Owen," disbelieving in "spirit, resurrection," and "future state." [15]

Commemorative institutions were established to testify to these facts, such as: the substitution of the first day of the week for the Jewish Sabbath day in token of Christ's resurrection, baptism for the remission of sins, and the "Lord's Supper." Here, Campbell said, we have not only a *"commemorative day,* but two *commemorative actions,* instituted to speak for the certainty and importance of this event." The Lord's Supper is commemorative of the *"sacrifice for sins,* indicative of the great *justification;* of *the reconciliation of a sinful world to* the character and government of God." Immersion, however, commemorated more than the *death* of Christ, for it commemorated His *"death, burial,* and resurrection." [16]

14. *Idem,* I, 185.
15. *Idem,* II, 29–36.
16. *Idem,* II, 44 ff., 62 ff.

Leslie's criteria apply to these facts in that they were sensible and public facts and commemorative institutions testify to them even unto the present day.

There was no contradictory testimony among contemporaries to lead us to reject the contents and authorship of the New Testament; yet non-Christian testimony of the period does verify the accounts. The New Testament was written by the *"persons whose names it bears, and at the time in which it is said to have been written"*; and it is the result of eight writers, "Matthew, Mark, Luke, John, Paul, Peter, James, and Jude," four of whom wrote "Memoirs or Narratives of Jesus Christ" and the others wrote "letters to different congregations and individuals, in Asia and Europe." [17]

In seeking to fortify ministers against skepticism in 1836, Campbell published the *Christian Preacher's Companion, or the Gospel Facts Sustained.* Its expressed design was "to furnish all preachers" with materials of the original opposers of Christianity for "reasoning against modern freethinkers and unbelievers." [18] In doing this, he gave brief accounts of the work and statements of Josephus, Tacitus, Suetonius, the Mishnah and Talmud, Epictetus, Arian, Emperor Adrian, Emperor Titus, Antoninus the Pious, Lucian of Samosata, Celsus, Porphyry, and "Julian the Apostate." This book of 156 pages is largely an extension of Campbell's extracts and deductions which he presented in the Owen debate. He drew freely from the comments of Lardner and Lightfoot.

In debating Owen, Campbell read at length from Chalmers' *Encyclopedia on Christianity* concerning Origen's dispute with Celsus.[19] He also cited the controversy between Trypho and Martyr and treatises written against Christianity by "Porphyry the philosopher," "Hierocles the philosopher," and "Julian, the

17. *Idem*, II, 9.

18. Alexander Campbell, *The Christian Preacher's Companion Or the Gospel Fact Sustained by the Testimony of Unbelieving Jews and Pagans* (Bethany, Va., M'Vay & Ewing, 1836), pp. 3–5.

19. *Campbell-Owen Debate*, II, 13–24. Thomas Chalmers (1780–1847) wrote an article on "Christianity" which was published in the Edinburgh *Encyclopedia* in 1813. It was reproduced in pamphlet form. Campbell stressed one of Chalmers' most noted points of view, namely, that the Bible is to be studied as a record of divine revelation according to the Baconian inductive method of scientific study. However, he might also have derived this from other theologians in Scotland and directly from his own reading of Bacon.

Roman Emperor" in order to prove that ancient skeptics of Christianity, including "infidel Jews, Pagans," and "apostates from the Christian faith," did not deny the facts recorded in the Christian Scriptures or question their reputed authorship.

Moreover Campbell claimed that an examination of the "internal evidence" of these writings shows that the authors were sincere in reporting facts because of the "labored minuteness" of their materials. Earmarks of deception do not appear in the Christian Scriptures. He quoted Chalmers to help substantiate his position.[20]

Prophecy

Prophecy is another historical evidence to support the divine facts upon which Christianity is founded. This "data is either the result of experience, of reasoning upon well established principles, or upon testimony." The foreknowledge of future events which the prophets possessed, Campbell declared, is not like the conjectures and probabilities which modern skeptics imagine but was the result of "supernatural knowledge."

He proceeded to outline "the direct, literal, and express prophetic annunciations of the fates" of "Egypt, Tyre, Ninevah, Babylon, and Jerusalem"; the "symbolic or figurative prospective institutions of the Jews' religion"; the "allusive and picturesque representations" which ultimately applied to "the Messiah and his Kingdom"; the "direct literal and express predictions of the Messiah and his kingdom, found in the Jewish scriptures"; and those "literal and symbolic prophecies of the New Testament, reaching down to our own times, and to the ultimate fates of all the nations now on the earth." He quoted Gulian C. Verplanck to show that the fulfillments of Biblical prophecies could not have been accidental. Verplanck accepted Rousseau's challenge through his Savoyard Vicar who would not believe in "divine interposition" unless its alleged "agreement of prophecy with event could not have been fortuitous."

In response to Hume's argument that prophecy could not prove to one's contemporaries that the prophet speaks by divine inspiration because the speaker is dead "at the time of its fulfillment," Campbell argued that this would hold true only in those occasions where such lapse of time has intervened between the

20. *Idem*, II, 24–29.

prophecy and the event. But it would not apply to Jesus and most of the prophets who foretold events which soon happened.[21]

The Bible

Another evidence which Campbell used to show that Christianity is divinely established is the Bible. He was unwilling to rest his position merely on the "external evidences" which support the supernatural facts of the Christian religion, for he insisted that the "internal evidences" of Scriptures themselves are sufficient to prove his proposition. If there were no other proof of the divinity of the Biblical oracles than

the contents of *the* book, (*Bible*), that alone would warrant us the conclusion, for we see the handwriting of the Almighty indelibly inscribed in the pages of this volume. The same grand developments displayed in the "pillar'd firmament," are to be found in the sacred volume; and they both proclaim with equal emphasis, that "the hand which made them is divine!" . . .[22]

Campbell asserted that the books of the Bible are the only ones of divine authority in the world and the historical and non-revelatory parts contain facts which "are necessary because of their intimate connection with the people to whom Divine Revelations were made." Thus they had to be "recorded and divinely authenticated." [23]

When asked how to *"ascertain the authorship of Job, some parts of the book of Deuteronomy, such as the death and burial of Moses, the authorship of the Epistles of the Hebrews etc.,"* Campbell responded that it is unnecessary to "prove the authorship of every particular piece" of the Bible "to prove" the "authenticity" of the Old and New Testaments.[24]

Campbell was also asked if we can be *"sure that we have the genuine works of these authors? Are there no interpolations?"*

21. *Idem*, II, 79–86.
22. *Idem*, I, 183–184.
23. *Idem*, II, 91–93.
24. *Idem*, II, 92–94. This was a pertinent question in view of the argument of that day. In a footnote, Campbell copied Bishop Watson's reply from his *Apology for the Bible* to Thomas Paine's charges that because of its anonymous parts, the Old Testament could not be authoritative. *Idem*, II, 92–93. Richard Watson (1737–1816), a distinguished English divine, wrote his *An Apology for the Bible* in 1796.

This query reminded Campbell of Soame Jenyns, a former skeptic who sought to study the Bible in order to write against Christianity by emphasizing its "fables and absurdities." As a result, however, Jenyns wrote a work on the Christian religion which "gave the world a short and unanswerable treatise upon the *truth* and *authenticity* of it." [25]

Campbell declared that numerous interpolations would not affect "the character of a single fact recorded in the New Testament." Interpolations have arisen through men who were more interested in presenting specific *"doctrines"* than *"facts"* in the Scriptures. Many such interpolations were made by ignorant monks and nuns during the "dark ages" but most of them were purged after the "revival of literature and the Reformation." Today rival sects safeguard the addition of new interpolations. [26]

At times Campbell was vague if not inconsistent in his tendencies toward interpreting the authority and inspiration of the Scriptures. To say the least, he was unsystematic. [27] He spoke of the Bible as being "dictated from heaven." The words of the Apostles "are as much the words of the Holy Spirit when in *written characters,* as they were when existing in the form of sound." [28] The writers were simply "guided in the selection of documents, and prevented from committing errors." In his more mature work, *Christian Baptism,* Campbell said that "God's

25. *Idem,* II, 94–95. Soame Jenyns (1704–1787), a distinguished English political leader and theological writer, wrote *View of the Internal Evidence of the Christian Religion* (London, T. Becket, 1776). He believed that the inherent truth of Christianity supported miracles and prophecy, rather than depending upon miracles and prophecy for the validity of Christianity. Revelation thinkers swayed back and forth between these two views in the eighteenth century. However, it is natural that Campbell combined the two focal points in the nineteenth century, for this work of Jenyns was also published with Leslie's *A Short and Easy Method* (London, printed for F. C. Rivington, 1801) in a single volume.

26. *Idem,* II, 95–96.

27. W. E. Garrison rightly points out this apparent inconsistency in Campbell and says that there "are many passages . . . which look in the direction of verbal inspiration, if indeed they do not directly affirm it." "Word and idea are conceived by Campbell, as by Locke, to be so inseparably connected that an idea cannot be said to exist without a word to represent it; much less can it be communicated without the use of the word which is the necessary means of making the requisite impression on the senses of the recipient." *The Sources of Alexander Campbell's Theology,* pp. 198–199.

28. *The Christian Baptist,* II, 11–16, 121.

Book" is "put into the hands of men as it was first spoken to man." [29]

On the other hand, there are tendencies in Campbell's thought which deny the spirit of Biblical literalism, for he held that all passages of the Bible are not equally important. All of the Bible is not properly a matter of revelations but only the religious information beyond the natural reason of man. The New Testament contains all that Christians need to know for their religious knowledge and salvation. Because of this, Campbell was charged with heresy by the Baptist Redstone Association in 1816 for his "Sermon on the Law," which stressed that Christians are not under the Old Covenant of Moses but the New Covenant of the Gospel of Christ.

Perhaps the key to his thought on the subject of inspiration and authority is turned in his debate with Owen. He affirmed that the question concerning the *"nature"* of inspiration "does not affect the problem of the authority of the Bible." Whether the Holy Spirit suggested "things entirely new" or merely revived a "remembrance" of things which the human writers had seen and heard, the writings of the "apostles and prophets are authentic histories written under the guidance of the Spirit of God; or, they are immediate and direct revelations of matters inaccessible to mortal man." [30]

The problem of whether the "Bible or the Book of Creation" is better suited to communicating spiritual knowledge to the human mind can be solved by answering these questions: Who knows God better, more clearly, rationally, and consistently? He who reads the Bible alone? Or the one who reads the Book of Nature alone? Revelation contains certain "intuitive principles which it presents to the honest student as Euclid does to his students." [31]

"On the Rules of Interpretation," he wrote that the Bible was "addressed to all classes of people" and "was interpreted" by the "aid of such principles, as other books are understood and explained." As each book of the Bible is read, we should ask the questions: Who wrote it? Why was it written? When was it written? To whom was it written? Where was it written? What does it say?

29. *Christian Baptism*, p. 50.
30. *Campbell-Owen Debate*, II, 91–92.
31. *The Christian Baptist*, V, 52–53.

So far as the Scriptures are designed to make known a *revelation* to us, respecting things that are above the reach of our natural understanding, just so far they are designed to communicate that which is intelligible. If you deny this, then you must maintain that to be a revelation, which is not intelligible; or, in other words, that to be a revelation, by which nothing is revealed.[32]

At the same time, one does not have to be magically enlightened by a direct act of the Holy Spirit in order to understand revelations. Two miracles are not necessary to accomplish one end. But there are "parts of the Scriptures which no unsanctified man can fully understand and appreciate in so far as they "relate to *spiritual* experience." Yet there is nothing unusual about this truth as far "as the *principle* itself is concerned," for it also applies to other books.

Who can read Newton's *Principia* or *Mecanique Celeste* of La Place, and understand them, unless he comes to the study of them with due preparation . . . Who can read intelligently even a book of mathematics, without sympathizing with the writer? . . . A demand for *religious feeling,* in order fully to enter into the meaning of the sacred writers, rests on the same principle as the demand for a poetic feeling in order to read Milton with success, or a mathematical feeling in order to study intelligibly Newton and La Place. . . . But still, it would be incorrect to say that Newton or Milton is unintelligible. . . .[33]

Campbell declared that when "God speaks to men" in the Bible, he speaks "in human language" in "condescension to our wants" and does not expect us to "understand the language of angels." The sacred writers always used human idioms and forms of speech "common to the Jewish nation and to individuals"; and they also employed their own "style and expression." [34]

In conclusion, he summarized his lifelong general view of the authority, nature, and the spirit of the Bible:

It is the *matter* rather than the *manner,* which characterizes the superiority of the Scriptures. The manner indeed is sublime, impressive, awful, delightful. But this is intimately connected with the elevated matter, the high and holy contents of the Bible. After all due allowances for this, we may say, that the manner *is the manner of men; it is by men and for men.*[35]

32. *The Millennial Harbinger,* 1832, p. 108.
33. *Idem,* 1832, pp. 108–109.
34. *Idem,* 1832, p. 110.
35. *Ibid.*

Prayer

Another evidence of revelation to Campbell is prayer, although he had relatively little to say about it in this connection. In 1843 he wrote:

Amongst the numerous and greatly diversified evidences, internal and external, of an early and direct communication of God to man, found in the world as well as in the Bible, prayer occupies a broad and a lofty place. Man's speaking to God is, to my mind, a demonstration that God has first spoken to man. . . .[36]

In this realm he seems to depart from his rigid conception that one must always have the correct and expressed word for a corresponding idea.

But there is more in prayer than speaking to God. There is more in prayer than a simple recognition of the divine existence. . . . It implies a knowledge of the attributes of God . . . that the being whom he addresses is an *omnipresent* God—that wherever he is, God is; and more than this, that God hears the voice of man; not merely the vehement, impassioned, and loud appeal, but the almost inaudible whisper of a contrite, fainting, dying heart. Oh! what language, what dialect of man, can express the eloquence of a sigh, a groan, a breathing of the human soul, pleading, wrestling, prevailing with God!

Prayer, therefore, implies much more than we have yet expressed, nay, much more than we can express. It implies, not only that God hears our, to human ears, inaudible whispers, but that he reads what we ourselves cannot read—the language of our agonies and unutterable sighs and emotions. . . .[37]

Sometimes Campbell wrote about prayer in the context of refuting both the implied determinism of deism and extreme Calvinism. He acknowledged that God "cannot be moved to greater love, for his love is always infinite . . . cannot be instructed in regard to our wants; for his wisdom is always infinite" and that the "true design and use of prayer is to bring a man under obedience to that divine will." But there is more to prayer than merely praying for a "resigned or holy state of mind." Campbell emphatically stated that "our Lord" said, knock, seek, ask; Elijah prayed for rain; Peter for Dorcas' life; James tells us,

36. *Ibid.*
37. *Idem*, 1849, p. 3.

the fervent prayer of a righteous man availeth much. . . . I do not believe that when God created the universe he made it like to an eight-day clock, to run just seven thousand years, and then stop. In that case, indeed, there would be no direct answer to prayer. One form of prayer would suffice for all cases. Instead of a daily prayer for our daily bread, or our daily health and safety, we might, with more propriety, say "thy will be done on earth as it is in heaven." This would be the only prayer necessary, in all cases, were prayer merely designed to produce acquiescence.[38]

In 1835 Campbell said that prayer,

like every other divine institution . . . has been much abused. . . . It is by some made the way of salvation, and it has been even substituted for the sacrifice of Christ . . . Even Deists themselves have been commanded to pray; and some of them, like Lord Herbert, have presumed to affirm that their prayers have been answered. Volney himself, in a violent sea storm, is represented as praying in an agony of *distress*—"*O God, (if there be any), save my soul, if I have any!*"

Campbell declared that prayer is more than invoking the name of God in times of distress, for, to be acceptable to God, the one who prays " 'must believe that he exists, and that he is the rewarder of them who diligently seek him' and that 'without faith it is impossible to please God.' " [39]

38. *Idem*, 1851, pp. 533–535.
39. *Idem*, 1835, p. 14.

CHAPTER XI

CHRISTIANITY IN HISTORY

W HEN Alexander Campbell rejected Robert Owen's analysis of the nature and influence of Christianity, he was challenged to present his own. He began by declaring that the three main facts of the Christian religion are that Jesus Christ was crucified, was buried, and rose from the dead. It was the design "of him 'whose ways are not as man's' " to "effect an entire moral revolution in mankind by the simple operation of the intrinsic weight, validity, and moral energy of these facts." They contain all the "principles necessary to make man happy" at his "highest point of dignity" and fearless of death.[1]

To form "correct ideas of the *genius* and tendency" of Christianity, we must heed "the genius and design of the former dispensation." Until Abraham's time all nations shared in the same general views of religion. The Persians, the Canaanites, the Philistines, and the Egyptians had not completely "apostatized" from the religion of Noah and Shem. The Chaldeans were the first peoples to lapse into complete idolatry and worship family gods.[2]

To save the world from idolatry, Abraham was called. His "posterity were erected into a nation" to "teach the unity, spirituality, and providence of God" and "introduce a new vocabulary by symbolic worship" to "prepare the world" for "the mission of his Son." Hence originated the theocracy.

God became a *"king of one nation"* and the "Sovereign and the Commander in Chief" of its armies primarily to make himself known before the other nations through "human relation and institutions." In the vegetable and plant kingdoms we "have a succession of stages of growth," each needing "special influences"

---

1. *Campbell-Owen Debate*, I, 176–177, 185.
2. *Idem*, II, 97. Campbell was the uncritical inheritor of Thomas Hyde's information concerning ancient Persian religion. Hyde (1636–1703), an English professor of Hebrew and a respected Oriental scholar, did not have access to some of the most important Persian documents which were then unknown in England.

and "treatment." In "the kingdom of God there is a similar progression of light, knowledge, life, and bliss." It had its infancy, childhood, and manhood with the "Patriarchal, Jewish, and the Christian Ages." [3]

The development of successive stages for the good of the human race was climaxed by the coming of Christ into the world. In both nature and morality the "Universal Benevolence" operates orderly in *"the fulness of time"* to "introduce the best possible order of things." Some ask why the Messiah was not "born immediately after the Fall." We ask,

Why does not the ripe ear of corn come up from the seed deposited in the earth? . . . One part of the human family is cultivated like a garden, and another part is left like a wilderness. . . . The vineyard, however, after a while produces, through an unavoidable degeneracy, no better grapes than the wild vines in the forest —and the hedge is torn down. A new order of things is developed, and the middle wall of partition crumbles to pieces. The Jews and Gentiles are alike degenerated, and the new order proceeds upon a levelling principle.

The covenant of the Jewish nation corresponds to a *"constitution,"* today similar to the *"national* compacts" in Scotland. This "constitution" was written *"by the Finger of God"* upon "two tables of stone." As long as the people lived to the *"letter"* of this constitution, their history was distinguished. When they departed from it, God ceased to reign over them and they fell into the hands of their enemies.

Under Christ a new constitution was established. This is the difference between the two. The former was *"pure* letter," a "constitution of law," pointing out a "rule of life" to man's "intellect." The "latter is pure *spirit,"* a *"constitution of favor,"* infusing "into the soul" a "disposition" "to these principles of action." [4]

In this sense Campbell said that Owen has some truth in his contention that the "letter or law" will not make men happy, since law is for the restraint of "evil doers." The law does not remove the disposition toward wrongdoing. If the disposition to do that which is unsocial is removed, morality, good order, and happiness can be more rationally expected. However, Owen should have known that the "Almighty" had given the Jews the best law pos-

3. *Idem*, II, 97–100.
4. *Idem*, II, 100–103.

sible and a *"social system"* in which a large surplus was created; the land was rested at least two out of every seven years and they had "the greatest share of social privileges enjoyed by any people." But what happened? They "became worse and worse." [5]

Campbell contended that "pure" Christianity is based "upon the most philosophic view of human nature." Its

immediate object is to implant in the human heart, through the discovery of divine philanthropy, a principle of love, which fulfils every moral precept. . . . Here is the grand secret. The religion of Jesus Christ melts the hearts of men into pure philanthropy. It converts a lion into a lamb. It has done this in our times in countless instances. Mr. Owen only dreams of reformations. Christianity alone changes, regenerates, and reforms wicked men. The materialists declare their system *"cannot make a wicked man good."* Scepticism never converted a wicked man since the days of Celsus till now. . . . Yes, the religion of Jesus sheds abroad in the human heart the love of God; and that love, purifying the heart, overflows in all good actions—kind, humane, benevolent; not only to the good, but to the evil. This is the true philosophy. Correct the spring—the fountain. *"Make the tree good."* Engraft a new scion on the old stock. Infuse new life. . . .[6]

Owen's plan is just the opposite, namely, to transplant

a crab tree and it becomes an apple tree. . . . What law could never do, though as holy, just and good as the constitution of Israel, through the weakness of the flesh, God, sending his own Son, in the likeness of sinful flesh, has done; he has condemned sin, wounded it, and killed it by a most transcendently glorious display of love. . . . This is the genius of Christianity.[7]

Without abstract opinions upon the principal facts of Christianity, this "saving faith" constitutes the simple belief *"that Jesus Christ rose from the dead."* A man cannot be condemned because he cannot comprehend the "metaphysical import of a prefixed *sub* or *supra,* or an intermediate" to "the word *lapsarian"* in theories which have divided speculative Christendom. The design of the Apostles' writings is that men might *"believe in the Messiah the son of God; and that believing you might have life through his name."* [8]

5. *Idem,* II, 103.
6. *Idem,* II, 105.
7. *Idem,* II, 105, 106.
8. *Idem,* II, 105.

Campbell's followers frequently interpreted such words more simply and rationalistically than he intended. Often "saving faith" was reduced to simple intellectual assent to the proposition. On account of using the word "faith" in several senses, Campbell was forced to clarify his meaning. In 1857 he wrote that a "cold assent to a speculative proposition, however orthodox or metaphysically true," never gave "faith, hope, and love" to man. It *never* "renovated" his

nature in the image of him whom we love and adore as "God manifest in the flesh. . . . For faith is the *confidence*—the *substantive existence* in the Soul of things hoped for, as well as the conviction and assurance of things unseen and unapprehended . . . Ours is not a *theory*. . . . It is a living, active and effective faith or confidence in the person, office, and work of the Lord Jesus Christ, a firm reliance on his person and offices and work as competent to our eternal redemption from the guilt, the pollution, and the power of sin.

When we speak of *faith* grammatically, it is the belief of testimony, neither more nor less. When we speak of it philosophically, it is confidence in a person, in an oracle, in a fact or event fully certified. When we speak of it religiously, it is confidence in God, in Christ, in the Holy Spirit as presented to us in the well attested, and fully substantiated facts. . . .[9]

In other words, the power and efficacy of faith is "not in itself but *in that which it apprehends, comprehends, and appropriates*."[10]

Campbell made the distinction between "objective and subjective faith" by calling them "faith" and "the faith."

Faith is confidence in testimony, or confidence in a person, or in a work. *The faith is the confirmed truth or facts of* the gospel. . . . Saving faith is not indeed a cold or formal assent to the historic records concerning the Messiah, the Lord Jesus Christ; but an implicit confidence in the person, offices and works of the Lord Jesus Christ, his work on earth and his work in heaven. . . .

The inspired writings of the Christian record are the periphery, or the circumference of the Christian faith, *objectively* contemplated; while the saving faith of the gospel age *subjectively* contemplated, is the firm conviction of the claims of Jesus of Nazareth as the true Messiah. . . . All true Christian faith, therefore,

9. *The Millennial Harbinger*, 1857, pp. 575–576.
10. *Idem*, 1857, p. 576.

centres in the Divine *person, office* and *work* of the Lord Jesus Christ.[11]

Although it has been questioned by his modern interpreters, Campbell was emphatic in his interpretation of the person, office, and work of Christ, for it involved the core of his conception of man as a sinner and the saving grace of God. In 1832 he wrote:

While the politician regards man rather as a subject of taxation; the merchant, as an article of trade; the naturalist, as a mere animal, governed by appetite and passion; while each profession regards him in reference to itself; the Christian preacher regards him as God's prodigal son, the fallen child of his love; as yet capable of immortality under a remedial constitution, and his soul travails for his salvation.[12]

In 1833, when the "Reformers" under Campbell were being accused of connecting themselves with "the unitarians and Arians of the West," Campbell retorted:

For my part, I regard no man as a believer in Jesus as the Messiah, who denies that he is a divine person, the only begotten of God. . . . I fellowship no man nor people under the heavens, and I am sure none in the heavens, who are unwilling to admit that Our Redeemer is Emanuel, God with us—God manifest in the flesh. . . .[13]

Campbell declared that the "genius of christianity is love"; the "tendency" of Christianity is "peace on earth and good will among men" and it "contemplates the reformation of the world upon a new principle . . . conquering men by love." [14]

He cited Soame Jenyns' views of "the moral character and tendency" of the Christian religion and classed *"valour, patriotism, and friendship"* as "false virtues" because they do not tend to produce purity in human hearts. Valor is largely "constitutional" and has no more moral merit than wit or beauty, health or strength; it tends toward the strong's plundering the weak. Patriotism leads to self-interest. Friendship, the nearest to Christianity, falls short of true merit because it is based upon the principle of loving those who love you.[15]

11. *Idem*, 1857, p. 577, 1859, pp. 640–644.
12. *Idem*, 1832, pp. 25–27.
13. *Idem*, 1833, p. 9.
14. *Campbell-Owen Debate*, II, 111.
15. *Idem*, II, 114–117.

Campbell said that Christianity teaches many unknown and hitherto untaught virtues which demonstrate its "divinity and excellent tendency." Following Jenyns, he listed such virtues as humility, forgiveness of injuries, repentance, and universal benevolence.[16]

Campbell affirmed that Owen must believe one miracle,

that a set of vile imposters . . . did give birth to the *purest* system of morality the world ever saw, did recommend the practice of every virtue which human reason in the most cultivated state of society can admire and approve . . . a miracle of a more incredible character than any one in the volume, especially when we take into view the circumstances attendant on the progress and sufferings of these wicked imposters.

"If weak thy faith, why choose the harder side?"

The Christian religion removes the guilt of sin and the fear of death; it gives to men joy and a good conscience. Monks and friars "invented the gloomy religion of modern times," but the first Christians "were commanded to *rejoice always*." [17]

Robert Owen listened to Campbell's defense of the genius and tendency of Christianity patiently. He replied that Christian society all over Christendom "abounds in vice and iniquity." What Campbell has said about the "purity" and "efficacy" of Christian doctrines "is disproved by the daily conduct of every christian in every quarter of the world." The fruits of the Christian tree are "pride and spiritual pride," "envy and jealousy," "ignorance," "presumption," "religious wars, massacres, and persecutions for conscience sake." [18]

As for the tendency of Christianity in history, Campbell said there is a "reflex light of this holy religion" which "affects almost every man in the region where it shines." The light shines directly into the hearts of some people and is "reflected" from their lives "as from a mirror" upon others of the community. Thus some are *"christianized,* more are *moralized,* and all are in some degree civilized." A "single pious man in a village is a restraint upon the wickedness and profanity of all the village." Owen himself

16. *Idem,* II, 118–121.
17. *Idem,* II, 121–123.
18. *Idem,* II, pp. 142–144, 155–157. The stenographer described "some stir among the audience." Owen invited those "afraid to hear the truth" to depart. "Here a lady almost fainted, and another had her foot bruised in the crowd."

is one who directly was *"moralized"* by the light of Christianity.[19]

He described Owen's "greatest error" as not learning what Franklin tried to teach Paine. When Paine submitted his *Age of Reason* to the "inspection of the greatest American philosopher," Franklin warned him "how much he was indebted for those principles of morality and benevolence which he possessed" to the "influence and genius of the religion he was about to attack." [20]

Campbell declared that there is neither a "necessary connection between Deism and a co-operative system" nor between socialism and atheism, for he argued that a New Testament society held "all things in common; but their happiness was not derived from a community of goods, but from the principle which issued, in their circumstances, in a community of goods." [21]

Campbell maintained that with Christian motivation men could cooperate toward the education of youth and improvement of their "social enjoyments." But Owen's system would "destroy social order and social happiness," for it "is at war with human nature as well as with religion, morality, and private property." On the other hand, Christianity has always tended toward making woman "not the inferior but the companion and the equal of man." Owen would destroy marriage, a natural and sacred institution, which weaves together "all the cords of affection" that "cement society." He would destroy the "most powerful of all natural affections" at the cradle by exempting woman "from the natural concern and care of her own offspring."

Campbell concluded that the trouble with Robert Owen's system is that there is no "inconsistency" in it, for "there can be nothing crooked unless there be something straight." He has the advantage over Christians for the latter have "something straight" in their system by which they can measure, compare, and be shown their "aberrations." Under Owen's views, if a child kills or honors its mother, it is all right as such action is resolved from nature or necessity. History, he asserted, proves that we "are indebted for all the great improvements in society to the philosophy of Christians and not to the philosophy of sceptics." The principle and practice of civil liberty has always made for the expansion and development of human intellect, arts, and social life.

19. *Idem,* II, 131–135, 167–168.
20. *Idem,* II, 132.
21. *The Christian Baptist,* V, 25, II, 133.

The Reformation from Popery gave the first shock to the despotism of Europe. The labors of the Reformers—and the more recent labors of Milton the poet, and Locke the philosopher, have done more to issue in the free institutions of Europe and America, than the labors of all the sceptics from Celsus to my friend Mr. Owen.[22]

Through his "Essay concerning Toleration," John Locke "laid the foundation" for a new era in the "cause of civil and religious liberty" more than "all the sceptics in Christendom." Similarly Bacon, in his *Novum Organum*, originated a new era in the field of physics. Along with "the Christian philosopher, Sir Isaac Newton," Lord Bacon propounded the "principles of investigation" for inductive philosophy. To John Locke we owe the imported American Constitution which "was a form of government for the Carolinas." [23]

Beginning with "the invention of the mariner's compass" in the fourteenth century, all the sciences and arts which have been introduced or perfected "have been given to us by men who looked through nature, society, and art up to nature's God." He listed numerous names, dates, and contributions to substantiate his position. Among these were Faust, Columbus, Copernicus, Galileo, Descartes, Boyle, Robert Fulton, and Sir Humphry Davy. He omitted La Place from the list on the grounds that he only entered the door which Newton had opened in the study of nature. He denied that Franklin should be given to the cause of skeptics on account of his acknowledgment of his "Creator and Benefactor" and hope for future life which was sketched by his hand for his epitaph.[24]

In 1858 Campbell proposed what he called a "new argument" against skepticism, namely, that "The Gospel must be true because no man could have invented it. . . . No philosopher or poet, known to the living world, ever drew a perfect character." No one ever imagined a perfect man until Jesus Christ was described in the four Gospels.[25]

But this was no new argument for Campbell. It merely indicates his later shift in emphasis in his defense of revealed religion. In

22. *Campbell-Owen Debate,* II, 5.
23. *Idem,* II, 4–5; see also *The Millennial Harbinger,* 1832, p. 40.
24. *Popular Lectures and Addresses,* p. 136–139; see also *The Millennial Harbinger,* 1858, pp. 144–146.
25. *Idem,* 1858, pp. 242–245.

his earlier years his chief stress was upon *miracles* and *prophecy* in his theory of knowledge; by now, it was upon the genius and tendency of the Christian religion and prophecy. His theory of knowledge was the same but his emphasis had changed. By 1852 he appealed mainly to the "simple character of Jesus" which "weighs more in the eyes of cultivated reason, than all the miracles he ever wrought." [26]

We shall examine this change in perspective in the next major part of this study.

In conclusion, no fairer description of Campbell's defense of revealed religion exists than his own words in 1858, in an article entitled "Faith versus Philosophy":

We know that there is "an empty and deceitful philosophy" and that there is a real and truthful philosophy, but the Gospel of Jesus Christ and his institutions are our philosophy truthfully so-called. We philosophize with philosophers. We preach the gospel to sinners. We teach the initiated and untaught. We debate with opponents, and cherish good will for all mankind. [27]

26. *Idem*, 1852, pp. 662–663.
27. *Idem*, 1858, p. 86.

PART THREE

PHILOSOPHY OF HISTORY

The coming events of apocalyptic vision are pressing our attention, and have strong claims for our grave consideration. . . . The signs of the times are ominous, and coming events cast their shadow before them, indicating to us the necessity of preparing for them. But for this purpose it is indispensible that we understand our own times, and their position on the chart of prophetic developments.

Alexander Campbell

CHAPTER XII

THE MILLENNIUM

HITHERTO, we have seen how Alexander Campbell concurred with the opponents of revealed religion in so far as their attack was against what he regarded as corrupt Christianity but not all Christianity. The counterfeits only rang notes of praise to genuine revealed Christianity which he defended.

Revelation was the dividing line which separated the sheep from the wolves. He would chastise the sheep that were astray and segregated into innumerable sects, each with its own subjective claims to be the one true flock. However, when the wolves crossed the line to destroy the ultimate premises of all the sheep, Campbell broke his controversial lance over their heads.

By the time of his debate with Robert Owen, the die was cast as to whether he would spend the rest of his life beating the sheep or defending them. Afterward, his chief concern was to seek more constructive solutions to the problems of the sheep. As a result, he became the founder and president of Bethany College, the president of a missionary society, a leader of the American Bible Society, and an advocate of national and public education.

Obviously his change was functional in that he moved from a conception of society and of the church which required complete individualism to one that required cooperative organization and planning. What is not obvious is that Campbell did not depart from his basic principles. Philosophically, his theory of knowledge remained the same. Theologically, his chief ideas of faith, redemption, and primitive Christianity did not change. Patriotically, his Americanism was more acute. His distrust of Roman Catholicism remained. These main patterns of thought deepened as he became more mature in reflective thought and more discriminate in controversial objectives. But the application of his principles radically changed; and so did his temperament. The "Infidel" type of temper of his *Christian Baptist* reform was modified in almost direct proportion to the extension of his defense of revealed religion and constructive churchmanship.

Moreover, the change was relatively contemporary with the decline in the radical individualism of the Jacksonian era of democracy. With the Western frontier changing, the cycle from settlement to organized community life was rapidly drawing to a close. Political, social, and religious life were requiring institutional expressions.

But does this adequately explain Campbell's move from complete individualism to organization? Does this adequately explain his new emphasis upon missions, education, culture, the mission and destiny of America, and his growing sense of discrimination between controversial objectives? In light of the evidence, it does not. Something else is needed for an objective interpretation of the sense of urgency, expectancy, and confidence which he had that a new order of society and the union of all Christians would take place.

Campbell had developed a philosophy of history which changed the whole perspective of the current struggle. The culmination of history was now at hand. The millennium was coming. World history and current events must be interpreted in the light of what was about to take place.

In the light of this new sense of eschatology, Campbell found an urgent place for missionary societies, educational institutions, Bible societies, an organized religious communion, and a mission for American and the whole Anglo-Saxon civilization. He became convinced that this was the divinely ordained climax and stage of history in which sectarianism, "popery," the union of kingcraft and priestcraft, skepticism, and paganism would be overcome in order that the millennium would arrive. They must be overcome through these institutions in a natural and normal manner. Christ was not to appear magically upon the physical clouds to accomplish it but he would ultimately reign in the hearts and lives of people.

How might this be effected? A defense of revealed religion would help to convince the world how impotent skepticism and natural religion are; but getting rid of sectarianism and Roman Catholicism would guarantee it. Primitive Christianity restored would eliminate both sectarianism and papalism. His Disciples of Christ followers would lead the way in restoring primitive Christianity and the union of all Christians. Bible societies and missionary organizations would convert paganism to New Testament Christianity. True education would help conquer sectarianism, skepticism, and Romanism simultaneously. America, especially, and the Anglo-Saxon world, through its language, its Protestantism, and its civilization would become the missionary and benefactor among the nations in ushering in the modern golden age.

The germ of this philosophy of history is evident earlier in his interests in prophecy and a history of salvation within the framework of the "three dispensations" of the Scriptures. Eschatology becomes more prominent in his work in the latter half of the 1820's and the key to it in the 1830's; it broadens into organization in the 1840's and 1850's; and it softens by 1860 when the discouraged Campbell decides that he is not as sure that the millennium is as near at hand as he had once supposed.

On January 4, 1830, Alexander Campbell published the first monthly installment of the *Millennial Harbinger* with the promise that its "range" would be "much greater" than the *Christian Baptist's*. He stated that "Christians" of every name should be interested in its object because it was perhaps the only work published in Christendom for that purpose. The first sentences of the "Prospectus" defined the "Comprehensive object" of the magazine:

This work shall be devoted to the destruction of sectarianism, infidelity, and antichristian doctrine and practice. It shall have for its object the development and introduction of that political and religious order of society called The Millennium, which will be the consummation of that ultimate amelioration of society proposed in the Christian Scriptures.

The outline of subjects which he gave as subservient "to this comprehensive object" deserves attention.

1. The incompatibility of any sectarian establishment . . . with the genius of the glorious age to come.
2. The inadequacy of all the present systems of education . . . to prepare man for rational and social happiness.
3. The disentanglement of the Holy Scriptures from the perplexities of the commentators and system-makers of the dark ages. . . .
4. The *injustice* which yet remains in many of the political regu-

lations under the best political governments, when contrasted with the *justice* which christianity proposes, and which the millennial order of society promises.

5. Disquisitions upon the treatment of African slaves, as preparatory to their emancipation. . . .

6. General religious news . . . of the proselyting spirit of the age.

7. Occasional notices of religious publications . . . bearing upon any of the topics within our precincts.

8. Answers . . . and notices of all things of universal interest to all engaged in the proclamation of the *Ancient Gospel* and a *Restoration of the Ancient Order of things*.

9. Miscellanea; . . . Much of the useful learning . . . will . . . be gleaned from . . . the most renowned Fathers of christian literature; and much aid is expected from a few of the more enlightened brethren of our own time, who are fellow-laborers and pioneers in hastening this wished-for period.[1]

The "Prospectus" represents a fair outline of the magazine's future course. However, the one striking subject omitted is the missionary enterprise which was given millennial prominence in the 1840's.

The Rise of Campbell's Millennial Thought

An important question is, when and how did Campbell's millennial outlook begin? The evidence reveals that it was the outcome of a gradual development which was rooted in his early studies of Biblical prophecy before 1816.

In 1856 Campbell wrote that he began his "studies in prophecy some forty years ago" with the writings of Joseph Towers and later added to the writings "numerous works of minor fame." He especially appreciated the works of Towers and Lord on "symbolic prophecy." [2] It took years for the millennial shoots of his interests in prophecy to push through the surface.

1. *The Millennial Harbinger*, 1830, pp. 1–2.

2. *Idem*, 1856, p. 188.

Joseph Lomas Towers (1757?–1831), the son of the English biographer, published his *Illustrations of Prophecy* in two volumes in 1796. He became insane in 1830.

David Nevins Lord (1792–1880), an American merchant and theological writer, graduated from Yale in 1817. His *Exposition of the Apocalypse* (New York, Harper & Brothers) appeared in 1847. He edited *The Theological and*

As early as August, 1823, "the millennium" was in Campbell's first list of proscribed "orthodox tenets" and "technical language rendered sacred." But by February, 1825, he himself employed the term in connection with the "restoration of the ancient order of things" and declared that "the millennium" has "commenced" to the extent that New Testament Christianity is restored.[3]

Campbell's specific references to the millennium are scanty in the earlier volumes of the *Christian Baptist* but his attention to the "ancient order of things" increased in the second, third, and fourth volumes. In his conclusion to the first volume's article, "The Conversion of the World," he wrote: "Christians, . . . as you desire and pray for the salvation of the world, the downfall of Antichrist, of Mahometan delusion, of Jewish infidelity, of pagan superstition;—return, return to the religion of our common Lord, as delivered unto us by his holy Apostles! . . ."[4] In this passage are his elementary outlines of the steps necessary for the arrival of the millennium, before he connects them with it or gives major emphasis to it.

In the second volume of the *Christian Baptist,* he wrote "The Apocalypse Explained," a vigorous refutation of Alexander Smyth's contention that the book of Revelation is a "pious forgery" by "Ireneus, who died A.D. 202." He noted that General Smyth claimed the discovery of a new infallible key to unlock the mysteries of the Bible and the Apocalypse but it is the same one which "the deists have worn out" and "welded a hundred times" without opening the lock.

In view of his writings and increasing following, it is not surprising that the trend toward Campbell's millennial thought deepened. By June, 1828, he reflected upon the success of his program and described this as "one of the most momentous and eventful periods" in "the religious world of the present century."

All religious denominations are shaking. . . . But of all the means which can be employed to promote peace on earth and good will among men, which have any influence to destroy sectarianism,

---

Literary Journal from 1848 to 1861; much of its space was allotted to an interpretation of the prophetic symbolism. He also wrote *The Duty and Advantage of Studying the Prophetic Scriptures* (1849), and *The Coming and Reign of Christ* (1858).

3. *The Christian Baptist,* II, 156.

4. *Idem* (Burnet ed.), I, 42.

or which are at all adapted to introduce the Millenium [*sic.*] there is none to compare with the simple proclamation of the *ancient gospel.*[5]

In his Preface to Volume VII of the *Christian Baptist* in 1829, he announced:

The prospects of emancipating myriads from the dominion of prejudice and tradition—of restoring a pure speech to the people of God—of expediting their progress from Babylon to Jerusalem —*of contributing efficiently to the arrival of the Millennium*— *have brightened with every volume of this work.* . . .[6]

In this light we can only conclude that the early seeds of study in prophecy, sown prior to 1816, gradually became millennial plants. They grew rapidly from 1823 until 1828 in the frontier wilderness which offered a favorable environment. The *Christian Baptist* and a greater popular following than Campbell had originally anticipated worked the soil for him.

Before he was prepared for it, the millennial plants were in full bloom; and then the harvest, or millennium, was *near* at hand. When Campbell had obtained the seeds of study in prophecy, he probably did not detect the elementary millennial seeds. As the first obscure millennial sprouts came up, he gave them little attention, for he was more interested in others. However, they grew so easily that Campbell's hopes for "the arrival of" "the Millennium" "brightened with every volume" of his magazine.

By 1829 he needed a larger and more technical instrument than the *Christian Baptist* for the care of the millennial plants which had his unreserved affection. It was all right for ploughing but not for cultivative purposes. Obviously the antiecclesiastical seeds needed no cultivation! all he had to do was to break open the field and let the New Testament scatter the seeds with the wind. Their growth and care would be automatic. But his particular type of millennial plants required constructive cultivation.

In the Owen debate, Campbell's garden variety of millennial plants were in full bloom. The millennium was nearer at hand

5. *The Christian Baptist*, V, 251–252.

6. *Idem*, VII, 6. The italics are mine. In his concluding remarks in the final volume of *The Christian Baptist*, Campbell admits that his conscious plans for reform were limited to restoring primitive Christianity within the confines of a local congregation until his surprising following that resulted from his debate with Walker in 1820.

than he had previously anticipated but he was not so sure of the order of the stages necessary for its introduction as he was later.

I have sometimes been ready to conclude with Bishop Newton, in his illustrations of the prophecies, that the unhallowed alliance between kings and priests, of church and state, is destined to be finally destroyed by a momentary triumph of infidelity; or, to come nearer to his own language, *before the millennial order of society can be introduced, there will be a very general spread of infidelity.* However . . . we would not be dogmatical. . . .[7]

In the meantime, Campbell had published two articles *"On the Millennium"* by Walter Scott of Steubenville, Ohio, in 1826. Scott wrote under the name of "Philip." These articles are important in signifying that Campbell had gained an invaluable millennial ally. Scott became second to Alexander Campbell in the leadership of the Disciples of Christ during their crucial early period.

The millennial temper and content of Scott's articles are somewhat different from Campbell's in spite of a similar eschatology and stages of history. In these articles Scott discussed three ages of the world: the *physical,"* the *"secular,"* and the *"millenial [sic.] evangelical,"* each of which is to be climaxed by an attendant judgment. He maintained that "the history of the world demonstrates" that man's knowledge of his relations to the natural world, to one another, and to God are "slow and progressive." The physical age, the "antediluvian period," is "characterized by the absence of all governmental arrangements." This age was swept away by "the flood" as God's judgment upon "the animal crimes of the race," for the gratification of "sexual and other appetites" formed its "chief guilt." [8]

The secular age, "the middle period of the world's history," was characterized by its "more remote order of relations" in such great empires as "the Babylonian, Persian, Grecian and Roman." It involved a complex corruption of "higher and more refined

7. *Campbell-Owen Debate,* I, 13–14. The italics are mine.

Thomas Newton (1704–1782), an Englishman, Bishop of Bristol, published the *Dissertation on the Prophecies Which Have Been Remarkably Fulfilled, and Are at This Time Fulfilling the World.*

Sir Leslie Stephen comments that Samuel Johnson "admitted that the 'Dissertation on the Prophecies' was 'Tom's great work: but how far it was great and how much of it was Tom's was another question.'" *Dictionary of National Biography,* XIV, 404.

8. *The Christian Baptist,* III, 270–272, IV, 25–26.

nature" of "those political and social relations which subsist in large communities."

The third or evangelical age is near at hand, for man has "nearly exhausted" the limits allotted "for pursuits purely physical and political." Scott maintained that the chief end of mankind is "happiness"; and, in time, man will learn by "the dint of long experience" that his happiness cannot be secured by "commerce and war." In the third or "millennial age" of the world, "the human race will enjoy great happiness," for "the relations which have been revealed as subsisting between men and their Creator and Redeemer, shall be fully investigated, developed, and enjoyed." The evangelical or millennial age, terminating "in the final judgment" and the "resurrection of the dead," will be affected by an immediate effort of the strong hand of Jehovah." [9]

It is worth noting that in spite of his prediction of the imminence of the millennium, Walter Scott was a religious, political, social, and economic critic of his age. His optimism was not rooted in a doctrine of inevitable human progress. He saw continuity in history and the unity of the human race but the millennial glory of man would come by the hand of God. [10]

Having a good millennial ally, in June, 1827, Campbell recommended Scott's prospective periodical, the *Millenium (sic.) Herald,* which Scott was planning to publish. [11]

The Stages of History and the Theory of Struggle

When Robert Owen announced his three stages of history and millennium, Alexander Campbell countered with his. For our purposes, this revealed that the basic materials of Campbell's later millennial thought were rapidly evolving, although not in a systematic form.

Campbell presented his most interesting effort to link popular economic and social theories with Biblical chronology and prophecy. He contended that Christendom expected a new order of things to pervade the whole race "perhaps in the present century." It will last for a thousand years and then "the present state of things" will end and "the multiplication of human beings" will cease. This confidence in Biblical prophecies is supported by "logic

9. *Idem,* III, 271–273.
10. *Idem,* III, 273, IV, 25–26.
11. *Idem,* IV, 263.

and arithmetic." Biblical data shows that only eight people were living "about four thousand years ago" but observe the ratio of increase in population in spite of wars, famines, pestilences, and all wastes of life. If eight people in four thousand years could fill half the earth as full of people as it can subsist, how long will *one thousand millions* be in filling the other half? Some desolation must empty the earth of its inhabitants or the human race must be extinguished.[12]

Campbell presented his three stages of history in the debate chiefly as evidences of Christianity as a divinely planned and developed religion, but he connected them with the millennium and a rapidly evolving theory of historical struggle through a series of falls of man. Viewed in the light of the completion of his millennial thought, a genuine philosophy of history was emerging.

When Owen spoke of the endless varieties of religion, Campbell resented the analysis and described the unity of the human race and religious development in history with Christianity as its divinely arranged outcome. In history there are only "three divine dispensations of but one religion," the patriarchal, the Jewish, and the Christian. The first, adapted to the "primitive state of man," formed "good individuals." The second, adapted to people "living under social and municipal institutions," made a "happy nation" and "comparatively a moral people." The third "fills men with peace, joy, and righteousness" and "will terminate in a pure and happy world." The "seed" of religion "was sown" in the patriarchal age; the plant sprang up and was cultivated in the Jewish; and it "ripened and was matured" in the Christian.[13]

Before the final state of human earthy existence, man must be fully developed; he is taught this through bitter experience and struggle. Little meaning can be detected in history from merely contemplating the present state of human existence. It is like placing a man in a room, ten feet square, through which a map of "ten thousand miles is passing." He sees "nothing but oceans of water" for many weeks; but, eventually, boundless forests, chains of mountains, deserts, flats, wastes, and wilderness come before him until "a succession of beautiful country passes before his eyes." After seventy years, the man may become impatient at

12. *Campbell-Owen Debate,* I, 106. Campbell did not mention T. A. Malthus in the debate but varieties of his population theory were as popular in those days as lists of the three stages of history.

13. *Idem,* I, 107, 185.

seeing only "specks" of that beautiful country. But wipe away his tiny room. He sees the whole map at one glance and the infinite wisdom and design of the moral Governor of the universe astound him!

Campbell was insisting that history has meaning and design but must be seen as a whole in which God plays the controlling part. It appears to be a "law of human nature that man can only be developed and brought into proper circumstances to please himself" by "experience." If Adam and Eve could have had the experience in the garden which they had after their exile,

they never could have been induced to taste the forbidden tree. . . . Every revolution of the earth, and all the incidents recorded in human history, are but so many preparations for the introduction of that last and most perfect state of society on the earth called the *Millennium*. First we have the germ, then all the blades, then the stem, then the leaves, then the blossoms, and last of all the fruit. Therefore, as Paul said, the apostacy came first.[14]

The last sentence of the above quotation deserves special notice, for it relates to Campbell's interpretation of the three stages of history which are filled with a series of falls of man. Man's tragic note of rebellion began with the fall in the garden and resulted in the exile. The fall in primitive society resulted in the Flood. The fall in Judaism, in relation to the divine attempt to produce a corporate and happy society by laws, resulted in the Dispersion. And the fall from primitive Christianity, in the form of Roman Catholic apostacy, resulted in the confusion of pure speech, creeds, useless metaphysical wrangling, schisms, sectarianism, and infidelity. The apostacy was literally foretold by Paul and "symbolized by John in the Apocalypse."

Nevertheless, in each of these successive falls, man learns by experience that God is working to overcome his deficiencies and to establish a final state of pure speech, happiness, spiritual and moral obedience, and the perfection of his plans in human history in terms of the Christian millennium. All the signs of the times "indicate . . . the near approach of this happy era." [15]

With this debate background, let us now examine what was occurring in the *Christian Baptist*. In a series of essays on "A

14. *Idem*, II, 88, 107, 185. See also Table XIII on "Prophetic Symbols" in *The Living Oracles*, 3d ed., pp. 41–51. By 1832 Campbell was concerned that *The Living Oracles* be read in the light of millennial perspective.

15. *Idem*, I, 88–90.

Restoration of the Ancient Order of Things," Campbell noted that many "reformations in religion have been attempted" since "the great *apostacy*," foretold and depicted by the holy Apostles, reached its prime. If any *"began in the spirit, they have all ended in the flesh";* yet they have benefited "mankind" politically and religiously.

There were differences between these reformations, for we owe "more to John Wickliffe than to Luther" and more, perhaps, to Peter Bruys than to John Calvin, just as we owe more to Columbus than to Americus Vespucius. While human systems of philosophy or religion are proper subjects of reformation, "Christianity can not be reformed." All we need to do is to restore the "ancient order of things" for the complete happiness of Christians and the millennium to come in fullness.[16]

This series of thirty-two essays was primarily devoted to his conception of primitive Christianity. Before its completion he began a series of sixteen "Essays on Man," which reveal that he no longer could write extensively on the restoration of "the ancient order of things" without emphasizing the stages of history in his growing millennial consciousness.

Four "Essays on Man" were on the "Primitive State" of man; four on the "Patriarchal Dispensation"; six on the "Jewish Age"; and the others were on the "Christian Age." As a whole, these essays contain the rudiments of his evolving religious philosophy of history, especially when one realizes that his later millennial emphasis was under a perspective which took in the whole world, its origin, its destiny, and its present and eternal course in history. He was headed toward a world historical view of things by which present events, institutions, and individuals derive their meaning.

In his first "Essay on Man" Campbell declared that the Bible engrosses the first chapter of self-knowledge. The Bible begins with man's creation and ends with his destiny. If the Bible were destroyed, man would not only be left as a savage but as ignorant of his origin as the beasts.

Man's *body* is built from the elements of the earth; his *soul* or *"animal life"* is given in common with all other created animals; but his *"spirit"* is infused by God—a purely intellectual principle. Jews, Greeks, and Romans have had the terms which correspond to the English *"body," "soul,"* and *"spirit"* respectively.

To the spirit belong the faculties of understanding which con-

16. *The Christian Baptist,* II, 153–156.

sist of reason, intelligence, and volition; to the soul or animal life belong the passions and affections; and to the body belong all the appetites and propensities of the body. Yet all three of these human constituents, body, soul, and spirit, are so combined that they act in concert, to the extent "that what one does the others do likewise." Originally man existed as a perfect being with the proper government in control of these three parts of his whole existence; consequently there was a perfect harmony existing between reason, passion, and appetites. The spirit was the ruling or governmental agency; man's passions were the servants of the spirit; and his whole body functioned in subordination to these two constituents.

Man was the last work of God and, judging from the gradation in the scale of creation, the "best" work of God. He was endowed with the powers of deriving pleasure from the material system by his senses and of deriving spiritual enjoyment from the spiritual system by his intellectual power. He was made a social creature and was given the power to communicate the enjoyments of these two worlds. Then God created a "co-ordinate being of the same endowments, but of more delicate organization" and kindred society resulted. The bliss of the primitive state was complete.[17]

In his second article of the series, Campbell presented his never-failing discourse on God's teaching our "first ancestors" speech and a vocabulary. But his chief interest was in the Fall. He declared that it makes *little difference* if this "arrangement" were literal or symbolic; the important thing is to know the nature of the "trial" of Adam, namely, "whether his spirit" would retain its God-given "sovereignty" or his "passions" would "usurp the government." Man fell through the triumph of passion and thus the original harmony and subordination were destroyed. Guilt, shame, and fear invaded his peace and overwhelmed him "in ruin and despair. . . . Thus, by the law of nature, death became necessary, as man was exiled from the Garden of delights and became the pensioner under a small annuity by the grace of God, until his physical energies should be worn out by the conflict of reason and passion."

Disorder, "confusion, and an awful reverse of curcumstances" resulted; and man became a slave to his appetite. Having been the son of reason, he now became the slave of passion. No chance is left of

17. *Idem* (Burnet ed.), VI, 7–9.

regaining his former standing; the controlling power is lost.
. . .[18] Adam begat a son in his own likeness, immediately after
"the Fall" This child was born in the likeness of fallen Adam—not
in the likeness of Adam in Eden. . . . Thus every child of Adam
begins its career, impelled and prompted by its appetites and passions, for a long time unchecked by reason; and when reason at
length appears, it is so weak and incapable of government, and
so unaccustomed to control, that it is continually baffled by the
fearful odds against it; and can never, by any effort of its own,
gain the ascendancy.

This is only part of the misfortune of the Fall, for man is no
longer afforded the environment which Eden afforded Adam. It
is as though a prince and princess were surrounded by the
grandeur, majesty, and education of an Oriental palace, only to
commit a crime worthy of imprisonment in some dreary dungeon
immediately after their marriage. The first child would be born
and confined there until its maturity. This illustrates the difference between our circumstances and those of Paradise.[19]

Campbell's third essay tells what Adam lost in other terms:
his personal glory, his conformity to the image of God, and the
loss of a correct idea of God's image—or moral character—which
is the "fountain of idolatry." After that, God cannot love man
with the "complacent affection" once possible, until his moral
image is restored. However, man did not lose his susceptibility
of being restored to the image of God and did not incur eternal
death. Pain, or "remorse and shame," is the consequence of moral
guilt which is carried over as inevitably as the physical consequences of sticking one's finger in a fire or of swallowing a
poison.[20]

In his fourth article, Campbell presented his distinctions between natural and revealed knowledge and an analysis of the
five senses, which are familiar. But also he presented three ages
in respect to man's religious relations: the patriarchal, Jewish,
and Christian, with religion and divine character being represented as progressively developed "and not consummated all
at once." Faith, "or confidence in God," has been the controlling
principle of "all religious homage." "Thus the patriarchal age
was the star-light of the moral world; the Jewish age was the

18. *Idem*, VI, 25–28.
19. *Idem*, VI, 25–28.
20. *Idem*, VI, 61–64, 88–91.

moon-light; the ministry of the harbinger was the twilight; and the Christian age was the sun-light of the moral world." [21]

The other "Essays on Man" cover essentially the ground which we have reviewed in our discussion of Campbell's defense of revealed religion. Biblical chronology and a heavy reliance upon Hyde are employed. In doing this he explains the confusion of languages as necessary before the eventual formation of Asiatic, African, and European nations. He also points out that the first religious economy, the patriarchal, was adapted to "families," with only a single family required for its usage; and the second was national, with accommodations to national institutions and societal organizations. As a consequence of the Fall, God withdrew his personal intimacies with the race and communicated through messengers, symbols, and human institutions thereafter, or "by things already known." [22]

In his "Prefatory Remarks" to the first volume of the *Millennial Harbinger,* Campbell linked his analogy of the starlight, the moonlight, the twilight, and the sunlight ages of the world with the expectancy of the millennium and with the tasks that must be done for its introduction.

Critique of Other Millennarians

The most convenient way to determine the boundaries of Campbell's millennial thought is to compare it with other types of contemporary millennial thought which he criticized, particularly the secularistic Owenite, the cataclysmic Millerite, and the theocratic Mormon systems.

The basic departure which he made from most of his contemporary millennarians was to insist upon a gradual and thorough triumph of Christ in the hearts of people on earth before the millennium would come fully, in contradistinction to those who proclaimed its sudden, if not altogether magical, arrival. One of his best efforts to clarify this difference of opinion was an article on the "Millennium" in 1856.

We are deeply penetrated with the idea that christianity, being a new dispensation of the Holy Spirit to Jews and Gentiles under Christ, a dispensation *not of letter,* but of Spirit, must continue till the *"Fulness of the Gentiles"* be consummated. But this clearly

21. *Idem,* VI, 61–64, 81–91.
22. *Idem,* VI, 109–112.

intimates that it is not to be forever, or to the final consummation of the drama of Christianity. That the Redeemer shall come out of Zion and turn away "ungodliness"—impiety, the fuel of unbelief—"from Jacob,"—is an express oracle indicative of some special and glorious interposition of the Lord Jesus—which may usher in what we usually call "the personal reign of Christ"— the subjection of all nations to him, of the moral certainty of such an interposition we should not dogmatically affirm in advance of a most cautious and prayerful investigation of both the Jewish and Christian oracles. . . .[23]

This is characteristic of Campbell's millennial outlook, roughly from 1829 until 1866. His effort to be objective in Scripture studies, with prayer and care, his desire to be cautious in observing current events and past history, and his emphasis upon the "fulness of the Gentiles" prevented him from predicting precise dates when the millennium would fully arrive. This also caused him to reject the "One Day Judgment" and other miraculous implications of the Millerite movement. His emphasis upon "the personal reign of Christ" heightened his disgust toward the Mormon theocracy. Moreover it tended to make the second coming of Christ *figurative*. He classed the Mormons, the Millerites, and the Owenites as "Bastard Millennarians." [24]

The greatest difference between Robert Owen's view of the millennium and Campbell's is that the former held that the millennium had already come, in part, on a secular basis, whereas the latter held that the millennium was approaching on a religious basis. Man had everything to do with it to Robert Owen; but Campbell held that the controlling part is wrought by the hand of God in the affairs and development of human history, although man's cooperation or lack of cooperation could check or accelerate its arrival. This involved their conflict over the plight and destiny of man which we have discussed.

Campbell declared that Owen speaks about a "divine system of legislation" to "place mankind under a modern Theocracy."

Sceptical as my friend is, I must infer that he is a *believer* in the millennium; and, for ought I know, he may be doing as much as a thousand missionaries to induce it. *Cyrus* knew not the God of Jacob; he had no desire to emancipate the Jews. . . . Mr. Owen tells us, that wars shall cease; that plenty shall follow us

23. *The Millennial Harbinger*, 1856, p. 697.
24. *Idem*, 1856, p. 698.

superabundantly as the waters of the Ohio; that there shall be no more need for accumulating property to answer our future exigencies, than there now exists for bottling up the waters of the Ohio? Now all this tends to bright anticipations of future glory and happiness to man. Mr. Owen's *millennium,* we suppose, has arrived; how long is it to continue? A millennium is a thousand years. . . .[25]

The first particular attention that Alexander Campbell paid to William Miller appears in the June 30, 1840, issue of the *Millennial Harbinger.* He had made an extensive northern trip which took him through New England in 1836 but was too occupied with the deists, skeptics, infidels, and Universalists to mention whether he had encountered any Millerite ideas.[26] He published and commented upon a copied letter of Miller to Himes, as follows:

The writings and preachings of a certain Mr. Miller, of New England, on the coming of the Lord during the present year, have given rise to some discussion and excitement in that quarter. Already a new periodical, called "The Signs of the Times," edited by J. V. Himes, Boston, is instituted on that subject, and has advanced to its third number. We think it due to the community to record the fact; and as Mr. Miller has given us a brief summary of his views on the whole subject, we shall not abridge them. We give them to our readers rather as one of the *signs of the times,* than because we regard them as scriptural or well-founded. The author of them is a little enthusiastic, perhaps; but be this as it may, we do not believe that his views are well founded, and yet they are more plausible than much of the most popular creeds of the last century. I have no objection that the present dispensation close during the present year. But were it to close, the fortunes of Christianity are vastly diverse from all that we have learned from both Testaments—especially from Daniel and John. A.C.[27]

This statement of Campbell charts the course for his consideration of the Millerite movement. The alleged interpretation that

25. *Campbell-Owen Debate,* I, 104–105.
26. In 1845 Campbell mentions that during the 1836 tour he quizzed Elias Smith in Boston concerning millennial views which Smith had published in 1808. Smith informed him that he had preached the personal reign of the Messiah in Jerusalem for eighteen months before he recovered " 'from the pleasing imagination' " but " 'it then expired within me.' " However, Campbell does not hint that he discussed Miller's views with Smith. *The Millennial Harbinger,* 1845, p. 50.
27. *Idem,* 1840, pp. 269–272.

Campbell changed the name of his magizine to the *Millennial Harbinger* on account of the influence of William Miller's popularization of the second coming of Christ [28] is as fantastic as other Disciples' explanations which have softened his eschatology.[29]

In 1841, in his first of a series of articles on "The Coming of the Lord," Campbell wrote that *"two* great impostures of the East and of the West have arisen," Mohammed and the Pope. But only the prophecies concerning the "rise of the pretended Prophet of God, and the infallible Vicar of Christ, have been fulfilled." However, the triumphs of the Gospel "over its four grand rivals,

28. B. L. Smith, *(Alexander Campbell*, p. 181), ignores the whole development of Campbell's millennial thought and consciousness before 1816, the time Miller began taking his Bible seriously. Miller kept his millennial light hidden until well into the 1820's and did not begin his public lectures on this subject until 1831.

29. W. T. Moore recognizes that the millennial note was Campbell's "predominant idea in naming his magazine" but presents no conception of how the millennial perspective overshadowed Campbell's change and future actions. In fact, he makes a mystery out of Campbell's millennial thought by saying, "It always has been somewhat difficult to understand just what were Mr. Campbell's views concerning the Millennial period . . . he evidently believed in the coming of the Millennial period, but he was never willing to commit himself to any definite time when it would begin. Nor is it clear that he took any particular side in the controversy between Pre-Millennialists . . . in no case was it ever made an important element in his teaching." He allots the subject a page and a half. *A Comprehensive History of the Disciples of Christ* (New York, Toronto, London, Edinburgh, Fleming H. Revell Co., 1909), pp. 303–305.

Robert Richardson allows the subject about a page, although he admits that Campbell was convinced that the "union of so many of different parties in the primitive faith" and the check of "infidel schemes" were leading to the "millennial period anticipated by the Church." *Memoirs of Alexander Campbell*, II, 302–303.

W. E. Garrison sees *The Millennial Harbinger* as the "symbol of change" from Campbell's *Christian Baptist* type of interest. But "The name of the new magazine . . . does not indicate any special interest in the second coming of Christ in a spectacular way or any marked devotion to either the premillennial or the postmillennial view. Apparently he uses the term in a quite loose and general sense. If any sort of millennium is ever going to arrive—meaning the triumph of the Kingdom of God on earth—it can only be by purifying and unifying the church. Therefore, as the harbinger of such a millennium, he proposed as the aim of his new periodical: (1) to restore the faith, ordinances, organization, and terms of admission of the apostolic church; (2) to do this by resting absolutely upon the authority of the Bible; (3) and by these means to arrive at what Thomas Campbell had called 'simple evangelical Christianity' and to make this the basis of union. This is all that Garrison allots to the subject." *Religion Follows the Frontier*, p. 147.

Mahometism, Papalism, Paganism, and Atheism, occupy a large space in the yet unfulfilled visions of Daniel and of John." [30]

This observation marks the departure of Campbell from other popular millennarians of his day and affords the list of four of his five "enemies" who must be won to Christ before the Millennium could come. He omits "Sectarianism" in this list but frequently included it. He felt that the most important question before the public is whether the Lord will come before or after the millennium. If he comes prior to the Gospel triumph over these five enemies, the millennium will be different from Campbell's suppositions. [31]

Therefore, Campbell discussed three theories of the millennium: "*Mr. Begg's Theory,*" "*Mr. Miller's Theory,*" and "*The Protestant Theory.*"

The first theory held that the Lord will make his descent from heaven and dwell in a rebuilt Jerusalem, reigning in personal presence "certainly 1000, and probably 365,000 years." The man of sin will be destroyed, the race of evildoers cut off, and a "resurrection of the saints and martyred witnesses of Christ precede the millennial reign," with a short apostasy succeeding that reign.

Campbell styled Miller's theory as

bolder and more intelligible than any of the moderns. . . . According to this view, the general conflagration of the resurrection of the dead saints, the transformation of the living, and the personal and glorious return of the Lord, must precede the Millennium. . . . The Millennium will commence, or rather this world will come to an end, in the year 1843, or 1847 at farthest. The day of judgment will then commence, and will continue for the whole thousand years; at the end of which the wicked shall be raised and sentenced to everlasting ruin. [32]

The Protestant theory corresponds roughly to Campbell's position, although he does not claim to agree with all of it.

The Millennium, so far as the triumphs of Christianity is concerned, will be a state of greatly enlarged and continuous prosperity, in which the Lord will be exalted and his divine spirit enjoyed in an unprecedented measure. All the conditions of society

30. *The Millennial Harbinger*, 1841, p. 7.
31. *Ibid.*
32. *Idem*, 1841, pp. 8–9

will be vastly improved; wars shall cease, and peace and good will among men will generally abound. The Jews will be converted, and the fulness of the Gentiles will be brought into the kingdom of the Messiah. Genuine Christianity will be diffused through all nations; crimes and punishments will cease; governments will recognize human rights, and will rest on just and benevolent principles. Conversions will not only be genuine, but early and general. Large measures of divine influence will be vouchsafed. One extended and protracted series of revivals will keep pace with the exigencies of society.[33] The seasons will become more mild; climates more salubrious, health more vigorous, labor less, lands more fertile, and the animal creations more prolific: for the knowledge and glory of God shall cover the whole earth as the waters cover the channel of the sea. The Millennium is to precede the coming of the Lord, the general conflagration, and the creation of new heavens and earth.[34]

Campbell judged that Miller's theory "promises the least blessing to the human race." The Lord comes on the "first day of Mr. Miller's Millennium" and conversion will end; the fruits are gathered in 1843 with the "number" of participants "sealed and registered for ever." For a thousand years not one child is to be born, one sermon preached, or one soul converted. Perhaps the church has been deluded in dreaming of converting a world of Jews and Gentiles; and "Paganism, Mahometanism, Papalism, Atheism, and Bibleism are all predestined to live till the Lord comes" and "die on the same day." This conception "seems to have no object in view, except the mere occupancy of this earth for a thousand years as a mere gratification to the saints before the wicked shall be raised." But if this be the "Lord's will . . . we acquiesce in it." [35]

He acknowledged that Begg's theory "promises more" but has "some inconveniences also." Campbell could not imagine the saints "eating spiritual food in Jerusalem, while they are ploughing and sowing, reaping and thrashing, grinding and eating earthly food in the country round about." The mixture of "immortal bodies" and mortal actions was too much for him! Furthermore, how

33. Note the nineteenth-century American frontier love of revivals in the millennial picture. Scott's friendship and revival interest are beginning to bear fruits to the Campbell who was once as nervous toward them as toward the formalities of ecclesiasticism.

34. *The Millennial Harbinger*, 1841, p. 9.

35. *Idem*, 1841, pp. 9–10.

can missionaries be sent out to foreign lands if conversion is to cease one day in 1843?

In 1841 Campbell presented his Biblical studies in the prophecies with a host of texts to support his positions. He described "four great events attendant" on the coming of the Lord: "the saints" would be raised, "the living saints would be immediately changed, a final judgment and separation of the "righteous and the wicked," and the changing of the structure of the material universe with a "new heaven and a new earth created." Campbell asked if the Advent occurs "within a few years, how shall all the promises and prophecies concerning Jews and Gentiles be fulfilled?" [36]

In his eleventh article on "The Coming of the Lord," January, 1842, Campbell announced that he would publish both sides of the Millerite question, for "our friends and brethren in the North" are spreading the contagion "to the West and South-West" that the millennial dispensation will arrive about September, 1843. He regretted that Miller's evidence seemed insufficient. However, later he described Miller as a sincere Christian who does not pretend to be a learned man in his view of Christ's coming literally in 1843.

In June, 1842, Campbell compared the conversions made from the Millerite excitement with those of "doubtful reputation" in deathbed "penitence." Such converts would relapse "in case of a disappointment." If they "hear not Moses and the Prophets, neither would they be persuaded though one rose from the dead." [37]

In August, 1842, Campbell's patience with the Millerite enthusiasts had "reached its end."

The Miller Millennarians, now the loudest, boldest, most confident in the field of discussion, are not so impartial and disinterested as I was at first so willing to believe. I gave their views so fully and so impartially that some thought that I not only favored them, but had actually gone over to their system of interpretation . . . they have not permitted their readers to see my reasonings against their visions. . . . Why is this studied and obstinate silence? Is it that of contempt, of fear, or of ignorance? Speak out, Elder Himes! . . . I still adhere to the theory that contemplates a *thousand years millennium*—not to one day of judgment millennium. . . . I am either literal or spiritual, not both, in inter-

36. *Idem*, 1841, 10–12, 49–54.
37. *Idem*, 1842, 42–44, 45, 97, 262

preting the first week, and in applying it as an allegoric sketch of the events of time. As were the first six days natural, so was the seventh. If any one of them were a diurnal revolution, or an age of ten thousand years, the others were. . . . If we have had six thousand years of labor and travail we shall have one thousand years of rest and peace. . . .[38]

In 1843 Campbell published twelve articles with the Millerite movement specifically in mind. He gave outlines and analyses of Miller's view and sympathy for the emotionally distraught. He concluded that he had written enough on the subject which time would settle and the world would go on the same in spite of the excited parties. In 1844 Campbell did not show enough interest to write a specific article about the movement.

Campbell was not long in writing about Mormonism. It was closer to him than the Millerite movement. Sidney Rigdon, one of the ablest leaders won by the Disciples from the Mahoning Baptist Association, deserted the ranks of Scott and the Campbells to become one of the organizing spirits of the new millennial theocratic movement.[39]

By July, 1831, Campbell was reporting an encounter with Mormonism on the Western Reserve, Ohio.[40] He attributed the current success of the movement not to the "lying spirit" which has "always been the spirit of false prophets," such as Joseph Smith and his "extravagant stories told of miracles, prophecies, and visits of angels, by the witnesses of the golden plates of Nephi" but to "Mr. Booth, a Methodist preacher of very considerable standing," and his conversion to "the New Bible." He was disgusted with Booth's reasoning that the *Book of Mormon* was four times better substantiated than the New Testament because "the disciples of Joseph Smith had *four living* witnesses to sustain

---

38. *Idem*, 1842, pp. 332–333.

39. How far Alexander Campbell influenced the Mormon movement through Sidney Rigdon is conjectural. He first met Rigdon in 1821 and talked with him about the dispensations that night and the next morning. Rigdon was present when Campbell spoke on "The Progress of Revealed Light" in which he gave his views on the dispensations and the starlight, moonlight, twilight, and sunlight ages before the Mahoning Baptist Association in 1826.

40. W. T. Moore claims that Scott had aroused many Disciples in that vicinity to an anticipation of the millennium. It is known that Rigdon himself sought to use Disciples churches around Kirkland, Ohio, for Mormon propaganda. *The Millennial Harbinger*, 1848, p. 523; W. T. Moore, *op. cit.*, pp. 176–177, 300–303.

the Book of Mormon." Only "starvation could cure" some of Smith's adherents.

Even Sidney Rigdon told me that "were Joseph to be proved a liar, or say himself that he never found the Book of Mormon as he has reported, still he would believe it, and believe that all who do not believe it shall be damned." But a very few, however, have attained to this faith of assurance; and it is more than probable that none of the late converts ever will.[41]

However, by January, 1835, Campbell realized that he had taken the movement too lightly and recommended the reading of E. D. Howe's *Mormonism Unveiled,* published in 1834. "Perhaps we were too sanguine when we thought that the fable was so barefaced that it could not stand upon its legs or palms in the face of day and the American people. . . ." [42]

In 1839 Campbell published Matilda Davison's account of the "Origin of the 'Book of Mormon' or 'Golden Bible' " from the *Boston Daily Advertiser.* The account told that Sidney Rigdon was connected with the printing establishment of Mr. Patterson of Pittsburg, the editor of a newspaper. There Rigdon had the chance to read a manuscript of the Reverend Solomon Spaulding of New York, who had written an imaginary account of *"a historical sketch of this long lost race"* (as evidenced by numerous mounds and forts at New Salem, Ohio, which were popularly supposed to be the "dilapidated dwellings and fortifications of a race now extinct"). The manuscript was not published. When the *Book of Mormon* appeared, friends acquainted with the manuscript discovered that the historical parts of it were "identical" with the work of Spaulding. Campbell commented that he had little doubt that Sidney Rigdon "is the leading conjuror in this diabolical affair" and the gullibility of the "present generation" has never been surpassed in history.[43]

From the years 1842 to 1845 Campbell published a few additional articles on Mormonism, chiefly in the form of extracts from the *Book of Mormon,* "exposures" of Mormonism, and anecdotes. His specific interest in the successful "Millennial Church" waned after he proudly concluded that Mormonism had not made headway among the Disciples of Christ.

41. *The Millennial Harbinger,* 1831, pp. 331–332.
42. *Idem,* 1835, pp. 44–45.
43. *Idem,* 1839, pp. 265–268.

CHAPTER XIII

THE INTRODUCTION OF THE MILLENNIUM

CAMPBELL left little doubt in the minds of his current readers as to the role of the Disciples in helping to introduce the millennium. The Disciples were to pioneer in the union of all Christians by a complete restoration of the New Testament creedless church. Even the most bitter of his former Baptist allies sensed Campbell's new millennial perspective. As early as 1830 Elder John Taylor wrote a pamphlet, "Campbellism Exposed," and likened Campbell to "Daniel's he-goat." [1]

In 1837 Purcell quoted the *Baptist Banner* which accused Campbell of being interested in reaping money, exhibiting his skill, and obtaining publicity from their debate: "The Campbellites will sip delicious wisdom from the lips of their leader. A new impulse will be given to their now drooping state. They will wage his high claims to competency to reform religion and introduce the Millennium." [2]

In the first of a series of articles on the "Millennium" in 1830, Campbell frequently used the expression, "The Millennial Church." He held that all creeds and speculative opinions are *"too* narrow and too weak" to be its foundation; they have never given peace and union to Christians. They require too much "intellectual operation." No larger societies can be based upon them than now exist. Campbell proposed, as a substitute, "the belief of gospel facts upon scriptural evidence" because the *"Ancient Gospel"* alone is "long enough, broad enough, strong enough for the whole superstructure called the Millennial Church." [3]

The restoration of original Christianity, not the reformation

1. *The Millennial Harbinger*, 1830, pp. 317–318.
2. *Campbell-Purcell Debate*, p. 59.
3. *The Millennial Harbinger*, 1830, pp. 56–58. Walter Scott, in his *Christian Baptist* articles on the millennium, had also used the term "Millennial Church."

of Popery or Protestantism, became the "polar star" of all his "aims and effort ecclesiastic." [4]

But his greatest hurdle was to show that the restoration of primitive Christianity is good churchmanship. When Campbell tried to establish a continuity of primitive gospel-minded "Protestants" throughout Christian history, Bishop Purcell aptly inquired where the Protestants were before Martin Luther. Campbell matched the query by asking where the popes and Roman Catholicism were before the time of Constantine. The Bishop subterfuged his own reply but Campbell had his.

The disciples were first called Christians at Antioch, he said, and call us "what you please, however, it does not change the nature of the race," [5] whether it be Galileans, Novations, Donatists, Paulicans, Waldenses, Albingenses, Protestants. ". . . we can find an unbroken series of Protestants—a regular succession of those who protested against the corruptions of the Roman church, and endeavored to hold fast the faith once delivered to the saints, from the first schism in the year 250, A. D. to the present day. . . ." [6]

Under his new eschatology, Campbell developed more constructive attitudes among the Disciples toward reform, church

4. *Idem*, 1853, p. 61. Campbell's view should be contrasted with A. Harnack in *What Is Christianity?* (New York, G. P. Putnam's Sons, London, Williams & Newgate, 1901). Upon considering the growth of early Christianity and its corresponding needs of organization and churchmanship, Harnack claims that *primitive Christianity* had to die in order that *Christianity* might live.

5. *Campbell-Purcell Debate*, pp. 77 ff. One of Campbell's inconsistencies is that he saw New Testament Christianity as a sect; yet he insisted that it is the true "church" and that there is no place for sectarianism. This is not a confusion of language on Campbell's part, for he knew the difference between a sect and a church. The same difficulty is evident in his speaking of the visible church and the invisible church interchangeably; apparently he saw the validity and necessity of both but was not quite willing to accept the paradox. He found it more convenient to speak of each in exclusive terms and demands.

6. *Ibid*. Purcell replied that Campbell was wrong in claiming an unbroken organic and doctrinal succession in these movements. They were heterogeneous sects and could not be proved Catholic "in *time*, in place, or in doctrine." He quoted two of Campbell's favorite historians to show the extravagances of the Cathari, Waldenses, and others. He advised Campbell to seek "more reputable religious ancestors" and not to make up a "monster-church."

Campbell sidetracked Purcell's references to the "monster-church" and shifted to the general theme that "Protestants" were usually reoccurring in church history. Campbell had slipped at the point of exalting ancient and medieval sects and of debasing modern sects, for he did not examine them all by the same criteria.

architecture, church organization, discipline, rites, orthodox theology, and speculative thought.

In his Preface to the 1833 *Millennial Harbinger* he wrote:

The Apostacy is in its dotage, and the Man of Sin tottering on the brink of the grave. The world is in travail; a new age is soon to be born; and the great regeneration is at hand. . . . Expectation is on tiptoe, stretching forth into the mysterious future, ready to hail with acclamation the harbinger of better times . . . The theory of reformation is, however, far in advance of the practice, *and to this fact special regard will be had in the volume which we have just commenced. . . .*[7]

Campbell, the patriotic American, appreciated the material improvements of his day. But he was as critical as Walter Scott of the social, moral, political, economic, and religious order. Their eschatology was not based upon perfectionistic, secular, or extremely supernatural millennial philosophies of history. Campbell and Scott were essentially reformers in their millennarian roles. They criticized their own religious group as well as other communions and secular trends. Of course, they favored their own communion as a hen would its chicks.

Campbell was a proud adopter of his brood but an uneasy and restless one. In the Preface to the *Millennial Harbinger* of 1838 Campbell wrote:

We teach that right thinking must precede right speaking and right acting; but should we stop at the end of right thinking, and be satisfied with ourselves, we should prove ourselves to be wrong thinkers of no ordinary type. We have had the Gospel and Christianity restored on paper and in speech: we want to see them living, moving, and acting on the stage of time, on a larger scale and with more brilliant light and power than has hitherto appeared. To this great end we devote supremely this second volume of the New Series.

The times are yet truly degenerate. It is, indeed, an age of improvement in every thing but moral and religious living. New roads, canals, cities, and projects innumerable engross the attention of the community; and benevolent schemes, domestic and foreign, have almost exhausted the copiousness of our vernacular for suitable designations. Against all these improvements we utter no complaint; but we do say, that the great multitude of professors are as carnal, selfish, sensual and worldly as ever:

7. *The Millennial Harbinger*, 1833, pp. 3–4; see also *idem*, 1832, pp. 138–139.

that living, talking, acting religion—vital piety—heaven-toned, heaven-taught, heaven-inspired piety and virtue are not the characteristics of the Christian profession in the present century. . . .

To *extend* the Christian profession, rather than to *elevate* it, has been too much the spirit of the modern enterprize . . . few seem to apprehend that to elevate it is the surer and speedier way to extend it. The boundaries between the church and the world are not sufficiently prominent to strike the attention of the truly inquisitive. . . .

The passion for wealth and power was never more active and impetuous in any community than it now appears to be in these United States. The very frame of our government, our constitution, laws, bills of rights, are all occasionally defied, and trodden under foot, and threatened with utter prostration and ruin at the impulse of these passions. Mobs, arson, murder, in order to put down offensive opinions, or to prevent the discussion of them, are now the order of the day. . . .[8]

In the 1830's Campbell advocated that the Disciples construct "Meeting-Houses" which would be as convenient and comfortable "as private dwellings for our families and friends." He retained his Calvinistic and Puritan note of simplicity and thrift. He complained at the way stoves were placed in churches which caused him to catch colds and a sore throat.

A Christian meeting-house ought to be humble, commodious, and free from all the splendor of this vain and sinful world. It should be a one story house, without steeple, galleries or pulpit. The floor should be an inclined plane, descending from the entrance one foot in every eight or ten. The Lord's table and seats for the elders of the congregation should be at the remote end, opposite to the entrance, and consequently on the lowest part of the floor, visible to every eye in the house. . . . More than half the expenses of erecting a meeting-house would be saved on this plan, inasmuch as the fashionable columns, galleries, and pulpits of this age constitute the chief items of expense. . . .[9]

In the meantime in the 1830's he wrote articles upon church organization and discipline. By 1842 he gave "Five Arguments for Church Organization" as necessary for: distributing the Bible abroad; cooperation on the mission fields; elevating the Christian ministry; checking, restraining, and removing "the flood of imposture and fraud committed upon the benevolence of the breth-

8. *Idem*, 1838, pp. 3–4.
9. *Idem*, 1834, pp. 7–8, 1839, pp. 55–56, 189.

ren" by irresponsible and deceptive persons; and for the cooperation of the tens of thousands of Israel.[10]

His articles on the subject increased during the 1840's and
1850's. The scope included "Conventions of Christian Churches"
which, he assured his former revolutionaries, implied no more
than organized and general cooperation. He urged the organization of state conventions and of yearly meetings, with the observation that "cases like it" occurred in the New Testament. Well
selected and ordained leaders should participate in these.[11]

In 1853, as the climax of the departure from his *Christian Baptist* position, he held that church organization is not named in the
Christian Scriptures but "is implied in the Apostolic Epistles."
He compared organization in the animal and vegetable worlds
with the essential growth of Christianity for its purposes. Another analogy suggested that as the official political grace is
vested in the president of the United States through its Constitution, every officer in the church is invested with grace and
authority in his office from the New Constitution (New Testament) in the kingdom of Christ. Emergencies, ordinary and ex-
traordinary, bring forth crises in the church requisite of judicial
and executive departments essential to the times and seasons.
"As a religious community, we have been in a transition state, and
are yet only partially organized. . . . We have grown and spread
with unprecedented activity. But a period has arrived when individual enterprise must yield to public concert and organized
effort." [12]

In the meantime, Campbell was elected president of the first
national convention of the Disciples of Christ in 1849.

Campbell urged attention to church discipline with the observation that good preachers rarely make good disciplinarians, just
as no good admiral, general, captain, or commander is "distinguished by much talking." Disciples' church difficulties, he
said in 1840, had not come out of doctrinal, speculative, and emo-
tional dogmas, as in "the species of sectarian alienations," but
from the maladministration or "error in discipline" in "every
case." He argued that age is not necessarily a requirement for
office, for it is a "relative term"; Timothy at thirty was an "older
man in the Lord than Sergius Paulus" at sixty.

10. *Idem*, 1842, p. 523.
11. For examples, see *idem*, 1845, p. 49, 1849, pp. 269, 271, 459, 689, 694,
1851, p. 605.
12. *Idem*, 1853, pp. 109, 120–127, 241–249, 488–493.

Appeals of local churches should be referred to special conferences or conventions "when exigencies may require" but the parties involved should have representation in the deciding tribunal in order that they may be more readily reconciled.[13]

In 1850 and 1851 he wrote two series of articles on "The Christian Ministry and Its Support" and "Support of the Christian Ministry." However, his old ghost haunted his steps. The *Christian Baptist* was quoted by former loyal supporters of his individualism to attack his *Millennial Harbinger* type of churchmanship. He tried to wiggle out of his former position without acknowledging his radical change. He insisted that his *Christian Baptist* essays on "Hireling Clergy" had been misunderstood and misapplied and he had been "placed on the wrong side of another question, while placing ourselves on the right side of that of the hireling clergy."

Nevertheless, Campbell's extreme sectarian followers knew what he had said and meant in his more turbulent days! His defensive maneuver never got the Disciples out of the jam of two incompatible patterns of thought and action.

Another important trend of Campbell's millennial pattern was to place a central place upon the "ordinances of the new institution." He had begun this early; for the Lord's Supper, baptism, and the Bible were stressed in his *Christian Baptist* days. In addition to numerous references on the importance of these, in 1830 he wrote extras of sixty and twenty-eight pages, respectively, on "Remission of Sins" and "The Breaking of the Loaf."

In 1843 Campbell's first article of the *Millennial Harbinger,* "The Ordinances," begins:

The current reformation, if conspicuous now or hereafter for anything, must be so because of the conspicuity it gives the Bible and its ordinances as the indispensible moral means of spiritual life and health. I would prefer to concentrate the peculiarities of our arguments with this generation into one grand characteristic, and with this as its differential attribute . . . That distinguishing characteristic is, A RESTORATION OF THE ORDINANCES OF THE NEW INSTITUTION TO THEIR PLACE AND POWER. Not a restoration of the world and the ordinances, as though distinct from each other; but simply a restoration of the ordinances; inasmuch as the Bible is one of these ordinances itself.[14]

13. *Idem*, 1840, pp. 34–35, 56–58, 120.
14. *Idem*, 1843, p. 9.

This tendency in Campbell's thought should be noted, for it has been assumed that he thought of the "ordinances," the Lord's Supper and baptism, as mere symbolic observances. On the contrary, he was close to a position of sacramentalism without priestly miracle, although he rejected the term "sacrament." As in other ideas, Campbell was closer to orthodox thought than his vocabulary legalism against orthodox jargon indicates.

Therefore, when Campbell speaks of the Bible as an ordinance, we must recall that he thought of the Bible as the vehicle of the word of God. Furthermore, he said:

In defining a law or ordinance of Nature, our masters of physical science, say, *"It is the mode in which the powers of nature act."* In religion I only amend its verbiage, while I retain its spirit. We say, a law or ordinance of religion is THE MODE IN WHICH THE GRACE OF GOD ACTS UPON HUMAN NATURE. The ordinances of Christianity are, therefore, the powers of the gospel of the grace of God. Every law of nature is a specific demonstration of divine power in reference to some effect no other way attainable. So every ordinance of the gospel is a specific demonstration of divine grace or spiritual power in reference to some effect no other way attainable. . . . No one ordinance of God in nature can ever be substituted by another. This when established in nature, shall be shown to be equally true in religion. . . .[15]

Nathan Rice was impressed with the marked similarity between Campbell's doctrine and that of Roman Catholicism in reference to baptism. After his debate with Walker, Campbell usually insisted that there is a necessary connection between immersion and the remission of sins, although he confessed that he cannot explain that connection.[16] Thus there is a great element of mystery in ordinances for Campbell.

Moreover, in his debate with Purcell, Campbell insisted that the ordinances of Protestants do not depend upon the efficacy of priestly ordination for their validity. He felt that no one could have assurance that a Roman Catholic priest was really ordained on account of the necessity of right intention, for the believer cannot know whether the priest has met the requirement or not. But Protestant ordinances are efficacious in themselves, independent either of the personal character or the office of the priest. The

15. *Idem*, 1843, pp. 9–10.
16. Yet he believed that unimmersed persons might be saved, but at the mercy of God through faith.

efficacy depends upon the nature of the ordinances and the faith of the receiver, without clerical interposal.

Alexander Campbell rapidly moved into more speculative, orthodox, and theological thought under his role as a churchman and defender of revealed religion. Yet he denied that he speculated except when dealing with the opponents of true Christianity. Two of his most maturely written short articles of reflective thought appear under the innocent titles, "Musings in Broadway, New York, Jan. 4, '58" and "Musings while on Board the Steamer 'Tempest," March 26, 1858." [17] He did not have to speculate. He mused.

Campbell sought to keep his movement from getting either too anti-Calvinistic or too anti-Arminian in flavor. In 1846 he held that both theoretic Calvinism and Arminianism were "equidistant from the true gospel." He observed that Peter was too Arminian for some Calvinists and Paul was too Calvinistic for some Arminians. "Much of Calvinism is true, and much of Arminianism is true. Let us, then, not place ourselves antagonistically to one of them, that we may not be regarded as partial to the other. Christianity is a few centuries older than either of them. . . ." [18]

He claimed that he never thought it

expedient to speculate, write, or teach . . . much on sectarian predestination or non-predestination. Still nothing is more evident than that the Bible teaches predestination. . . . I do not say that it teaches Calvinian or Arminian predestination . . . there is a scriptural election and reprobation . . . *persons, places, and things* are elected and reprobated by God. . . .[19]

In 1853 he reviewed "A Discussion" of 1852 between the Reverend James Matthews and Elder Benjamin Franklin on "Predestination and Foreknowledge of God." Campbell declared that the *"epistolary* debate" was as much as his nerves could stand in one session.

The theme is one of such height and depth, and of such length and breadth, I never could bring my mind to debate on a stage, or before a promiscuous auditory. Election and foreknowledge are words found in the common version of the New Testament, and, therefore, ought to be understood. But for some reason, which I cannot now develop, I have always felt that these matters, as

17. *The Millennial Harbinger,* 1858, pp. 144–145, 241–244.
18. *Idem,* 1846, p. 173.
19. *Idem,* 1846, p. 326.

well as the doctrine of "the trinity," ought to be debated rather on the knees, than before a promiscuous auditory.[20]

Campbell's post-*Christian Baptist* thought moved into a somewhat Calvinistic atmosphere. Especially is this seen in connection with the sovereign will of God as the cause of all things. Also his analysis of the nature of man, as a war of elements, passion, and reason in "chaotic confusion and disorder," is suggestive of Calvinism, for "self-love" is the "mother" of the passions, vanity, avarice, and ambition, which are always present in the triumph of the *"human"* over the "divine" in human nature.[21] But there were too many other elements in his thought to restrict it to Calvinism.

In 1855 Campbell noted that "Dr. Edwards, the first of American metaphysical Doctors, and Dr. Dwight, the second of American Rabbis, mainly concur in their sublime metaphysics of theology." He reviewed an article dealing with their conception of regeneration and said that he could "fully subscribe" to it. Yet on a higher authority than Edwards or Dwight we do not have to reason, but *"By faith we understand* that the worlds were framed *by the word of God."* [22]

In 1855, upon being accused of changing since his *Christian Baptist* days, Campbell characteristically replied: "I am not conscious of any change in any Christian doctrine since I wrote the first volume of the Christian Baptist. That my horizon has been much enlarged during the last thirty years, I should be ashamed not to avow." [23]

That was not the first transition for Alexander Campbell. In the third volume of the *Christian Baptist,* when "An Independent Baptist" was too individualistic even for him, Campbell had confessed:

I have tried the pharisaic plan, and the monastic. I was once so straight, that, like the Indian's tree, I leaned a little the other way . . . for I was once so strict a Separatist that I would neither pray nor sing praises with any one who was not as perfect as I supposed myself . . . until I discovered the mistake, and saw that on the principle embraced in my conduct, there never could be a congregation or church on the earth. . . .[24]

20. *Idem*, 1853, p. 233.
21. *Idem*, 1858, pp. 144–145, 1842, p. 6, 1843, p. 11, 1854, pp. 275–279, 1861, p. 3, 1863, pp. 241–243, 1864, p. 82.
22. *Idem*, 1855, pp. 664, 668–678.
23. *Idem*, 1855, p. 343.
24. *The Christian Baptist*, III, p. 228.

In the 1840's and 1850's Campbell resented the heretical implications of the nickname, "Campbellism." He tried to prove that his followers were "evangelically more orthodox" and more in line with Christian history than his opponents superficially supposed.[25]

The man who had been too straight to bend with a local congregation became flexible enough to join a sect of congregations. Later he tried to organize a church of sects. His "horizon" had "enlarged during the last thirty years" on the background of a growing millennial consciousness.

Catholicism in its Millennial Perspective

Three particular emphases of Campbell show the millennial role of New Testament forces in conquering "Papalism": Catholicism's apocalyptic status in history and prophecies, its anti-American aspects, and the need for the organization of Protestant hosts to combat it.

His third proposition in the debate with Bishop Purcell in 1837 stated that the Roman Catholic Church "is the Babylon of John, the Man of Sin of Paul, and the Empire of the Youngest Horn of Daniel's Sea Monster." He placed his millennial eye upon the seventh chapter of Daniel and saw amazing results. The four sea monsters of "the Mediterranean" were taken to be God's symbol of tyrannical governments. He concentrated upon the "fourth beast," which had ten horns, for these horns symbolized the Roman Empire which was divided into ten kings or kingdoms

after the barbarian invasion . . . and another (THE LITTLE HORN) shall arise AFTER them. And he shall be DIVERSE (not merely political) from the first (ten) and he shall subdue the three kings . . . he shall destroy the antagonist power of the three empires that preceded this. "He shall speak great words against the Most High, and shall *wear out* the saints of the Most High, and think to *change* times and *laws*. (These three never met in any beings save the popes of Rome.) And they shall be given into his hand until a time, and times, and the dividing of a time."

He estimated that "a time, and times, and the dividing of a time" meant that the Little Horn would sustain its world empire

25. *The Millennial Harbinger*, 1854, pp. 166 ff., 1857, pp. 75–82; see also the references in the "Evangelical Alliance" given later.

for twelve hundred sixty years. There were never but four "great universal empires on earth," the Catholic Empire being the fourth. The Messiah's will be the fifth.[26]

Moreover, he found that "John's Babylon the Great" (a seven-headed, ten-horned savage beast which resembled a lion, a bear, and a leopard, and also Daniel's vision, to Campbell) was the Latin-Empire beast out of which the "Little Horn grew." He took pleasure in citing Irenaeus and his identification of Babylon and the Mother of Harlots.[27]

Giving a familiar exposition of II Thessalonians, he showed that Paul's "Man of Sin" answered the descriptions of Daniel and John; and that he foretold the great "Apostacy." [28]

Bishop Purcell was not convinced. He retorted: "When my opponent stated . . . *'She* is the *man* of sin,' I imagined that he meant no more than an innocuous laugh at the expense of the 'Mother Church,' by making a man of her in her old age." He was surprised that Campbell would dash himself headlong upon "this rock of commentators around which are scattered the wrecks of many learned lucubrations for the last 1800 years!" He observed that both Catholics and Protestants, from Papias to Newton, have floundered upon this hidden shoal of controversy; and the symbolism could apply to Protestants as well as to Roman Catholics.[29]

In the last proposition of the debate, Campbell endeavored to prove that Roman Catholicism is anti-American. He argued that the naturalization laws of the United States require that the potential citizen "entirely renounce all allegiance and fidelity to every foreign prince, potentate, state, or sovereignty"; and yet Catholic bishops have to swear allegiance to Rome, which exercises political and temporal authority in Europe as well as spiritual authority. He described the papacy as a persecuting monarchy which accommodates itself to the customs of a country until it is powerful enough to reach its end. No countercouncil since Trent had acted against its oath to suppress heresy.[30]

As compared with the *Christian Baptist,* the *Millennial Harbinger* represents a concentrated attack upon Roman Cathol-

26. *Campbell-Purcell Debate,* pp. 225–227.

27. *Idem,* pp. 228–230.

28. *Idem,* p. 234.

29. *Idem,* pp. 237–246. It was a nip and tuck debate and Purcell won the count on proposition three.

30. *Idem,* pp. 311–350; see also *The Millennial Harbinger,* 1844, p. 410.

icism. As the reader will recall, the anti-Catholic program in the former publication was to "unmask" the clergy and Catholic elements in Protestantism. Now Roman Catholicism is isolated and the attack against Catholic elements in Protestantism becomes more discriminate.

Campbell watched the formation of the American Protestant Association with favor. It was not anti-Catholic enough for him but he urged "Protestant Popes" to unite and witness against the "Grand Papa," with the hopes that they would lessen their strife among themselves. In 1843 he printed the Constitution of the American Protestant Association with this interesting comment:

Such an association I have long thought the peculiar signs of the times loudly call for. Deeply penetrated with the conviction that the plan was profoundly concocted . . . in the very bosom of the Papal See, to subjugate all America to the Catholic faith and tyranny of its ambitious and tyrannical Pontiff, I proposed to Dr. Beecher, of Cincinnati, and some others, about the time of my debate with Bishop Purcell, to have an association got up in the valley of the Mississippi, and to hold state annual meetings for the very purposes displayed in the Address following the Constitution. . . .

However, Campbell related, Beecher thought that the times were not ripe for the organization then.[31]

The Role of Education

Alexander Campbell opened the "Buffalo Seminary" in his home at Bethany, Virginia, in 1818. Although he obtained more students than he could accommodate, his purpose failed and the school disbanded by 1823. He founded it to offer a classical and religious education, hoping to train young men who would enter the ministry, but too many ventured into law and medicine.[32]

One can scarcely imagine his conducting a seminary in 1823. Then he had much to say about the failure of others in seminary training and little to say about his own.

Under his new perspective, however, Campbell was devoted to organized education. He began in 1830 a series of articles on "Education," describing its millennial role.

31. *Idem*, 1843, pp. 182 ff., 351–353.
32. Robert Richardson, *Memoirs of Alexander Campbell*, I, 491 ff.

In the millennial order of society a system of education in accordance with the true philosophy of the whole man, mental and corporeal, will doubtless universally obtain. I have doubted, seriously doubted, for at least fifteen years, whether the present mode of training the human mind in common schools—whether for infants or young men—was not almost anti-podes to reason, and sailing against the wind and tide of human nature. It is worse than wrong end foremost. We begin in metaphysics, and end in physics. The *natural* sciences, in the present course, are for young men, the last years of their academic, and the *unnatural* sciences (pardon the antithesis) are for infants and children! . . . We want another class of *infant* schools for *young men*. I made something like an experiment of this sort when superintending a classical school, in which mathematics, and what are called the natural sciences, were taught, some seven or eight years ago. It was sufficient to convince me that more than half the time spent in the collegiate way was lost, and less than half the acquisitions were made during the whole course, which might, under a rational system, be obtained at the age of from sixteen to eighteen. I rejoice to see the advances which every year is making towards that perfection of education which is necessary to the millennial order of society.[33]

He claimed that traditional education teaches children "views of the divine character" which "generally alienate" them "from the life of God." Total depravity, stressing *"that infants naturally, perfectly and cordially hate God,"* is avoidable under the Christian "economy." There is no such innate hatred, for "the enmity or love to God conceived in the mind of a child, depends upon the character of God drawn out and figured forth to its mind." There is no reason why children should be "corrupted by education," for their "minds" are "capable of being shaped after almost any model and cast into any mould, universal testimony and observation prove." [34]

In 1834 an address on "Education" before the "Western Literary Institute and College of Professional Teachers" in Cincinnati depicted his basic conception of education. He cited Locke, Milton, Lord Kames, St. Pierre, and others to support his position that giving direction to the interest, mind, and morals of a student is more essential than beginning his education by drum-

33. *The Millennial Harbinger*, 1830, p. 252.
34. *Idem*, 1830, pp. 252–255.

ming his mind full of rote memorizations. Moral culture is *"almost wholly neglected"* in current education. It should precede formal intellectual education, accompany it, and follow it. Benevolent feelings can be trained by presenting benevolent objects before the infant.

He contrasted the French spirits such as Voltaire, Diderot, D'Alembert, and Rousseau with Bacon, Locke, Newton, Boyle, Addison, and others to show the difference that moral education, accompanied by intellectual education, makes for the good of society.[35]

In 1840 he gave his *"beau ideal* of education."

With me *education* and *the formation of moral character* are identical expressions. An immoral man is uneducated. . . . We contemplate a scheme in which the formation of the physical and intellectual man shall not be neglected, but which shall be always held in subordination to the moral man. In which, in one word, the formation of moral character, the cultivation of the heart, shall be the Alpha and Omega, the radical, regulating, and all-controlling aim and object in all the literary and scientific studies, in all the exercises, recreations and amusements of children and youth.[36]

In April, 1840, he announced the granting of a charter by the Commonwealth of Virginia for the incorporation of "Bethany College." The last section of the charter fulfilled the dreams of his vocabulary legalism with the provision that "the establishment of a Theological Professorship in the said college" would be unauthorized.[37] He became the president of Bethany College and held the office until his death. Four professors were appointed. Alexander Campbell taught "Mental Philosophy, Evidences of Christianity, Morals and Political Economy." He could teach theology by not calling it theology but "plain facts."

Campbell's addresses on education continued with a plea for a common public school system for the good of Virginia and the nation.

His new educational experiment was to contribute toward "the advancement of the great cause of human redemption from ignorance, immorality, superstition, and error." By 1846 he

35. *Idem,* 1840, pp. 157–158.
36. *Ibid.*
37. *Idem,* 1840, p. 179.

ranked "scholastic education" as "second only to the ministry of the word" in importance.[38]

As a fair example of his baccalaureate addresses at Bethany, in 1848 Campbell maintained that railroads, telegraphs, electricity, steam, new discoveries, galvanism, mesmerism, Owenism and Fourierism would not "save mankind from ignorance and crime, from disease and poverty." Science and learning "dissociated from Christian religion and morality" are a curse, as illustrated by "a Spinoza, a Hobbes, a Voltaire, a Gibbon," or a Volney.[39]

In 1850 Campbell defined education as "the full development of man in his whole physical, intellectual and moral constitution, with a proper reference to his whole destiny in the universe of God." He believed that two erroneous opinions were common in Christendom: that "religious instruction is necessarily sectarian" and that "morality can be taught as well without religious instruction as with it." Education cannot be "properly conducted or perfected" without nature and the Bible used as the two great textbooks of God. Without the study of the Bible, a school or college is a "grand imposition on the community." The Bible can be taught as the textbook of "moral science or religion" without sectarianism because we have a catholic Protestant faith, hope, and Bible. Enough Protestant latitude and longitude should be allowed to teach the Bible as *inductively* as any other science and not "in the scholastic way." It should be read and its facts observed and classified.[40]

A school or college without the Bible . . . is not in accordance with the wants of society, with the genius of human nature, with the interest of the State, with the progress of civilization, with the advancement of the church, with the glory of God, or with the happiness of man.

Religion is not a free and spontaneous thing which springs up voluntarily in the human breast. It is the result of education and authority.[41]

In 1856 Campbell asked students to prepare "to meet infidelity in any and every guise" in its "chameleon like" forms. Infidels

38. *Idem*, 1841, pp. 272–379, 1846, p. 62.
39. *Idem*, 1848, pp. 427–430; see also *idem*, 1850, p. 511.
40. *Idem*, 1850, pp. 123–125, 169–172.
41. *Idem*, 1850, pp. 173–174.

should be met on their "own premises, and with their own weapons," "reason and science." [42]

As a defender of revealed religion he testified: "We teach Paley's Evidences of Natural and Revealed Religion after Butler's Analogy has been carefully read and digested . . . at Bethany. . . ." [43]

His familiar *Lectures on the Pentateuch; Delivered before the Morning Class of Bethany College during the Session of 1859–60,* edited by W. T. Moore in 1867, resound with his familiar defense of revealed religion. He stressed that it is essential to study the "Volume of Revelation" before examining Butler and Paley but all three are "cardinal books" for his lectures on sacred literature. He used Butler to show that "there is nothing wrong in religion" and Paley to "learn the power and wisdom of God." However, they offer no sound arguments for revealed religion; unsound reasoning upon them produces many "infidels." Analogy can offer no positive proof of revelation, yet Butler's work is useful for showing that all the arguments used against revealed religion apply with equal force against the laws of nature. Natural religion, in itself, is "pure deism." Butler and Paley are good to stop "the mouths of those who are continually saying, we look up through nature to nature's God." [44]

Campbell argued that colleges are not essentially "leagued with error and immorality," for the "Luthers, the Calvins, the Wesleys, of all ages and nations of Christianity, have come out of these great centres and seats of learning." [45]

In his 1853 baccalaureate address he declared that every son of Romanism and infidelity will hate and abhor American Protestantism which is to be English and German Protestantism "enlarged and improved." This

spirit . . . has occasioned the war against the common school system. It is not Webster's spellingbook, nor Webster's dictionary. It is not Murray's grammar, nor Ray's arithmetic, nor Gummere's Surveying, nor Euclid's Elements, nor Virgil, nor Homer, nor Hesiod; nor is it our American geography nor European astronomy.[46]

42. *Idem,* 1856, p. 409.

43. *Idem,* 1857, p. 350.

44. *Familiar Lectures on the Pentateuch* (Cincinnati, Bosworth, Chase & Hall, 1871), pp. 374 ff.

45. *The Millennial Harbinger,* 1843, p. 215.

46. *Idem,* 1853, pp. 423–429.

Campbell was enabled to combat his millennial foes of natural religion, sectarianism, and papalism, which to him thrive upon ignorance, through a college of his own and organized education in general.

The Role of Foreign Missions and Interdenominationalism

In the meantime Campbell, particularly in the 1840's, stressed the need for foreign missions. As an outcome of the first national convention of the Disciples of Christ in 1849, "The American Christian Missionary Society" was organized. Campbell served as its president for the rest of his life.

In 1851 he urged:

We want Bibles, missionaries, pastors and teachers. We want men to meet the crisis and the age. Infidelity, superstition and error, ancient and modern, are everywhere around us and in our midst. Paganism, papalism, infidelity, and every form of error and heresy, are still struggling for the ascendency. . . .[47]

He favored the Disciples' missionary activities in Jerusalem as his "first choice." Jerusalem's "future rise and glory occupy a large space in the visions of the future." It is the "duty of all to distribute the Gospel in the land of the Jews and Moslems." [48]

Campbell welcomed the formation of the American Bible Society, of which he was one of the first vice-presidents. He was happy to help it promote the translation of a modern version of the Bible and he worked on the revision of Acts. He thought that it would work toward the union of all Christians but the implications of sprinkling as a form of baptism should be dropped. In an address to the "Bible Union Convention" in 1852 he said, ". . . is it not contrary to theory, to faith, to experience, to history, to think of a millennium—of a union of all Christians—on Pedobaptist principles? In order, then to pray, or to teach, or to labor, *for a millennium,* we must have a Bible that is most explicit on this great subject. . . .[49]

In 1847 Campbell cherished the "Evangelical Alliance" along

47. *Idem,* 1851, p. 695. We shall discuss Campbell's millennial relations to missions and interdenominational activities in more detail under the next theme of the destiny and mission of America. We are merely establishing the connection with specific organizations now.

48. *Popular Lectures and Addresses,* pp. 524 ff.

49. *Idem,* p. 594.

with "The Bible Society" as "great initiatory institutions" for "a more rational and scriptural scheme of Christian co-operation and communion" on the basis of great fundamental truths. The human mind, he said, never takes "but one short step at a time." This is like the principles of his father's "Declaration and Address," even if it is connected with "Pedobaptists." It is properly "a step" or "alliance" of Protestants and not a real "union." [50]

The Destiny and Mission of America

Alexander Campbell's expedient view of the State underwent a similar change as did his conception of organized religion. During his *Christian Baptist* days, his chief positive interest in Christian religion and American democracy was in the freedom they guarantee to individuals and to institutions. Under the millennial perspective, it was upon the responsibilities which they imply for religious citizens.

His nervousness toward the State subsided somewhat in the 1830's and early 1840's. Later, his millennial perspective demanded a fundamental place for the destiny and mission of America—its democracy, its education, its Protestantism, its missionary enterprises, and its government—as the fulfillment of human history and the hope of the introduction of the millennium.

Campbell ventured into politics as a delegate from Brooke County to the Virginia Convention in 1829, which was called to amend the state's constitution. It was represented by such figures as John Marshall, James Madison, John Randolph, James Monroe, and Philip Doddridge. He backed the western Virginia block of the easterners' attempt to reestablish the old constitutional provision that each slave owner would be entitled to an extra vote for every three of his slaves.[51] He proposed an article in the Virginia constitution for the gradual emancipation of slaves, with compensation to the owners at a price set by the State and also that slave importation should cease.[52]

50. *The Millennial Harbinger*, 1847, pp. 31–33.

51. It is said that he provoked John Randolph to remark, "That man is never satisfied. God Almighty could not satisfy him with the Bible which He gave and Mr. Campbell went and wrote a Bible of his own." (Robert Richardson, *op. cit.*, II, 304–310.)

52. While the convention was meeting, Campbell held nightly religious services in the Sycamore meeting house. James Madison is reported to have admired Campbell for his skill in debate at the convention. But he said, "It

The importance of Campbell's position on slavery, for our purpose, is that his millennial perspective was prominent at this period. The convention was held after his debate with Robert Owen. The fifth subject which Campbell outlined as subservient to the comprehensive object of the *Millennial Harbinger* for the "developement [*sic.*] and introduction of that political and religious order of society called The Millennium" reads: "Disquisitions upon the treatment of African slaves, as preparatory to their emancipation . . ." This was published in the same month that the convention voted upon the provisions of the Virginia constitution.

Campbell never sanctioned slavery and was never an abolitionist. His constant position was the third alternative, antislavery with discrimination, rather than yielding to sweeping generalizations.

Campbell's "An Oration in Honor of the Fourth of July, 1830" is basic for understanding his changing conception of the role of the state. In this, he described four historical chapters of society. The first was without civil government; the second was without religious associations; the third was a state of society under a "politico-religious government"; and "in the fourth chapter, a scheme began which contemplates the government of men by religion without politics, by the efficacy of one principle alone." [53] He declared that *"Jesus Christ will yet govern the world by religion only, and that by the operation of a single principle."* When that triumph comes, the "admirers of American liberty and American institutions have no cause to regret such event, no cause to fear it." It will be "but the removing of a tent to build a temple—." [54]

In this context, Campbell promised that the victory of the Revolution of 1776 was only the "precursor of a revolution of infinitely more importance to mankind," which will "make men free indeed." It will be greater than

is as a theologian that Mr. Campbell must be known. It was my pleasure to hear him very often as a preacher of the gospel, and I regard him as the ablest and most original expounder of the Scriptures I have ever heard." *Idem*, p. 313.

Madison's comment is particularly interesting concerning Campbell as a theologian, for Madison had studied theology while at Princeton and for a year after that at his home.

53. *Popular Lectures and Addresses*, pp. 368–372.

54. *Idem*, pp. 372–374.

the substitution of a representative democracy for an absolute or limited monarchy. . . . Talk not of a liberty which only makes men greater slaves. Under the monarchies of the Old World men are more free from themselves than under the free government of these United States. The reason is, under this free government the citizens have the opportunity of improving and bettering their circumstances to such an extent to engross all their energies, to call forth all their powers hence, upon themselves they impose such tasks and inflict such toils and privations as few monarchs of the East would be so cruel to impose upon their subjects. Here in this land of liberty we see all men striving for power . . . the more successfull, the more eager to commence again. . . . Yet they boast of being free! Free!—yes free to make slaves of themselves! If the Son of God has made them free, they would not thus toil till the last pulsation of their hearts. . . .

To introduce the last and most beneficial change in society, it is only necessary to let the gospel, in its own plainness, simplicity and force, speak to men. . . .[55]

Readers have been misled by not realizing the millennial perspective under which this address was made. It conforms to the basic imagery of his millennial thought without containing the word "Millennium." He had an urgent place for the American system of democracy, even though the millennium itself would not have human politics. He never assumed that the millennium had arrived. His was only the period in which the great battle was being won for its introduction.

In 1839, after a tour through Washington, D. C., Campbell ruefully described the rising "worldly pomp and splendor." If it were representative, the spirit of the American people is the spirit of pagan Rome; the symbol of the American eagle is to be compared with the English lion—as a beast of prey. "I have never spoken the word of the Lord in Washington. Among other reasons, one is—that I know of nothing more anti-podal to the gospel than politics. The *meum* and *teum* of the American statesmen are the truest antagonistic powers in society against the philanthropy of Christ's gospel." [56]

This does not mean that Campbell was antagonistic toward all material and symbolic expressions of Americanism. In the same year, he paid his respects to the American patriot whom he ad-

55. *Idem*, pp. 375–377.
56. *The Millennial Harbinger*, 1839, pp. 7–8.

mired, Thomas Jefferson, at Charlottsville, Virginia. He pleaded that nation, state, or country should leave a suitable monument and give adequate care to Jefferson's grave as befit the "author of the Declaration of Independence"; they now appear as though he were some " 'Arnold guilty of his country's blood.' " He described the house and grave as in near ruins and "the site" as the only interesting thing at Monticello.[57]

In 1840 Campbell advised Christians not to take an active part in American politics because of the mercenary and ambitious interests of politicians who try to deceive the people.[58]

By 1846 Campbell expressed his personal political duty as non-participation "in local politics and strife" but to "support principles and measures" for the best interest of the community "in national concerns." He would conduct his magazine impartially in political matters.[59]

He declared that the civil throne and government are bestowed in the world by the grace of God. God ordains magistrates who are under the law of God. Man has no right to kill or punish. Motives are men acting in the masses; and "nations can only do those things which every individual man has a right to do, anterior to the national form of society." He preferred capital punishment by the government rather than life imprisonment, because he thought it was more likely to get a change in the individual. However, capital punishment is countenanced by Biblical precedents, decrees of God, the Judge of all, and not "because it chances to fall in with our theories of what is expedient, useful, or consonant to the genius of our age and government." [60]

He would have capital punishment on the Biblical basis of responsibility of every state according to divine precept. He would have no soft allowance that a minor punishment is more effective than a greater one. Divine law calls for the life of the murderer.

In 1846 Campbell, contemplating the "Prospective Glory of the United States," asked who could conceive the result of the "experiment of millions of men living under a republican government, and left to the fruition of an unfettered body and free mind,

57. *Idem*, 1839, p. 60.
58. *Idem*, 1840, p. 413.
59. *Idem*, 1846, pp. 4–5.
60. *Idem*, 1846, pp. 20, 124, 129, 147, 151.

joined together in advancing the interests of humanity, and accomplishing the highest perfection our nature" is capable of ? [61]

In 1848 he commented upon Great Britain:

. . . the efforts of her Protestant population to civilize, evangelize, and bless the human race, in every barbarous land where her power is felt, . . . have never been equalled. . . . On these accounts, notwithstanding her great national sins and transgressions, the blood that she has shed, the cruelties sometimes inflicted upon the people she has conquered, and if not commanded, yet winked at by her government, England stands upon the proudest eminence, and has reached the highest acme of national glory ever attained by any nation or people. . . .[62]

Campbell advocated the emendation of the Constitution of the United States to limit the reign of sovereigns to one term of eight to ten years and inhibit reelections; or else the people must be converted to Christianity. "Our policy, our interests, our morality, our religion, are subjected to a crisis every four years, from which every true patriot and Christian in the nation prays to be delivered." [63]

Yet he would not sell his "political rights and privileges of American citizenship for all the honors and emoluments that cluster around the stateliest and most aristocratic subject of any European or Asiatic crown now worn on earth." [64]

By 1853 Campbell was saying that the American, of all governments, is the nearest approximation of Christianity, for it offers "no utopian theory of politics or religion" and is more "Protestant." However, Christianity itself offers the only panacea for all the ills and folly of man, as it reconciles man to live under every form of government until it can be "constitutionally, rationally, or providentially reformed, and made to work in unison with the genius of humanity." As Christians, we live under a *"Christocracy."* [65]

In 1855 Campbell asked his students at Bethany College what further glory remains to be achieved by our colleges, English and American—*"the full development, decoration, and aggrandizement of the moral man."* This is particularly needed in America,

61. *Idem*, 1846, p. 356.
62. *Idem*, 1848, pp. 548–549.
63. *Idem*, 1848, p. 678.
64. *Ibid.*
65. *Idem*, 1853, p. 487.

he said, because of the "vigor, the boldness, the energies, and the independence of the Anglo-Saxon American." [66] Two years later, in another address at Bethany, Campbell said that the United States citizens have the highest value of education of any nation in the world with more schools and colleges that are outgrowing themselves. This, he said, "speaks loftily for Young America." [67]

In 1857 Campbell said that every man in America and its Government should vote for good and against evil, or for the lesser of two evils. Every Christian is constrained by letter and spirit to do good to mankind as far as God has given him the opportunity.[68]

This sketch of Campbell's changing emphasis from individualism and nervousness toward civil government shows that by 1836 he was giving an increasing importance to the destiny and mission of Anglo-Saxon America. The value of this for his millennial thought can especially be seen in three of his greatest public addresses that occurred before our sketch ends.

In 1849 Campbell delivered an "Address on the Anglo-Saxon Language: Its Origin, Character, and Destiny." In this most of his main millennial notes emerge. He held that John Wycliffe and William Tyndale were the "morning stars, the rising dawn of Protestantism."

Luther was a Saxon and Calvin was a Frenchman but Tyndale "was an Anglo-Saxon." The Protestant Reformation "was the regeneration of literature, science, art, politics, trade, commerce, agriculture." The more Protestant the progress is, the more *"self-thinking and self reliances,"* not in the sense of "confidence in the flesh, pride, self-conceit," but in the "confident application of our minds to the means of intellectual, moral, political, and religious improvement, in the hope of improving ourselves and our conditions." [69]

He reminded his hearers that the Anglo-Saxon language, commerce, and power dominate the globe; all this God has given the Anglo-Saxon people. The destiny of the Anglo-Saxons, under God, is to Christianize the world. The Anglo-Saxon peoples are the givers of science and learning which could not be expressed in Hebrew, Greek, Latin, or any other language hitherto spoken by many; and it may be alleged "that our religion will be a passport

66. *Idem*, 1855, pp. 5–13.
67. *Idem*, 1858, p. 363.
68. *Idem*, 1857, p. 174.
69. *Popular Lectures and Addresses*, p. 32.

yet to our language into all the nations of the earth." The Anglo-Saxon language has "fabricated a myriad of new words from dead languages" and has formed "thousands of new combinations of the words of dead and living tongues, to express all our Anglo-Saxon sciences, arts, and literature."

These predictions and observations were surveyed under the range of his philosophy of history; and, on the basis of his population estimates, he figured that by one hundred fifty years the Anglo-Saxons

must direct and control the energies and destiny of the world. . . . On these premises the tongue of skepticism must falter, and its face turn pale. All must concede to Noah the spirit of inspiration, as well as to the Apocalyptic John . . . By what other spirit could the Apostle John have foretold the rise, the progress and the fall of empires, and a Christian triumph over all her foes? . . . we may hope that, as there was at first but one language, there will be at last but one language amongst the sons of Adam. . . . Hence we strongly affirm the conviction, that for the sake of these, and in honor of those who, by Bible translation, Bible-distribution, in all lands and languages, missionary enterprise, missionary zeal, and missionary success in the cause of human advancement and human redemption, the Anglo-Saxon tongue will ultimately triumph . . . Peace and universal amity will reign triumphant. For over all the earth there will be but one Lord, one faith, one hope, one language. . . . No event in the future, next to the anticipated millennial triumph, appears more natural, more probable, more practicable, or morally certain and desirable, than this Anglo-Saxon triumph in the great work of human civilization and redemption.[70]

Campbell's "Address on the Destiny of Our Country" 1852 at Canonsburg College, Pennsylvania, rings with the same note as the Anglo-Saxon language address. He began with God and Creation and ended with his characteristic millennial note.

There is a reason for everything, if there be any reason for anything. . . . All Christendom has its special mission . . . into the world. . . . Britain and America are of one destiny. They stood by Luther, by the first Protestants, in the times that tried men's souls; and however perverted upon and around the throne, the heart of England has ever sympathized with young America, and with all the Protestants of Europe. . . . To the Saxons in Europe, to the Anglo-Saxons on this continent, God has given the sceptre

70. *Idem*, pp. 2–45.

of Judah, the harp of David, the strength of Judah's Lion, and the wealth of the world. . . . To Britain and America God has granted the possession of a new world; and because the sun never sets upon our religion, our language and our arts, he has vouchsafed to us, through these sciences and arts, the power that annihilates time and annuls the inconveniences of space. Doubtless these are but preparations for a work which God has in store for us. . . .[71]

In 1848, in an "Address on War" [72] at Wheeling, Virginia, Campbell maintained his pacifist position that: there are no real Christian nations; a Christian has no right to wage war upon his neighbor unless he can wage war upon himself; the men that fight are not the men that make the war; and distinctions between defensive and aggressive wars are mere quibblings. Although he depicted the horrors of war in destruction of life and property, his greatest protest was its moral destruction. He argued that the Bible, philosophy, and history teach that disputes should be settled by umpires, for no man is a proper judge of his own case:

Could not a united national court be made as feasible and as practicable as the United States? . . . Why not . . . have a congress of nations and a high court of nations for adjudicating and terminating all international misunderstandings and complaints, redressing and remedying all wrongs and grievances? [73]

Campbell's conclusion rings with a millennial tone: "the time will not be far distant when

> No longer hosts encountering hosts
>   Shall crowds of slain deplore:
> They'll hang the trumpet in the hall,
>   And study war no more." [74]

To grasp the paradoxical growth of Alexander Campbell's conception of the destiny and mission of America under his focusing millennial perspective, we must recall that in 1839 he decried the "worldly pomp and splendor" of Washington, D. C., and had not spoken the word of the Lord there because of nothing being "more anti-podal to the gospel than politics." In June, 1850, as a result of an invitation from the Congress of the United States, Campbell

71. *Idem*, pp. 163–170.
72. This address was reprinted in the Congressional Record of November 22, 1937, at the request of the Honorable Joseph Shannon of Missouri.
73. *Popular Lectures and Addresses*, pp. 342–365.
74. *Idem*, pp. 365–366.

addressed a joint gathering of both houses for an hour and a half on "the Divine *Philanthropy.*" After that he wrote of the "magnificence" of European architecture which he had seen and compared it with

our great National Metropolis. . . . Our capitol in Washington, and our President's palace transcends in beauty, in fine taste, if not in real grandeur, any capitol parliament house, court, or legislative hall, in Europe. . . .

Having spent some three hours in the Senate Chamber, so replete with wisdom and eloquence, viewing and hearing the great men of the day—some of them, indeed the greatest statesmen of the world; satisfied that the eye was never to be satisfied with seeing, nor the ear with hearing, I hied away to the cars. . . .[75]

Another symbol of Campbell's change is seen in his appeal for contributions toward the erection of "a place of worship in Washington City, the great metropolis of this great nation," in order that the "principles of the present Reformation be annually laid before all" who "desire to know them." [76] By then, in 1851, the Disciples had members in Congress and other prominent governmental posts.

75. *The Millennial Harbinger,* 1850, pp. 447–450.
76. *Idem,* 1851, pp. 53–54.

CHAPTER XIV

THE POSTPONEMENT OF THE MILLENNIUM

T HE full picture of the millennial influence upon Campbell's life and program can be seen by summarizing its chronological development and final outcome.

Rising from an earlier interest in prophecy, his eschatology reached its peak in the late 1820's and early 1830's as a result of the unexpected success of his reform program. Expectancy heightened when he thought of the possibilities of restoring primitive Christianity beyond the confines of local congregations and believed the millennium was near at hand.

Soon the restoration of "the ancient order of things" called for greater social planning before the awaited introduction of "the new order of things" and his eschatology broadened in terms of organization in the 1840's and 1850's. In these decades the program, which looked forward to the introduction of the millennium, was extended to include the destiny and mission of America and the Anglo-Saxon world, organized education, missionary enterprises, Bible societies, an organized Disciples of Christ communion, and an organized Protestant effort to overcome Roman Catholicism. The task of conquering the citadels of infidelity, papalism, sectarianism, Mohammedanism, and paganism was not as individualistic and simple as was formerly conceived.

His high eschatology declined as his millennial outlook broadened into organized efforts to speed the fulfillment of the prophecies which must occur before the ultimate millennium or triumph of Christ which would precede the thousand years of peace and harmony.

Unwelcomed millennial allies went further in eschatology than he. In 1833 his readers were reminded with "what caution we have spoken on the prophecies and millennial matters" as he introduced an essay by "S. M. M'Corkle, *a Layman*," on "Signs of the Times." M'Corkle advocated that men should be informed of an immediate and literal coming of Christ. From 1833 until 1836 Campbell, ex-

changing replies with him, attacked the view of a literal coming
of Christ in the clouds before the millennium. He concluded that
M'Corkle's "whole theory is air-built and imaginary with much
less labor than I at first anticipated." [1]

By 1840 Alexander Campbell's attention was so concentrated
upon education, Christian ordinances, attacks on infidelity, and
efforts to get the Disciples of Christ organized that some of his
readers lost the threads to the millennial import of such energies.
Consequently, he answered the querists who imagined

that a *millennial harbinger* must be always discussing or preaching millenniary affairs. When we put to sea under this banner we
had the port of Primitive Christianity . . . in our eye; reasoning that all the Millennium we could scripturally expect was not
merely the restoration of the Jerusalem church in all its moral and
religious characters, but the extension of it through all nations
and languages for one thousand years. To prepare the way for
such a development of Christianity several things are essential—
1st. The annihilation of partyism.
2nd. The restoration of a pure speech.
3rd. The preaching of the original gospel.
4th. The restoration of the Christian ordinances.
5th. Larger measures of the Holy Spirit, as promised to those
who seek for it in the appointed way.
To these five points, as means of the triumph of the gospel over
idolatry, infidelity, impiety, immorality, and corrupt religion, we
have for years been directing the inquiries of our readers.[2]

By 1843 Campbell's eschatology had softened. In reacting
against Millerite and kindred views of conversion on the basis
of an immediate and magical millennium, his once swift, moving
expectancy was slowing down.

Although we did not expect that our title of *Millennial Harbinger*
was to be so literally and coincident with the fact of an immediate
Millennium, as some of our brethren, and all the Millerite school
would have us to think; still I expected, as I yet expect, a Millennium—a thousand years of a triumphant Christianity, and at no
very distant day. I never have been, and am yearly less disposed
to be, dogmatical in affirming how, or by what means and instruments this glorious period is to be ushered in, nor what it is to be
in all its developments. . . .[3]

1. *The Millennial Harbinger*, 1833, p. 5, 1835, pp. 5–11, 197, 1836, p. 13.
2. *Idem*, 1840, pp. 561–562.
3. *Idem*, 1843, pp. 73–74.

His sense of urgency was not abandoned but was taking a new form. In the late 1840's his millennial perspective was at its mature peak. Bethany College was thriving; organization was developing in the Disciples of Christ; a missionary organization was being achieved; cooperation with Protestant-minded groups in respect to Roman Catholicism, Bible distributions, and alliances on basic principles with interdenominational societies were being extended. His battle with the many varieties of natural religionists had reached its apex. His interpretation of the destiny and mission of Anglo-Saxon civilization was coming into its fullness. Campbell knew where to fight in the millennial battle against papalism, Mohammedanism, paganism, sectarianism, slavery, and infidelity.

In fact, his zeal on a trip to Europe in 1847 brought him popular acclaim and a stay in jail on the charge of libel in remarks about an antislavery antagonist. In Liverpool, his speeches were a success on the catholic subjects, the *"Evidences of the Christian Religion"* and the *"Holy Spirit."* He spoke in the crowded Concert Hall, a building constructed by the "Owenites, *alias* Socialists," which held around two thousand people. From the evidences of Campbell's letters, it seems that he enjoyed his martyrdom of imprisonment; but his greatest discomfort came after addressing the "Sceptics, or Socialists in their Hall of Debate" in London. Some of the skeptics were too unruly for Campbell. He was in a hurry to leave. When quizzed concerning the existence of God, he replied that he was unaware that they had not yet decided whether there is a God. After one of them derided the Bible, Campbell gathered his hat and bearing and walked out on the gentlemen.[4]

Campbell's millennial outlook remained on an even keel from 1849 until 1856 when he was still writing articles on "The Millennium" and defining it as "the consummation of the Christian dispensation." In 1858, in his baccalaureate address at Bethany College, he informed his audience that they were "standing upon the experience of 5862 years, lacking only 138 years of the Millennial Age." [5]

But there is a marked change in Campbell's millennial outlook by 1860. His former vertical eschatology, which had softened and leveled so extensively into organizational enterprises,

4. *Idem*, 1847, pp. 433, 515, 555.
5. *Idem*, 1858, p. 422.

had almost run its course. The tendency to postpone the arrival of the millennium more definitely to around the year two thousand probably had something to do with it. However, at this time, Campbell was a tired, discouraged, and physically broken old man. The Civil War was at hand. Peace, as well as the union of all Christians on New Testament principles, looked further away than he had hoped since the early 1820's.

He was beginning to resign prophecy to finding its sum total in Jesus Christ "as the spirit of prophecy" and the preaching of Christ as the central key and end of all prophecy. These two elements had been in his millennial thought all along but not with such concentrated and exclusive emphasis. With perhaps a heavy heart, he confessed:

It has, in days past, occurred to us, that the long cherished and yet unsatisfied inquisitiveness, as to the unaccomplished promises and prophecies, concerning the career of the Christian Institution; or, in other words, as to the conquests and triumphs of the gospel, has not been, is not now, nor is it likely soon to be, perfectly satisfied. And along with this conviction, there is a waning of confidence in many minds as to the advantage, or the propriety of concentrating the Christian mind, upon this subject; or, in other words, of devoting our energies, our whole minds to the special study of the types, and symbols, and imagery of Moses, Daniel, Ezekiel, Isaiah, Jeremiah or the Apocalypse of John.

It has, however, after frequent and long protracted thought and reflection upon the premises, occurred to us that these readings, reflections, and efforts should not be abandoned; but that another course should be instituted and prosecuted. To be fully understood, we submit one prominent oracle as THE SUN of the whole system of prophecy. It is, too, the consummation of the whole Apocalyptic Revelations. Properly translated it thus reads in our living vernacular—*For the testimony of Jesus is the spirit of the prophecy.* Apocalypse 19th chapter, 10th verse. To the same effect we quote the Redeemer's own summary, John v. 39: "The Scriptures testify of me." [6]

In addition, Campbell summoned John the Baptist, Mark, and John to support his new position. He recommended that fulfilled prophecy is the safe index to the unfulfilled prophecy of all dispensations. ". . . the Family, the National, and the Ecumenical. Our motto shall be, as before said, the testimony concerning

6. *Idem*, 1860, pp. 121–131.

Jesus—or the testimony relating to Jesus, is the spirit of the prophecy. . . ."[7]

Not only can the reader detect the sudden change in Campbell's feeling and concern for the millennium in this quoted material of the year 1860 but also it furnishes a fair sample of the lack of former power, style, and challenge which characterize his writings of earlier years. This accounts somewhat for the great decline in the number of subscribers to the *Millennial Harbinger*— a fact which had discouraged Campbell. However, the ill and aged Alexander Campbell did not go down so easily, for flashes of his old form reappeared here and there before his death in 1866.

Also, in 1860, Campbell proposed to investigate the "whole field of Bible prophecy," for he said that he had never seen or read a "lucid and satisfactory interpretation of the Patriarchal, Jewish, and Christian dispensations," nor of any one of them in "its whole import and bearings."[8] That was a promise. But, at best, he only rehashed part of his old stuff.

In 1861 Campbell maintained a note of mystery but it is different from his old emphasis regarding prophecy.

The future of anything, indeed the entire future of everything, is hid from mortal man. Known to God alone is the future destiny of the entire universe, and of every atom of it. . . . And one day being with the Lord of the universe as a thousand years, and a thousand years being as one day, we may on all our premises anticipate a glorious consummation of the present campaign in some *one hundred and forty* years hence. . . .[9]

It is difficult to imagine his underlining those words two decades prior to this!

In the same year, he emphasized that Christology (a word which he formerly detested but a study which he had always stressed in all but the formal name) is indispensible to understanding Christocracy. It, he said, is essential to have a perfect and complete development of the *"person,* the *mission,* the *character, and the work* of the Lord Jesus," which involve

four transcendently splendid ideas—1st, the God man, personally *Divine* as his Father; perfectly human as his Virgin Mother. His fourfold office, 1st. The *Oracle* of Jehovah—2nd. The *Prophet* of eternal future—3rd. *The High Priest* of the celestial temple—and

7. *Idem,* 1860, p. 127.
8. *Idem,* 1860, p. 670.
9. *Idem,* 1861, pp. 18–20.

lastly, and loftiest of all, *The King Eternal*, invisible, immortal, omniscient, and omnipresent. . . . The Christology is, at our angle of vision, the true and proper basis of the Christocracy. Before the *Christocracy*, or the actual reign of the Messiah over all the nations, kindreds, tongues, and people, can culminate in all its glory and grandeur, the gospel must be announced to all the nations and peoples on this earth.

The true and real Millennium cannot be fully developed till Papalism, paganism, Mohammedanism, and Protestant Sectarianism, shall be annihilated, either by the personal return of the Lord Jesus Christ or by the spread of the power of the gospel in its original purity and power. The judgments threatened by Daniel, by Paul, and by John the apostle, against Paganism, Mohammedanism, Papalism, and all the apostacies from pure, original apostolic christianity must be consummated in their full import and significance, antecedent to the triumphant reign of the Lord Jesus over a ransomed world. . . .[10]

This is the old Campbell emerging from his hard-knocked corner with plenty of fight left. In 1863, overwhelmed to a great extent by the Civil War, he was still fighting as is indicated in his Preface:

We see in the confusion and anarchy of the public mind, much to excite the anxiety and fears of the true disciple of Christ, and we are not without the hope that, with the temper and moderation of a true Christian charity, we may do and say much to aid in keeping the ship of our Zion not only rightly directed and trimmed for weathering the storm, but with her bow ever directed to the polar star of our Christian hope. . . .[11]

In 1864 the mixture of the old and new millennial thinker emerges:

We claim . . . no prophetic infallibility, but yet, we are sure that we have looked long and steadfastly at the interests of the church, and weighed with an anxious if not often heavy heart the signs of the times, and the shadows of the coming struggles and fortunes, which of late have been thrown thick and dark upon the horizon. We are not ready, the great Master knows, nor willing to see these gloomy portents. We would rather see only the rosy dawn of a peaceful and triumphant procession of a golden age for the church —to imagine her going forth in her bridal adornments to meet the coming of her Espoused in the garments of joy. But it may not

10. *Idem*, 1861, pp. 462–465; see also *idem*, 1862, pp. 218–221.
11. *Idem*, 1863, p. 4.

be. Darkness and tempest are round about the habitation of His Throne, and the aspects of the future for the church are darkly militant. For forty years we have been not an unfaithful nor an unwatchful sentinel upon the walls of Zion, and we had, with perhaps unwarranted fondness, cherished the hope of closing our service beneath peaceful and hopeful skies. . . . The times are full of corruption, and the church is contaminated with the times. We need to be reminded, in tones of tenderness, coming as from the world-renouncing agonies of the cross, that *we, the people of the living God, are not of the world.* . . . Let us not forget the weapons of our warfare, nor distrust the wisdom and power of our Leader. . . .[12]

Current events shook Alexander Campbell but they did not shake his philosophy of history. It stood the severest test. He had to discard his interpretation of current events by postponing the final climax of human history beyond his generation. For decades he had steered dangerously near the extremes of optimism and pessimism but he finished his course in confidence and without illusion in regard to his progress, day, and age. When the storm came, he headed from the shallows into the deep. He was a tough seaman.

12. *Idem*, 1864, pp. 3–4.

CHAPTER XV

CONCLUSION

ALEXANDER CAMPBELL was a product of the European Enlightenment transplanted upon nineteenth-century American soil. He was primarily a revelation thinker. He was both a skeptic and a believer in the Enlightenment but he resolved these tensions by placing his total faith in primitive Christianity.

His attacks against ecclesiasticism and natural religion were practical expressions—right- and left-hand actions—of this intellectual background. They derived their vigor and authority from his conception of revelation. Revelation, to him, was the purposeful and progressive self-disclosure of God who alone affords man adequate knowledge and allegiance for his temporal welfare and eternal salvation, as affected in Jesus Christ and in the essential New Testament facts concerning his person and mission as the word of God. The whole course of history finds its meaning in the Bible. The Spirit of God reveals and confirms this meaning to anyone who freely examines and trusts the evidence of the Bible.

Campbell's attacks against ecclesiasticism and natural religion were based upon the conviction that both, as popularly conceived, were unreliable. The union of all Christians upon a universal faith in the revealed truths of the Bible, in terms of the restoration of primitive Christianity, was his alternative to both ecclesiasticism and natural religion. If the false presumptions of the former were abolished, with its resulting sectarianism, skepticism would perish because of its inherent negative character.

He refused to tolerate the claims of infallibility by traditional believers either in Christian revelation or in natural religion. Both, to him, deprived the masses of people of their rights and potentialities.

His conception of revelation led him to denounce formally the final authority of philosophy or pure reason for all truth. His prejudice against philosophy was grounded in his rejection of a rationalism which led to natural religion and away from faith in revelation. This rationalism he deemed corrupt, for it was based solely upon human authority and imagination which are always subjective and limited. Equally severe was Campbell in rejecting the traditional speculation and creeds of Christians and on the same principles. His distrust of formal theology was rooted in its acceptance of innate ideas, intuition, or authoritarianism, which, on the basis of his eighteenth-century principles, made revelation logically unnecessary, if not untenable.

However, his life's interests were in the problems and subjects of both theology and philosophy. He was proficient in these fields when employing them as tools to defend revealed religion and the first principles of Protestantism. Yet he often denied that he was employing theology and philosophy in his advocacy of simple "Bible Christianity."

But his Disciples of Christ admirers had and still have difficulty in following his pattern. Their tendency has been to reject all theology and philosophy as proper subjects of reflective thought, without distinguishing the particular types of theology and philosophy which Campbell rejected. Their departure from Campbell is largely based upon their failure to discriminate between his formal words (and natural tendency to overstate the applications of his principles) and his actual objectives and life program. Consequently, as a group, the Disciples have remained suspicious of theology and philosophy without becoming as proficient in them as Campbell was in time. As an evidence of this, they have not produced a seasoned Christian theologian of distinction for a hundred years.

Moreover, the Disciples have tended to split into rival thought groups in efforts to follow either Campbell's left-hand or his right-hand trends. Consequently, their extremes have tended toward rationalism in so far as they have become reflective-minded, on the left, and toward antiecclesiasticism in so far as culture and reason have been rejected, on the right. However, the broad or latitudinarian group has tended to stay in the middle of the road and to remain only mildly reflective and antiecclesiastic.

This calls for a reexamination of Alexander Campbell. His followers have tended to divide and subdivide into over twenty groups, most of whom claim to be the true followers of Campbell. Much of this claim is true because of his two distinctive periods and perspectives in life. However, most of the divisions have occurred over conceptions of the form of church organization. This is partly because of the tensions existing between an assumed single pattern of New Testament church organization and doctrine and a loose constructionist view of the proper New Testament church for the modern world. The former is strict and sectarian; the latter is less rigid and more churchlike.

Thus Campbell's "Christian Baptist" type of antiecclesiasticism has ever been at war with his "Millennial Harbinger" type of churchmanship. Campbell made the change without exploding because of the sheer strength of his body, his toughness of mind, his basic theological principles, and the religious orientation of his life. In other words, Campbell changed but his basic principles did not. His emphasis changed according to his changing conceptions of the proper structure of a modern New Testament church and his philosophy of history. His philosophy of history and conception of faith are the keys which unlock this change, for they involve his growing sense of mission in life. The change was not a departure from his fundamental ideas so much as it was a matter of more maturity of thought and of strategy in applying them. He deepened but he did not splinter.

Lesser men did not understand the significance of his transition; and the movement of movements, which united in 1832, exploded when the stable Scotts, Stones, and Thomas Campbells left the scene. Alexander Campbell was too apologetic and busy to see far enough into the future of the movement to make his position clear and his energies more effective in holding the tensions together. He never frankly and objectively admitted his changes of emphasis. Obviously, he did not think he had changed, for he thought in terms of his lasting principles, not his changing emphasis in applying those principles.

Any effort to explain Alexander Campbell in terms of single and simple causation will fail. It is not enough to interpret him in terms of any of the following: John Locke, Sandeman, the Haldanes, Ewing, John Walker, Alexander Carson, the Scotch theologians and philosophers, the Dutch Covenanters, or a mere private study of the Scriptures. Campbell did not have that sort of mind and temper. For the sake of a summary and convenience, the main sources of Alexander Campbell's theology, philosophy, and program are outlined as follows:

1. *Method:* Bacon, Newton, Locke, Scotch theology, and the effort to use the Baconian scientific method in the

study of religion but the rejection of natural science *as the basis* of religion.

2. *Theology:*
   A. Main-line Protestant principles: Luther, Calvin, Wesley.
   B. Sect-line Protestant principles: Walker, the Haldanes, Carson, Ewing, and a study of church history in regard to the sporadic reoccurrences of primitive Gospel sects in Christian history.
   C. Biblicism: firsthand study of the Bible based on Locke, the Dutch Covenanters, and both sect and church types of men whom he admired as well as Scotch theologians.
3. *Philosophy:* Locke, Hume, Mirabaud, and others.
4. *Philosophy of History:*
   A. Dutch Covenant theological view of religious dispensations.
   B. Hyde, Watson, Bishop Thomas Newton, Boothroyd, Leslie, and others.
   C. Malthusian theories of population growth.
   D. The Bible (Daniel, Revelation, etc.).
5. *Antiecclesiasticism:*
   A. French Revolution: Voltaire, Rousseau, Paine, etc.
   B. Sectarians: Walker, the Haldanes, Carson, Ewing, etc.
   C. Controversialists proper: Leslie, Chalmers, Jenyns, George Campbell, Hume, Hobbes, Paley, Butler, etc.
   D. Primitive gospel studies in the Bible and in church history.
6. *Anti-Catholicism:* Leslie, sectarians, French Revolutionaries, and Locke.

Regardless of his egotism, his superficialities, and his intolerance, he had the strength of character, the religious depth, and the genuine interest in truth for its own sake which enables such men to hold together paradoxical and even incompatible views. So far, he has occupied a provincial place in modern history.

But somewhere among the apologists and defenders of the universal Christian faith Alexander Campbell has a rightful place; just where is doubtful. Whether he belongs with the more established figures is now relatively unimportant, if not superficial. At least, he was the most effective critic among the leaders of the American primitive gospel movement of the naturalism which was emerging in the nineteenth century. In line with the leaders of the "Second Great Awakening" in the Eastern states, the "Great Revival" of the West, and the Methodist movement, Alexander Campbell helped American Christianity to recover an interest in and commitment to revealed religion.

Whether he was a transitional figure at the threshold of a new age or merely a figment of the end of a passing age is a matter for the future to decide. If international government appears, if world union and cooperation of the churches occur in the ecumenical movement, if modern men reject natural religion— *if the millennium comes*—Campbell, having his eyes set in these directions, may be one of the transitional figures. Campbell lived when devotees of technical science, industrialism, new social systems, nationalism, and internationalism were making their claims upon the modern mind.

Campbell was a fighting pacifist who was convinced that no Christian, though he cannot walk by sight, need be ashamed of his faith and of the reasonableness of his cause in the modern world. Science, reason, and organized Christianity had humble roles as servants of faith and human society. But advocates of absolutism in religion, science, and philosophy had no place in his admiration.

APPENDIX

ALEXANDER CAMPBELL (1788–1866), was born in County Antrim, Ireland, on September 12, 1788. He is known chiefly in connection with the rise of the movement in nineteenth-century America which calls itself "The Disciples of Christ," the "Churches of Christ," or the "Christian Church." It is one of the largest Protestant bodies of the United States and it claims a total world membership of 1,867,591 persons. Residents of the United States comprise 1,404,955 of these. The other members live in Canada and thirty-nine countries abroad.[1]

We shall briefly sketch the rise of this movement in relation to Alexander Campbell and his historical context.

Thomas Campbell (1763–1854), the father of Alexander, was born in County Down, Ireland, on February 1, 1763, from the direct line of "The Campbells of Argyle, Scotland." His father, Archibald Campbell, served in the British Army; it is claimed that General Wolfe died in his arms at the close of his siege of Havana and Quebec.[2]

Archibald Campbell, reared as a Roman Catholic, became a member of the Church of England. His son, Thomas, reared in the Church of England, became a member of the strict sect-type of Seceder or Antiburgher Presbyterian Church which had three synods in Scotland and the one in Ireland to which he belonged.

Thomas Campbell was well educated. He attended the University of Glasgow from 1783 until 1791 and graduated with honors after studying three years in the School of Arts and five years in the Seceder Divinity Hall. He also attended the lectures in medicine as an aid to his student pastoral work in Seceder Presbyterian churches in northern Ireland. In 1787 he married Jane Corneigle of French Huguenot ancestry. About eleven years later he became the minister of a Seceder congregation at Ahorey, County Armagh, Ireland.

Thomas Campbell carefully directed Alexander's education in hopes that he would become an accomplished scholar. Because of the lad's consuming interest in athletics, the discouraged father curbed Alexander's love of exercise by making him do hard manual labor on the farm. Soon he was well on the way in Greek, Latin, English, and literature. By the time Alexander was seventeen, his father opened an academy at Rich Hill and made him his assistant. Alexander was specializing in studies in church history and theology in the event that he would finally decide to follow his father's wishes and enter the ministry.

He memorized long passages of poetry and sections of the Bible. Decades later, while writing articles during his travels on the American frontier, he

1. *Year Book, 1945,* of the Disciples of Christ (Indianapolis, the Year Book Publication Committee of the International Convention of the Disciples of Christ and its related organizations), pp. 590, 623.

2. Alexander Campbell, *Memoirs of Elder Thomas Campbell* (Cincinnati, H. S. Bosworth, 1861), p. 7.

often quoted selections from Milton, Pope, and Cowper with the apology that he had to rely upon his memory. Out of the most influential works of his youthful acquaintance were John Locke's *Letters of Toleration* and the *Essay Concerning Human Understanding*. Thomas Campbell directed him in these studies.

Two characteristics became ingrained in Alexander Campbell: The love of the art in competition and the desire to excel. When interested chiefly in physical endeavors, he won the reputation among his playmates of hurling the biggest snowballs. When laboring on the farm, he tried to become the best sower of grain. He achieved the reputation of being an expert swimmer, an expert hunter, and an expert fisherman. In his intellectual world, as put into his own words, he aspired to be "one of the best scholars in the kingdom."

That was merely Alexander Campbell the youth before he became a religious leader. The characteristics, love of competition and the ambition to excel, never left him. When applied later in religious controversy, they had both tragic and beneficent effects upon his personality and the history of the Disciples of Christ. More is involved in the interpretation of these early experiences of Alexander Campell than historians of the Disciples have allowed.

Thomas Campbell was a peaceful figure in a turbulent Ireland. In 1804–05 he attempted to help unite the Burgher and Antiburgher Seceder synods of Ireland. Although he failed, the union was effected in 1820.

The combined task of pastoral work and teaching impaired his health and upon a physician's advice he went to the United States in 1807. He was assigned to minister to some small Seceder Presbyterian churches in Washington County, Pennsylvania.

Soon Thomas Campbell's catholicity of spirit caused trouble when he invited some non-Presbyterians, who had no churches of their own in that vicinity, to share in the Seceder communion services. The Chartiers Presbytery charged him with violating the standards of the Seceder Presbyterian Church. He appealed his case to the Seceder Synod of North America. The Synod mildly censored him. However, so much feeling was aroused in his vicinity that he withdrew from the Synod but continued his preaching. He preached Christian liberality, union, and the infallible right to do and say the things read in the Bible.

Sympathizers followed him until their relations were practically severed from the Seceder Church. In 1809 the group formed "The Christian Association of Washington" and Thomas Campbell drew up the principles adopted by the Association under the title of a "Declaration and Address." These principles advocated a rejection of the authority of all human opinions; the acceptance of the Bible alone as the original and required standard of faith and practice; the Holy Spirit, as their teacher; and Jesus alone, as exhibited in the Word of God, as their salvation.

The expressed aim of the "Declaration and Address" was to promote a simple evangelical Christianity on that basis, supporting a pure Gospel ministry and considering themselves not as a church but merely as a group of "voluntary advocates for church membership." All forms of doctrine, worship, discipline, and government were reduced to the words of the Bible. A "Thus saith the Lord" was to stand behind every matter of faith and duty in this "Second Reformation," as its advocates styled it, in seeking to restore **primitive Christianity.**

In the meantime, in 1808, Thomas Campbell had summoned his family to come to the New World. The family, which consisted of Alexander, who was then twenty-one years of age, Dorothy, Nancy, Jane, Thomas, Archibald, Alicia, and their mother, set sail on October 1, 1808. Their vessel was wrecked off the coast of Scotland. Two important results came from this crisis: Alexander Campbell decided to enter the ministry and the delay enabled him to attend the University of Glasgow for eight months before the family left for America on a successful voyage.

At this time the University of Glasgow was still seething from the effects of the French Revolution, the new sciences, the issues of revealed versus natural religion, the Common Sense philosophy, and the double effort of Scotch theologians to apply the Baconian method of inductive science to the study of religion and yet to discourage the tendencies toward making natural science the basis of religion. The Covenant theology of the Dutchmen, Cocceius and Witsius, with its development of the conception of successive religious dispensations, had influenced the University of Glasgow.

The year at Glasgow further familiarized Alexander Campbell with the writings of Locke, Beattie, Buffon, Young, and Johnson and enabled him to study writings of Thomas Reid, Dugald Stewart, Francis Bacon, Isaac Newton, David Hume, William Godwin, Rousseau, and other political and social philosophers. He took courses under Professor Ure in experimental philosophy, Professor Jardin in logic and belles lettres, and Professor Young in Greek. He continued his studies in Latin and French.

Years later Alexander Campbell quoted all of these men to support his views. Also, it is important to observe that he became acquainted further with Greville Ewing, whose Sabbath evening school he attended, and Robert Haldane, in whose home he frequently visited. Ewing, a personal friend of the Campbell family, introduced Alexander to his professors. Haldane's religious and social awakening had come chiefly from interest occasioned by the French Revolution. Both of the Haldane brothers had preached at Rich Hill and Thomas Campbell had been a member of the Evangelical Society in which they participated. Moreover, such independents as John Walker, Rowland Hill, Alexander Carson, and Robert Sandeman had influenced both of the Campbells at Rich Hill.

When Alexander Campbell came to America in 1809, he was in sympathy with his father's views and with "The Christian Association of Washington," although he insisted that the "Declaration and Address" implied logically a rejection of infant baptism. James Foster, who had also come over from Rich Hill, had already made the same observation, along with Andrew Monroe, another member of the Christian Association. Temporarily, the problem was postponed.

By October, 1810, the Campbells feared that they were becoming the leaders of another sect in their efforts to abolish sectarianism; therefore, they sought to unite their Christian Association with the Presbyterians at large. But the Synod of Pittsburgh declared that on the basis of the principles of the "Declaration and Address," the Christian Association was really saying that parts of the Westminster Confession were non-Biblical and such emphasis would only disturb the peace of the Presbyterian Church.

Consequently, in May, 1811, the Christian Association reorganized itself into a regular church. The new church, located at Brush Run, celebrated the

Lord's Supper weekly but soon encountered its unsettled baptismal problem when Joseph Bryant refused to participate in the communion services unless he were immersed. Alexander Campbell had been worried over the problem in connection with both his future ministry and family policy. After studying the Greek New Testament, he decided to practice immersion. On July 4, 1811, Thomas Campbell consented to immerse Joseph Bryant.

On June 12, 1812, Alexander Campbell and his wife were immersed. His father had already taken this step. Shortly, as Errett Gates says, ". . . the church consisted of none but immersed believers. Those who did not ask immersion withdrew from the church, so that in many respects during the year 1812 it became a Baptist church without the name." [3]

As a natural result, the Brush Run Church of immersed believers became acquainted with the Baptists in that vicinity; and by 1813 a formal union was adopted with the Redstone Baptist Association. The Campbells were granted permission "to teach and preach whatever they learned from the Holy Scriptures." But fundamental differences between the two groups were inherent from the beginning. The union was contracted primarily upon the mutual sympathy over similarity chiefly "in church polity and the form and subjects of baptism." [4] The Campbells and their movement did not subscribe to the Philadelphia Confession of Faith which the Redstone Baptists upheld and there were other differences which are not within our scope to state.

This union with the Baptists lasted roughly from 1813 until 1830 when the Campbell movement separated from the Baptists to form a communion of its own—with its purpose, in part, to rid the world of denominationalism by a complete restoration of primitive Christianity. However, during their union with the Baptists, the Campbells never accepted the name "Baptist," for they preferred the titles, "Disciples of Christ" or the "Reformers." These two titles were used to distinguish the adherents of the Campbell movement from the regular Baptists. But there was an overlapping of church membership and leadership.

In 1832 the "Disciples of Christ" or "Reformers" were informally united with about an equal number of Barton W. Stone's followers who were called "Christians." The union was not as formal as the earlier union of the Campbell group with the organized Redstone Baptists Association of churches; neither the "Disciples" nor "Christians" had an organized association of churches. However, the union was more genuine, for the two groups had more in common.

Traditional scholarship has tended to distort the history of the origin of the Disciples of Christ, Churches of Christ, or Christians by writing as though the union of the Disciples and Christians in 1832 is to be compared with a branch running into a river. It makes Alexander Campbell's movement the river and Stone's movement the branch. A more accurate analysis is to be derived from the analogy of two streams merging to form the one river. No river existed until the union of the two smaller streams in 1832.

Barton W. Stone (1772–1844) was born near Port-Tobbacco, Maryland. He was reared in Pittsylvania County, Virginia, where, at nine years of age,

3. Gates, *The Early Relation and Separation of Baptists and Disciples,* p. 15.

4. *Idem,* pp. 20–21.

he could hear the guns from the battle of Guilford Court House in the Revolutionary War. He was stirred by the spirit of freedom. Stone also was greatly influenced by several religious denominations. He was more interested in what communions had in common than in their differences. He was born into the Church of England and appreciated it, yet he was profoundly impressed by Baptists, Methodists, and Presbyterians.

An example of his spirit can be noted by his reaction to Baptist ministers in Virginia; he traveled for miles to behold the novelty of their immersions: "Great and good was the reformation of society. Knowing nothing better, I considered this to be the work of God. The preachers had the art of affecting their hearers by a tuneful or singing voice in preaching." [5]

Also, he was struck by the arrival of Methodist ministers in his community:

"Their appearance was prepossession—grave, holy, meek, plain, and humble . . . their zeal was fervent and unaffected, and their preaching was often electric on the congregation. . . . The Episcopalians and Baptists began to oppose them with great warmth. The Baptists represented them as denying the doctrines of grace, and of preaching salvation by works. They publicly declared them to be the locusts of the Apocalypse, and warned the people against receiving them. Poor Methodists! They were then but few, reproached, misrepresented, and persecuted as unfit to live on the earth. My mind was much agitated and was vacilating between the two parties." [6]

Stone aspired to be a lawyer. He attended an academy in Guilford, North Carolina, under David Caldwell, a Princeton graduate and Presbyterian minister, who ultimately taught fifty ministers and five governors of states. Finally, Stone was ordained in 1798 as a Presbyterian minister but only after critical struggles with his lifelong objections to extreme Calvinistic views of conversion and speculations upon the Trinity. He agreed to receive and adopt the Westminster Confession of Faith as long as he could see it as consistent with the Bible.

He was the minister of two small Presbyterian churches at Cane Ridge and Concord, Kentucky, when he attended the Kentucky camp meeting of Logan County in 1801. Although he became a leader in the revival, his analysis and written record of the curious phenomena are reminiscent of Jonathan Edwards' study of the Great Awakening in which he was a leader. Stone considered the excesses as disgusting but was convinced that God worked mysteriously through the camp meeting because, as a whole, more good was done than evil in freeing men from sin and from sectarian competition.

As a result of the Great Revival in the West, Stone and four other Presbyterian ministers deviated from the Westminster Confession of Faith enough to preach "free grace." When one of the ministers was tried before his synod on such charges, they withdrew from its jurisdiction and formed the "Springfield Presbytery" in an effort to abandon all creeds by taking the Bible as their only authority and rule of faith and practice. Soon they feared that the Springfield Presbytery was developing all the earmarks of the institutionalism from which they had revolted. Therefore, in 1804, they drew up "The Last

5. John Rogers, *Biography of Barton W. Stone Written by Himself, with Additions and Reflections* (Cincinnati, J. A. & N. P. James, 1847), p. 4.
6. John Rogers, *op. cit.*, p. 5.

Will and Testament of the Springfield Presbytery." The evolution and content of this document were similar to Thomas Campbell's "Declaration and Address" of five years later.

Stone became the key leader of the new group which reorganized under the name "Christians." The proposal for the name came from the same Rice Haggard who had led the former Republican Methodists in Virginia and North Carolina to adopt that name for their reorganized movement which had revolted from the Methodists because of Asbury's refusal to democratize the Episcopacy.

Meanwhile, Elias Smith and Abner Jones had emerged with similarly minded groups in New England known as the "Christian Connection." The "Christians" of the West, the North, and the South were drawn together in an unofficial union under Stone's leadership. Although he was immersed, Stone insisted that the form of baptism should not be made a test of fellowship and the principle held among the group. In 1832 about half of these Christians followed Stone into the informal union with the Disciples of Christ.

Another figure, Walter Scott (1796–1861) of Scotland and the University of Edinburgh, needs to be mentioned to complete our sketch. It was he who helped to check the extreme tendencies of Alexander Campbell. He persuaded him to avoid prejudices and to increase subscriptions by naming his first periodical the *Christian Baptist.* He insisted that the Campbells' Disciples should not abandon the name "Christians" after their break from the Baptists in 1830. And he reinforced Alexander Campbell's philosophy of history at the critical crisis in the early development of the Disciples in the 1830's.

Consequently, when the Disciples and Christians united forces in 1832, they had four types of gifted leaders in Thomas Campbell, Alexander Campbell, Barton Warren Stone, and Walter Scott. The movement was welded together in part by the personalities of these men and by the periodicals of Alexander Campbell, Stone, and Scott.

The apparent relation of the four main figures of the early origin and development of the Disciples can be expressed in an analogy. Thomas Campbell brought the infant Disciples into the world and Alexander Campbell became their guardian. Stone reared the infant Christians and Alexander Campbell tried to adopt them.

Alexander Campbell never made an objective effort to understand Stone. Stone never yielded to him in their differences but refused to quarrel with him.

It is difficult to conceive that Alexander Campbell could have successively kept the Disciples from anarchy without the crucial assistance of Walter Scott, Barton W. Stone, and Thomas Campbell. Alexander Campbell had a commanding personality which enabled him to become the outstanding leader of the four men but he lacked the temperament which made for the stability of the group. A contemporary friend in the movement observed, "Brother Campbell's weakness was in his ambition; he could not brook the idea of having a rival; he would rather have been the first man in a village, than the second man in a city." [7]

Alexander Campbell was willing to feed the young movements after they got into the world and he wanted the credit. But he needed the advice and help of Scott, Stone, and his father or he would have strangled the infants with

7. Elder W. D. Frazee, *Reminiscences and Sermons* (Nashville, Gospel Advocate Publishing Co., 1892), p. 115.

excessive and irregular feedings. He knew better about the protection, defense, and inspiration of the children than about the more stabilizing elements of their inner growth. His force and power of intellect were not sufficient. The others had the humility, the sympathy, and the consistency which help to sustain the growth of churches in Christian history.

I. *THE EARLIER PICTURE: MEN AND MOVEMENTS*

A. *CHRISTIANS*
1. NEW ENGLAND, OR NORTH
Elias Smith (1769–1846),   "CHRISTIAN CONNECTION"
   ex-Baptist   in New England
Abner Jones (1783–1832),
   ex-Baptist

2. SOUTHERN (ex-Republican Methodists)
James O'Kelly (1735–1826)
Rice Haggard (1769–1819) (joined Stone)

3. WESTERN
William Kinkade (1785–1832),
   ex-Presbyterian   "THE CHRISTIAN CHURCH"
David Purivance (1766–1847),   or "CHRISTIANS" of the
   ex-Presbyterian   West, from Stone's original
Barton W. Stone (1772–1844),   movement
   ex-Presbyterian

B. DISCIPLES OF CHRIST, or Reformers
Thomas Campbell (1763–1854),
   ex-Seceder Presbyterian, and
   real founder of this stream   "DISCIPLES OF CHRIST,"
Alexander Campbell (1788–1866),   "Reformers," or "Campbell-
   ex-Seceder Presbyterian   ites" of Pennsylvania, Ohio,
Walter Scott (1796–1861),   Kentucky, and Virginia
   ex-Baptist, the evangelist
   and revivalist of this stream

Dr. Chester Bullard (Va.) [8]   "The Bullardites"

II. *THE LATER PICTURE: MOVEMENTS*
"Christian Connection"   *"Churches of Christ,"*
   of *New England*   *"Christian Denomination in*
                                    America" [9]

8. Dr. Chester Bullard led an independent movement in southwestern Virginia known as the "Bullardites." Bullard claimed that he reached his position through independent Bible study. The group was highly prejudiced against the "Campbellites" until Bullard met Campbell in 1840.

9. Many of the "Christians" of this group eventually united with the Congregationalists in 1930 under the name Congregational-Christians. Stone's influence was so great among the "Christians" at the 1930 union that, when asked to present the principles of their beliefs, the "Christians" presented the six fundamental principles on which he had led the union of the Chris-

II. *THE LATER PICTURE: MOVEMENTS* (*continued*)
  "The Christian Church" or
    "Christians," West and South   1832

  "Disciples of Christ," or   "Disciples of Christ,"
    "Reformers"   "Churches of Christ," or
                                       "Christians," of 1832 ff.

  "The Bullardites"
  (United with the Disciples
  through A. Campbell in 1840   1840

---

tians of the North, South, and West. This fact should not be taken too lightly in estimating the surviving Stone influence among the Disciples of the post-1832 union. However, not all of "The Christians" or "Churches of Christ" united with the Congregationalists in 1930 and many now exist under the title, "The Christian Denomination."

In 1906 the Disciples officially split into two sections, the smaller of which is now known as "Churches of Christ." This group is conservative, following the lines of Alexander Campbell's earlier antiecclesiasticism, disapproving of organ music and having other distinctive symbols of differences from the Disciples. They are popularly known as "the Antis," meaning "Anti-organists." There is still much overlapping between the "Antis" and the "Disciples" in the form of limited cooperation, exchange of pulpits, and members of both groups whose allegiance is divided. The fact that both groups in some sections of the country employ the titles "Churches of Christ" and "Christians" adds to confusion.

BIBLIOGRAPHY

I. *Writings of Alexander Campbell*

A. BOOKS

Campbell, Alexander, *Christian Baptism, With Its Antecedents and Consequences.* Bethany, Va., Alexander Campbell, 1851. 444 pp.

—— *The Christian Preacher's Companion, or the Gospel Facts Sustained by the Testimony of Unbelieving Jews and Pagans.* Bethany, Va., M'Vay & Ewing, 1836. 153 pp.

—— *The Christian System in Reference to the Union of Christians, And a Restoration of Primitive Christianity, As Plead in the Current Reformation.* 3rd. ed., Pittsburgh, Forrester & Campbell, 1840. 354 pp.

—— *A Connected View of the Principles and Rules by Which the Living Oracles May Be Intelligibly and Certainly Interpreted, of the Foundation on Which All Christians May Form One Communion, And of the Capital Positions Sustained in the Attempt to Restore the Original Gospel and Order of Things, Containing the Principal Extras of the Millennial Harbinger, Revised and Corrected.* Bethany, Va., M'Vay & Ewing, 1835. 404 pp.

—— *A Debate between Rev. A. Campbell and Rev. N. L. Rice, on the Action, Subject, Design, and Administrator of Christian Baptism; Also on the Character of Spiritual Influence in Conversion and Sanctification, and on the Expediency and Tendency of Ecclesiastic Creeds, as Terms of Union and Communion.* Lexington, Ky., A. T. Skillman & Son, 1844. 912 pp.

—— *A Debate on Christian Baptism between the Rev. W. L. Maccala, a Presbyterian Teacher, and Alexander Campbell, Held at Washington, Ky., Commencing on the 15th and Terminating on the 21st Oct., 1823, in the Presence of a Very Numerous and Respectable Congregation. In which Are Interspersed and to Which Are Added Animadversions on Different Treatises on the Same Subject, Written by Dr. J. Mason, Dr. S. Ralston, Rev. E. Pond, Rev. J. P. Campbell, Rector Armstrong, and the Rev. J. Walker.* Buffaloe, Va., Campbell & Sala, 1824. 420 pp.

—— *A Debate on the Roman Catholic Religion, Held in the Sycamore-Street Meeting House, Cincinnati, from the 13th to the 21st of January, 1837, between Alexander Campbell of Bethany, Va., and the Rt. Rev. John B. Purcell, Bishop of Cincinnati.* Cincinnati, J. A. James & Co., 1837. Vol. I, 359 pp.

—— and Owen, Robert, *A Debate on the Evidences of Christianity; Containing an Examination of the "Social System," And of All the Systems of Scepticism of Ancient and Modern Times; Between Robert Owen, of New Lanark, Scotland, and Alexander Campbell, of Bethany, Virginia, with an Appendix Written by the Parties.* Bethany, Alexander Campbell, 1829. Vol. I, 251 pp., vol. II, 301 pp.

—— "The Disciples of Christ" (typewritten copy for *The Encyclopedia of Religious Knowledge*). Brattleboro, Vt., Fessenden & Co., 1836. 3 pp.

—— and Skinner, A., *A Discussion of the Doctrines of Endless Misery and*

Universal Salvation in an Epistolary Correspondence between Alexander Campbell, of Bethany, Va., and Dolphus Skinner, of Utica, N.Y., Utica, C. C. P. Grosa, 1840. 436 pp.

—— *Familiar Lectures on the Pentateuch; Delivered before the Morning Class of Bethany College, During the Session of 1859–60, Also Short Extracts from His Sermons during the Same Session.* W. T. Moore, ed., Cincinnati, Bosworth, Chase & Hall, 1871. 379 pp.

—— *Infant Sprinkling Proved To Be a Human Tradition; Being the Substance of a Debate on Christian Baptism, between Mr. John Walker, a Minister of the Secession, and Alexander Campbell, V. D. M., a Regular Baptist Minister, Held at Mount Pleasant, Jefferson County, Ohio, on the 19th and 20th June, 1820, in the Presence of a Very Numerous and Respectable Congregation, to Which Is Added a Large Appendix.* Steubenville, Ohio, James Wilson, 1820. 216 pp.

—— *Lawrence Greatrakes Calumnies Repell'd.* Buffaloe, Va., Alexander Campbell, 1825. 60 pp.

—— *Letters to a Skeptic, Reprinted from the Christian Baptist.* Cincinnati, H. S. Bosworth, 1859. 57 pp.

—— *Memoirs of Elder Thomas Campbell, Together with a Brief Memoir of Mrs. James Campbell.* Cincinnati, H. S. Bosworth, 1861. 319 pp.

—— *Popular Lectures and Addresses.* Philadelphia, James Challen & Son, 1863. 647 pp.

—— *The Sacred Writings of the Apostles and Evangelists of Jesus Christ, Commonly Styled the New Testament. Translated from the Original Greek, by George Campbell, James Macknight, and Philip Doddridge, Doctors of the Church of Scotland. With Prefaces to the Historical and Epistolary Books; And an Appendix, Containing Critical Notes and Various Translations of Difficult Passages.* Buffaloe, Va., Alexander Campbell, 1826. 478 pp. 2d ed., same title, place, and publisher, 1828. 456 pp. 3d ed., same title through "Doddridge," then the following change is made: *With Prefaces, Various Emendations And an Appendix, Containing Various Translations of Difficult Passages—Some Critical Notes on the Language, Geography, Chronology, and History of the New Testament—and Miscellaneous Tables Designed to Aid Every Candid Reader of the Volume in Acquiring a Satisfactory Knowledge of Its Contents.* Bethany, Va., Alexander Campbell, 1832. 517 pp.

—— *Strictures on Three Letters Respecting the Debate at Mount Pleasant Published in the Presbyterian Magazine in 1821; signed Samuel Ralston.* Pittsburgh, Eichbaum & Johnson, 1822. 76 pp.

B. PERIODICALS

Campbell, Alexander, ed., *The Christian Baptist.* Buffaloe Creek, Va., printed by Solomon Sala at the Buffaloe Printing Office, 1823–1824. Vol. I, 300 pp.

—— ed., *The Christian Baptist.* Buffaloe, Va., Buffaloe Printing Office, 1824–1826. Vol. II, 288 pp., vol. III, 288 pp.

—— ed., *The Christian Baptist.* Bethany, Va., printed and published by the Editor at the Bethany Printing Office, 1826–1830. Vol. IV, 284 pp., vol. V, 284 pp., vol. VI, 286 pp., vol. VII, 286 pp.

—— *The Christian Baptist, Edited by Alexander Campbell. Revised by D. S.*

Burnet, from the Second Edition, with Mr. Campbell's Last Corrections.
13th ed., Cincinnati, H. S. Bosworth, 1867. 670 pp.
—— ed., *The Millennial Harbinger,* I–XXXV. Bethany, printed and published by the Editor, 1830–1864.
Pendleton, W. K., ed., *The Millennial Harbinger,* XXXVI–XLI. Bethany, printed and published by the Editor, 1865–1870.

II. *Additional Sources*

A. BOOKS

Abbott, B. A., *The Disciples, an Interpretation.* St. Louis, The Bethany Press (Christian Board of Publication), 1924. 271 pp.
Aaron, R. I., *John Locke.* London, New York, Toronto, Oxford University Press, 1837. 328 pp.
Ainslie, Peter, *The Message of the Disciples for the Union of the Church, Including Their Origin and History.* New York, Fleming H. Revell Co., 1913. 212 pp.
Athearn, C. A., *The Religious Education of Alexander Campbell, Morning Star of the Coming Reformation.* St. Louis, The Bethany Press, 1828. 204 pp.
Bates, E. S., *American Faith, Its Religious, Political, and Economic Foundations.* New York, W. W. Norton & Co., Inc., 1940. 445 pp.
Barrett, J. Pressley, *The Centennial of Religious Journalism.* 2d ed. Dayton, Christian Publishing Association, 1908. 656 pp.
Battenfield, J. A. and Pendleton, Philip Y., *The Great Demonstration, A Harmony of All the Prophetic Visions of the Holy Bible, Daniel, and Revelation.* Cincinnati, Standard Publishing Co., 1914. 462 pp.
Baxter, William, *Life of Elder Walter Scott* (The Walter Scott Centennial Edition, Abridged by B. A. Abbott). St. Louis, The Bethany Press, 1926. 215 pp.
Billington, R. A., *The Protestant Crusade 1800–1860; A Study of the Origins of American Nativism.* New York, The Macmillan Co., 1838. 514 pp.
Boles, H. Leo, *Biographical Sketch of Gospel Preachers.* Nashville, Gospel Advocate Co., 1932. 455 pp.
Borden, E. W., assisted by Showalter, G. H., *Church History—Showing the Origin of the Church of Christ, and Its History from the Days of the Apostles to Our Time.* Austin, Texas, Firm Foundation Publishing House, 1939. 408 pp.
Bury, J. B., *A History of Freedom of Thought.* New York, Henry Holt & Co.; London, Thornton Butterworth, 1913. 253 pp.
Brougham, Henry Lord, *Works of Henry Lord Brougham,* "Natural Theology, Dialogues on Instinct, Observations on the Structures of the Cells of Bees and Fossil Osleology Vol. VI." Edinburgh, Adam and Charles Black, 1872. 455 pp.
—— *Opinions of Lord Brougham on Politics, Theology, Law, Science, Education, Etc.* Philadelphia, Lea & Blanchard, 1839. Vol. 1, 243 pp., vol. 2, 251 pp.
Butler, Joseph, *The Analogy of Religion, Natural and Revealed, To the Constitution and Course of Nature, To Which Are Added Two Brief Disserta-*

tions. Prefix by Samuel Halifax. London, printed for Scott & Webster, 1734. 303 pp.

Campbell, Selina Huntington, *Home Life and Reminiscences of Alexander Campbell, by His Wife.* St. Louis, John Burns, 1882. 503 pp.

Cauble, Commodore Wesley, *Disciples of Christ in Indiana, Achievements of a Century.* Indianapolis, Meigs Publishing Co., 1930. 305 pp.

Chalmers, Thomas, *Evidence and Authority of the Christian Revelation.* Hartford, Sheldon & Goodrick, 1816. 180 pp.

—— *Evidence of the Christian Revelation and Lectures on Paley's Evidences.* Edinburgh, Edmonston & Doughlas; London, Hamilton, Adams & Co., 1863. 582 pp.

—— *Discourses on the Christian Revelation Viewed in Connection with the Modern Astronomy, Together with Six Sermons Embracing the Loss Occasioned by the Death of Princess Charlotte of Wilson.* Andover, Mark Newman, Flagg, & Gould, 1818. 344 pp.

—— *Bridgewater Treatises,* "On the Power, Wisdom, and Goodness of God as Manifested in the Adaptations of External Nature to the Moral and Intellectual Constitution of Man, Vol. I." Philadelphia, Carey, Lea & Blanchard, 1833. 308 pp.

—— *The Works of Thomas Chalmers, D.D., Minister of the Tron Church, Glasgow, Complete in One Volume.* Philadelphia, Hogan & Thompson (stereotyped by L. Johnson), 1833. 469 pp.

Christopher, Hiram, *The Remedial System; Or Man and His Redeemer.* Lexington, Ky., Transylvania Printing & Publishing Co., 1876. 436 pp.

Clayton, Mary Black, *Reminiscences of Jeremiah Sullivan Black.* St. Louis, Christian Publishing Co., 1887. 256 pp.

Cole, G. D. H., *The Life of Robert Owen.* London, Macmillan & Co., 1930. 350 pp.

Combe, George, *A System of Phrenology.* 3d American ed., from the 3d Edinburgh ed. Boston, Marsh, Capen, & Lynon, 1835. 664 pp.

Creed, J. M. and Smith, Boys J. S., *Religious Thought in the Eighteenth Century, Illustrated from Writers of the Period.* Cambridge, Cambridge University Press, 1934. 301 pp.

Cudsworth, Ralph, *The True Intellectual System of the Universe: Wherein All the Reason and Philosophy of Atheism Is Confuted and Its Impossibility Demonstrated.* A Treatise on Immutable Morality with a Discourse Concerning the True Nature of the Lord's Supper: and Two Sermons. 1st American ed. New York, Gould & Newman. Vol. I, 1837, 804 pp., vol. II, 1838, 756 pp.

Davis, M. M., *How the Disciples Began and Grew, A Short History of the Christian Church.* Cincinnati, The Standard Publishing Co., 1915. 244 pp.

Dayton, Amos Cooper, *Pedobaptist and Campbellite Immersions: Being a Preview of the Arguments of Doctors Walker, Fuller, Johnson, Wayland, Broadus, and Others.* Introductory Essay by J. R. Graves. New York, South-Western Publishing House, Graves, Works & Co., 1858. pp. 13–270.

DeGroot, A. T., *The Churches of Christ in Owen County, Indiana.* Spencer, Ind., Samuel A. Guard & Co., Inc. 181 pp.

—— *The Grounds of Divisions among the Disciples of Christ.* Chicago, privately printed, 1940. 228 pp.

—— and Dowling, E. E., *The Literature of the Disciples of Christ*. Advance, Ind., Hustler Print, 1833. 78 pp.

Egbert, James, *Alexander Campbell and Christian Liberty. A Centennial Volume of His Controlling Ideals—Enforced by His Own Words*. St. Louis, Christian Publishing Co., 1909. 338 pp.

Farrar, Adam Storey, *A Critical History of Free Thought in Reference to the Christian Religion*. New York, D. Appleton & Co., 1880. 487 pp.

Ferguson, C. W., *The Confusion of Tongues, A Review of Modern Isms*. Garden City, N. Y., Doubleday, Doran & Co., 1929. 464 pp.

Fortune, A. W., *Adventuring with Disciple Pioneers*. St. Louis, The Bethany Press, 1942. 78 pp.

—— *The Disciples in Kentucky*. St. Louis, The Convention of the Christian Churches in Kentucky, Christian Board of Publication, 1932. 415 pp.

—— *Origin and Development of the Disciples*. St. Louis, The Bethany Press, 1924. 186 pp.

Frazee, Elder W. D., *Reminiscences and Sermons*. Nashville, Gospel Advocate Publishing Co., 1892. 396 pp.

Fuller, Andrew, *The Gospel, Its Own Witness: On The Holy Nature, and Divine Harmony of the Christian Religion, Contrasted with the Immorality and Absurdity of Deism*. New York, printed for Cornelius Davis, 1800. 288 pp.

Gabriel, R. H., *The Course of American Democratic Thought, An Intellectual History since 1815*. New York, The Ronald Press Co., 1940. 330 pp.

Garrison, J. H., *Memories and Experiences, A Brief Story of a Long Life: An Autobiography*. St. Louis, Christian Board of Publication, 1926. 269 pp.

—— *et al.*, *The Reformation of the Nineteenth Century, A Series of History Sketches Dealing with the Rise and Progress of the Religious Movement Inaugurated by Thomas and Alexander Campbell, From Its Origin to the Close of the Nineteenth Century*. St. Louis, Christian Publishing Co., 1901. 515 pp.

—— *The Story of a Century; a Brief Historical Sketch and Exposition of the Religious Movement Inaugurated by Thomas and Alexander Campbell, 1809–1909*. St. Louis, Christian Publishing Co., 1909. 278 pp.

Garrison, W. E., *An American Religious Movement*. St. Louis, The Bethany Press (Christian Board of Publication), 1945. 167 pp.

—— *Catholicism and the American Mind*. Chicago, Willett & Clark & Colby, 1928. 267 pp.

—— *Religion Follows the Frontier—A History of the Disciples of Christ*. New York, London, Harper & Brothers, 1931. 317 pp.

—— *The Sources of Alexander Campbell's Theology*. St. Louis, Christian Publishing Co., 1900. 302 pp.

Gates, Errett, *The Disciples of Christ, the Story of the Churches*. New York, The Baker & Taylor Co., 1905. 346 pp.

—— *The Early Relation and Separation of Baptists and Disciples*. Chicago, The Christian Century Co., 1904. 124 pp.

George, E. A., *Seventeenth Century Men of Latitude, Forerunners of the New Theology*. New York, Charles Scribner's Sons, 1908. 199 pp.

Grafton, T. W., *Alexander Campbell, Leader of the Great Reformation of the Nineteenth Century*. St. Louis, Christian Publishing Co., 1897. 234 pp.

Gregory, Olinthus, *Letters to a Friend on the Evidences, Doctrines, and Duties of the Christian Religion.* From the 4th London ed., revised and slightly abridged. New York, American Tract Society, 1822. 480 pp.

Haley, J. J., *Debates That Made History, The Story of Alexander Campbell's Debates with Rev. John Walker, Rev. W. L. McCalla, Mr. Robert Owen, Bishop Purcell, and Nathan L. Rice.* St. Louis, Christian Board of Publication, 1920. 249 pp.

Hall, Thomas Cuming, *The Religious Background of American Culture.* Boston, Little, Brown & Co., 1930. 348 pp.

Hanna, William Herbert, *Thomas Campbell, Seceder and Christian Advocate.* Cincinnati, The Standard Publishing Co., 1935. 222 pp.

Harnack, Adolph, *What Is Christianity?* New York, G. P. Putnam's Sons; London, Williams & Norgate, 1901, 322 pp.

Haydon, A. S., *Early History of the Disciples in the Western Reserve, Ohio, With Biographical Sketches of Principal Agents in Their Religious Movements.* Cincinnati, Chase & Hall, 1876. 476 pp.

Hinsdale, Burke Aaron, *The Genuineness and Authenticity of the Gospels: An Argument Conducted on Historical and Critical Grounds.* St. Louis, Christian Publishing Co., 1872. 276 pp.

Hudson, John Allen, *The Man and the Movement, A Study in the Life of Alexander Campbell.* Cincinnati, Christian Leader Co., 1927. 148 pp.

Hume, David, *The Philosophical Works of David Hume.* Boston, Little, Brown & Co., 1854. Vol. IV, 580 pp.

Humphrey, Edward F., *Nationalism and Religion in America, 1774–1789.* Boston, Chipman Law Publishing Co., 1924. 536 pp.

Jarrell, W. A., *The Gospel in Water, or Campbellism, Being an Exposition and a Vindication of the Gospel and the New Testament Church.* St. Louis, National Baptist Publishing Co., 1886. 605 pp.

Jennings, Walter Wilson, *A Short History of the Disciples of Christ.* St. Louis, The Bethany Press, 1929. 236 pp.

—— *Origin and Early History of the Disciples of Christ.* Cincinnati, The Standard Publishing Co., 1919. 344 pp.

Jenyns, Soame, *View of the Internal Evidence of the Christian Religion.* 3d ed. London, T. Becket, 1776. 32 pp.

Jones, Allen Bailey, *The Spiritual Side of Our Plea.* Cincinnati, Christian Standard Publishing Co., 1901. 394 pp.

Jones, Thomas Rymer, ed., *The Bridgewater Treatises on the Power, Wisdom, and Goodness of God, as Manifested in the Creation.* London, Henry G. Bohn, 1852. Vol. I, 372 pp., vol. II, 404 pp.

Keith, Alexander, *Demonstration of the Truth of the Christian Religion.* From the 2d Edinburgh ed. New York, Harper & Brothers, 1839. 336 pp.

Kellums, Jesse R., *Alexander Campbell and the Disciples.* New York, Richard R. Smith, Inc., 1930. 409 pp.

Kersher, F. D., *How to Promote Christian Union; An Historical and Practical Handbook.* Cincinnati, The Standard Publishing Co., 1916. 235 pp.

Koch, G. Adolf, *Republican Religion: The American Revolution and the Cult of Reason.* New York, Henry Holt & Co., 1933. 334 pp.

Latourette, K. S., *A History of the Expansion of Christianity,* "The Great Century A. D. 1800–A. D. 1914 Europe and the United States of America"

Vol. IV. New York, London, Harper & Brothers, 1941. 516 pp.

Lefanu, Philip, trans., *Letters of Certain Jews to Monsieur Voltaire, Containing an Apology for Their Own People, and for the Old Testament with Critical Reflections, and a Short Commentary Extracted from a Greater; With Christian Notes and Additions on Various Parts of the Work.* 2d American ed., with corrections. Two vols. in one. Paris and Covington, Ky., G. G. Moore & J. L. Newby, 1845. 612 pp.

Leslie, Charles, *A Short and Easy Method with the Deists, With a Letter from the Author to a Deist upon His Conversion by Reading His Book.* London, printed for F. C. Rivington, booksellers to The Society for Promoting Christian Knowledge, 1801. 127 pp.

—— *A Short and Easy Method with the Deists.* 1st American ed. from the 8th London ed. Windsor, Vt., T. M. Pomroy, 1812. 134 pp.

—— *The Theological Works of the Rev. Charles Leslie.* London, W. Bowyer, 1721. Vol. I, 810 pp., vol. II, 883 pp.

Locke, John, *An Essay Concerning Human Understanding, Knowledge, Opinion, and Assent.* Edited with an Introduction by Benjamin Rand. London, Toronto, J. M. Dent & Sons, 1924. 242 pp.

Longon, G. W., *Origin of the Disciples of Christ, A Review of Prof. W. H. Whitsitt's Volume Entitled, "Origin of the Disciples of Christ," To Which Is Added an Appendix Containing Extracts from Reviews of Prof. Whitsitt's Book by Baptist Writers.* St. Louis Publishing Co., 1889. 195 pp.

Lord, David N., *An Exposition of the Apocalypse.* New York, Harper & Brothers. 1847. 542 pp.

Lutz, Henry F., *To Infidelity and Back, A Truth-Seekin's Religious Autobiography.* Cincinnati, The Standard Publishing Co., 1911. 231 pp.

Madelin, Louis, The French Revolution. *The National History of France,* F. Funck-Brentano, ed., "The French Revolution." New York, G. P. Putnam's Sons, 1925. 662 pp.

McGiffert, A. C., *The Rise of Modern Religious Ideas.* New York, The Macmillan Co., 1915. 315 pp.

—— *Protestant Thought before Kant.* New York, Charles Scribner's Sons, 1942. 261 pp.

McLachlan, H., *Religious Opinions of Milton, Locke, and Newton.* Manchester, Manchester University Press, 1941. 221 pp.

McLean, Archibald, *Alexander Campbell as a Preacher; A Study.* New York, Fleming H. Revell Co., 1909. 46 pp.

Milligan, R., *Reason and Revelation; The Province of Reason in Matters Pertaining to Divine Revelation Defined and Illustrated; And the Paramount Authority of the Holy Scriptures Vindicated.* 8th ed., Cincinnati, Central Book Concern, 1880. 564 pp.

Mode, Peter G., *Source Book and Bibliographical Guide for American Church History.* Mensha, Wis., The Collegiate Press, 1921. 735 pp.

Moore, W. T., *A Comprehensive History of the Disciples of Christ, Being An Account of a Century's Effort to Restore Primitive Christianity in Its Faith, Doctrine, and Life.* New York, Toronto, London, Edinburgh, Fleming H. Revell Co., 1909. 830 pp.

Morais, Herbert M., *Deism in Eighteenth Century America.* New York, Columbia University Press, 1934. 203 pp.

Morrill, M. T., *A History of the Christian Denomination in America 1794–1911 A.D.* Dayton, Ohio, The Christian Publishing Association, 1912. 407 pp.

Morris, W. A., *The Writings of Alexander Campbell: Selections Chiefly from the Millennial Harbinger.* Austin, Texas, Eugen Von Boechmann, 1896. 271 pp.

Mossner, Ernest C., *Bishop Butler and the Age of Reason.* New York, The Macmillan Co., 1936. 271 pp.

Niebuhr, H. Richard, *The Kingdom of God in America.* Chicago, Willett, Clark & Co., 1937. 215 pp.

—— *The Social Sources of Denominationalism.* New York, Henry Holt & Co., 1939. 304 pp.

Owen, Robert, *The Life of Robert Owen by Himself* (with an Introduction by M. Beer). New York, Alfred A. Knopf, 1920. 352 pp.

—— *Robert Owen's Opening Speech, and His Reply to the Rev. Alex. Campbell, In the Recent Public Discussion in Cincinnati, To Prove That the Principles of All Religions Are Erroneous, and That Their Practice Is Injurious to the Human Race, Etc.* Cincinnati, published for Robert Owen, 1829. 226 pp.

Paine, Thomas, *The Age of Reason.* London, R. Carlile, 1822. 246 pp.

—— *Common Sense.* Philadelphia, R. Bell, 1776. 79 pp.

—— *Rights of Man.* London, J. S. Jordan, 1791. 162 pp.

Paley, William, *Evidences of Christianity*, "The Works of William Paley, D.D.," Vol. IV. London, printed for Thomas Tegg, 1825. 440 pp.

Post, Albert, *Popular Free Thought in America, 1825–1850.* New York, Columbia University Press, 1943. 249 pp.

Power, Frederick D., *Sketches of Our Pioneers.* Chicago, Fleming H. Revell Co., 1898. 148 pp.

Prideaux, Humphrey, *The Old and the New Testaments Connected in the History of the Jews and Neighboring Nations from the Declensions of the Kingdoms of Israel to the Time of Christ, Etc.* 1st American ed. from the 16th London ed. Charlestown, Mass., J. M. 'Kown, 1815–16. Vol. I, 339 pp., vol. II, 439 pp., vol. III, 499 pp., vol. IV, 424 pp.

Richardson, Robert, *Memoirs of Alexander Campbell, Embracing a View of the Religious Reformation Which He Advocated.* Cincinnati, Standard Publishing Co., 1913. Vol. I, 560 pp., vol. II, 688 pp.

Robertson, J. M. A., *A History of Freethought in the Nineteenth Century*, Vol. I. New York, G. A. Putnam's Sons, 1930. 312 pp.

Rogers, John, *The Biography of Barton W. Stone, Written by Himself with Additions and Reflections.* Cincinnati, J. A. & N. P. James, 1847. 404 pp.

—— *The Biography of J. T. Johnson.* Cincinnati, published by the Author, 1861. 408 pp.

Rowe, John F., ed., *Biographical Sketch and Writings of Elder Benjamin Franklin.* 8th ed. Vol. I. Cincinnati, G. W. Rice, 1881. 511 pp.

Rowe, F. L., *Pioneer Sermons and Addresses.* 3d ed. Cincinnati, published by the Author, 1925. 295 pp.

Schlesinger, A. M., *Political and Social History of the United States, 1839–1925.* New York, The Macmillan Co., 1925. pp. 1–150.

Sears, Clara E., *Days of Delusion, A Strange Bit of History.* Boston, Houghton, Mifflin Co., 1924. 264 pp.

Seth, Andrew, *Scottish Philosophy, A Comparison of the Scottish and German Answers to Hume.* 3d ed. Edinburgh & London, William Blackwood & Sons, 1894. 222 pp.

Shuckford, Samuel, *Sacred and Profane History Connected, from the Creation of the World to the Dissolution of the Assyrian Empire at the Death of Sardanapalus, and to the Declension of the Kingdoms of Judah and Israel, Under the Reigns of Ahaz and Pekah. Including the Dissertation on the Creation and the Fall of Man.* 5th ed. Revised, corrected, and greatly improved by James Creighton. London, Charles Wood, 1919. Vol. I, 331 pp., vol. II, 459 pp., vol. III, 477 pp., vol. IV, 316 pp.

Smith, Benjamin L., *Alexander Campbell.* St. Louis, The Bethany Press, 1930. 399 pp.

—— *The Millennial Harbinger Abridged.* Cincinnati, The Standard Publishing Co., 1902. Vol. I, 588 pp., vol. II, 690 pp.

Snowden, J. H., *The Truth about Mormonism.* New York, George H. Doran Co., 1926. 369 pp.

Stephen, Leslie. *History of English Thought in the Eighteenth Century.* New York, G. P. Putnam's Sons, 1876. Vol. I, 466 pp., vol. II, 469 pp.

Stevenson, Dwight E., *Walter Scott, Voice of the Golden Oracle, A Biography.* St. Louis, Mo., Christian Board of Publication, 1946. 240 pp.

Stiles, Joseph C., *A Letter to Alexander Campbell in Reply to an Article in the Millennial Harbinger.* Lexington, Ky., Intelligencer Printers, 1838. 57 pp.

—— *Reply to an Article in the June Number of the Millennial Harbinger.* Frankfort, Ky., A. G. Hodges, 1838. 55 pp.

Sweet, W. W., *Makers of Christianity from John Cotton to Lyman Abbott.* New York, Henry Holt & Co., 1937. pp. 272–334.

—— *The Story of Religions in America.* New York & London, Harper & Brothers, 1930. 542 pp.

Tullock, John, *Rational and Christian Philosophy in England in the Seventh Century.* Edinburgh & London, William Blackwood & Sons; New York, Scribner, Welford & Armstrong, 1872. Vol. I, 463 pp., vol. II, 500 pp.

Tyler, A. F., *Freedom's Ferment.* Minneapolis, University of Minnesota Press, 1944. 608 pp.

Tyler, B. B., *The American Church History Series,* "A History of the Disciples of Christ." New York, The Christian Literature Co., 1894. pp. 1–162.

Walker, Williston, *A History of the Christian Church.* New York, Charles Scribner's Sons, 1940. pp. 298–624.

Ware, Charles C., *Barton Warren Stone, Pathfinder of Christian Union; A Story of His Life and Times.* St. Louis, The Bethany Press, 1932. 399 pp.

Warburton, William, *Letters from a Late Prelate, William Warburton, to One of His Friends.* 1st American ed. New York, E. Sargeant, 1809. 337 pp.

Watson, R., *An Apology for the Bible, In a Series of Letters, Addressed to Thomas Paine, Author of a Book Entitled "The Age of Reason," Part the Second, Being an Investigation of True and of Fabulous Theology.* Cambridge, Hillard & Brown, 1828. 173 pp.

Weigle, Luther A., *American Idealism.* New Haven, Yale University Press, 1928. 356 pp.

Welshimer, P. H., *Concerning the Disciples, A Brief Resume of the Movement to Restore the New Testament Church.* Cincinnati, The Standard Publishing Co., 1935. 205 pp.

Whitham, J. Mills, *A Biographical History of the French Revolution.* London, George Routledge & Sons, 1930. 493 pp.

Whitsitt, W. H., *Origin of the Disciples of Christ (Campbellites), A Contribution to the Centennial Anniversary of the Birth of Alexander Campbell.* 4th ed. Louisville, Chas. T. Dearing, 1899. 112 pp.

Wilett, H. L., *et al., Progress, Anniversary Volume of the Campbell Institute on the Completion of Twenty Years of History.* Chicago, The Christian Century Press, 1917. 329 pp.

Williams, J. A., *Life of Elder John Smith, With Some Account of the Rise and Progress of the Current Reformation.* Cincinnati, The Standard Publishing Co., 1904. 476 pp.

B. PERIODICALS

The Christian-Evangelist (national weekly of the Disciples of Christ). St. Louis, Christian Board of Publication.

The Christian Standard (devoted to the restoration of primitive Christianity). Cincinnati, The Christian Standard Publishing Co.

The Scroll. Chicago, published monthly (except July and August) by The Campbell Institute.

C. DICTIONARIES AND ENCYCLOPEDIAS

Cyclopedia of Biblical, Theological, and Ecclesiastical Literature. Prepared by J. M'Clintock and James Strong. New York, Harper & Brothers, 1869–1877.

Dictionary of American Biography. Allen Johnson and Dumas Malone, eds. New York, Charles Scribner's Sons, 1928–1937.

Dictionary of National Biography. Leslie Stephen and Sidney Lee, eds. London, Smith, Elder & Co., 1908 ff.

Encyclopedia of Religion and Ethics. James Hastings, ed. New York, Charles Scribner's Sons; Edinburgh, T. & T. Clark, 1908–1927.

D. REPORTS

Minutes of the General Assembly of the Presbyterian Church in the United States from A.D. 1821 to A.D. 1837 Inclusive. Philadelphia, Presbyterian Board of Publication and Sabbath-School Work. 678 pp.

Proceedings and Debates of the Virginia State Convention of 1829–30, To Which Are Subjoined, The New Constitution of Virginia, And the Votes of the People. Richmond, Samuel Sheperd & Co., 1830. 919 pp.

Year Book, 1945, of the Disciples of Christ. Indianapolis, Publication Committee of the International Convention of the Disciples and Its Related Organizations.

INDEX

ADAMS, JOHN, 3
Age of Reason, 63, 84, 157
Albigenses, 16, 186
Alexander Campbell, 9, 47, 177
American Bible Society, 163, 201, 202
American Protestant Association, 41, 196
American Revolution. *See* Revolution
Americanism, viii, 3–4, 48, 123, 158, 163, 184, 187, 194, 195, 202–210, 221. *See also* Millennium and Revolution
Analogy of Religion, Natural and Revealed, 66, 200
Apology for the Bible, 145
Apostles' Creed, 36, 37, 47
Architecture. *See* Disciples of Christ
Arian, 17, 35, 42, 45, 122, 155
Aristotle, 113
Arius, 42
Arminian, 17, 42, 45, 46, 102
Asbury, Francis, vii
Athanasian Creed, 37
Athearn, C. R., 47
Atheism, vii, 6, 57, 58, 68, 85–88, 97, 105, 108, 117, 157; types of, 64, 113–116, 131, 181. *See also* Problem of evil and Problem of knowledge
Augustine, Saint, influence of, 43–44, 98

BACON, FRANCIS, 61, 91, 143, 158, 198, 225; method of, 143, 158, 220, 225
Baptism, 33, 67, 97, 191, 226. *See also* Immersion
Baptist Banner, 185
Baptist Recorder, 38
Baptists, 10, 15, 17, 30, 67; Associated or Regular, 14, 16, 46, 49, 51, 60, 137; Independent, 14–16, 46, 49, 193; influence upon Barton W.

Stone, 227; Mahoning Association, 15, 183; Pedobaptists, 20, 37, 38, 43, 50, 201–202; Redstone Association, 147, 226; Two Seeds in the Spirit, 33; union with Disciples of Christ, 14–17, 51, 226, 227
Berkeley, Bishop, 76
Bethany College, 3, 4, 31, 131, 163, 198–202, 206, 207
Bible, and deism, 107–112; and education, 199–200; and ignorance of skeptics, 62–65, 96; King James translation, 33, 43, 47, 121; language of, 31–40, 90–91, 117, 165; mistranslations of, 33, 61, 146; and natural religion, 53, 112, 132–134; and natural sciences, 134–135; and natural theology, 112, 133–135; and nature, vii–viii, 53, 108; nature of, 38, 145–148; and phrenology, 124–125; and prophecy, 144–148, 170; and revelation, vii–viii, 53, 68, 90–91, 95–98, 102–104, 143, 152, 173; societies, 12, 13, 17, 46, 163, 164, 201–202, 211; and Spiritualism, 127–128; use of, 8, 10–11, 13, 39, 103, 138, 147. *See also* Living Oracles and Primitive Christianity
Bible Union Convention, 201
Biography of Barton W. Stone Written by Himself, 227
Book of Mormon, 183–184
Bradstreet, Stephen J., 29
Bridgewater Treatises, 130
Brougham, Henry Lord, 130–139
Buffalo Seminary, 196
Bullard, Chester, 229; and Bullardites, 229, 230
Butler, Joseph, 66, 200, 221

CALVIN, JOHN, 43, 111, 171, 200, 207, 221

Calvinism, 35, 42, 45, 46, 47, 149, 192–193; and deism, 110–111

Campbell, Alexander, vii–ix, 218–222; and defense of revealed religion, 57–162; and ecclesiasticism, viii, 3–58, 67, 90, 218–222; and similarities with natural religionists, 45–53. *See also Christian Baptist*, Debates; Disciples of Christ, and *Millennial Harbinger*

Campbell, Archibald, 223

Campbell, George, 31, 137, 138, 141, 221

Campbell, Thomas, 67, 179, 220, 223, 224, 228, 229

Campbellism, 45, 194

Campbellism Exposed, 148

Campbellites, 6

Campbell's New Testament, and *Campbell's Translation*, 27, 31, 47, 69. *See also Living Oracles*

Camp meetings, 28

Canonsburg College, 208

Capital punishment, 205

Chalmers, Thomas, 143, 221

Christian Association of Washington, 224, 225

Christian Baptism, With Its Antecedents and Consequences, 32, 51, 146

Christian Baptist, and policy of, 3, 4, 5, 22, 28, 31, 51, 53, 57, 58, 67, 68, 90, 110, 136, 163, 165, 166, 167, 168, 172, 179, 189, 190, 193, 202, 228

Christian Connection, 228–229

Christianity, genius and nature in history, 85–86, 101, 151–159, 171, 206; *See also* History and Primitive Christianity

Christian Herald, 45

Christian Preacher's Companion, 58, 143

Christian System in Reference to the Union of Christians, 32, 39, 51

Christocracy, 206, 215, 216

Christology, 117, 215, 216

Churches of Christ, 229

Cicero, 38, 105, 138

Cincinnati Chronicle, 69

Clack, Spencer, 38, 39

Clarke, Adam, 107, 118, 132, 141

Clay, Henry, 11, 18

Clergy, and alliance with the state, 7–8, 13, 19, 48, 87, 196; kingdom of, 7–11, 196; organization of, 26–29, 48, 52; as a "priesthood," 7, 9, 13, 16, 20, 29, 30, 47, 48, 50, 87, 164; and skepticism, 142; special call of, 8–11, 19, 29; and support of, 7–9, 11, 18, 19, 22, 23, 26, 30, 52, 190; and titles, 11, 25–28. *See also* Theological seminaries

Combe, George, 123–124, 129

Comprehensive History of the Disciples of Christ, 179, 183

Congregationalism, 18, 20, 29, 44, 229

Connection of the Old and New Testament, 140

Constantine, 42

Conventions. *See* Disciples of Christ

Conversion, 10, 33, 167, 182; *See also*, Holy Spirit, Jesus Christ, Regeneration, and Salvation

Council of Nicaea, 36, 42

Creeds, charges against Alexander Campbell, 38–40, 46; and pure speech, 31–37; and sectarianism, 13, 30, 42, 59, 60, 185–186

Cudworth, Ralph, 113

DAVISON, MALTIDA, 184

Debate between Rev. A. Campbell and Rev. N. L. Rice, 10, 49. *See also* Debates

Debate on the Evidences of Christianity, 48. *See also* Debates (Campbell-Owen)

Debate on the Roman Catholic Religion, 37. *See also* Debates (Campbell-Purcell)

Debates, attitudes toward, 67; publication of, 5, 11; and Campbell-Maccalla, 66; Campbell-Owen, 46, 49, 51, 54, 57, 60, 66–89, 91, 101, 104, 138, 141, 142, 143, 150, 151, 153, 163; Campbell-Purcell, 37, 41–43, 60, 186, 191, 194–196; Campbell-Rice, 10–11, 35, 39–40, 44, 46, 60,

91, 97–98; Campbell-Skinner, 118–121; Campbell-Walker, 66, 168, 191

Debates That Made History, 67

Decartes, 158

Declaration and Address, 202, 224–225

Deism, vii–viii, 17, 45, 57, 58, 97, 105, 121, 122, 131, 138; types of, 52, 107–112, 200. *See also* Millennium and Problem of knowledge

Demonstration of the Truth of Christian Religion, 66

Determinism, 52, 69. *See also* Nature of man

Diderot, 63, 64, 198

Disciples of Christ, 46

Disciples of Christ, vii, 6, 46, 47, 49, 50; and architecture, 187–189, 210; conventions of, 189; and Mormonism, 183–184; and ordinances of, 190–191, 212, 226; and organization of, 14–15, 40, 67, 185–194, 201–202, 212–213, 219–220; sketch of, 223–230; and theology, 39–40, 88, 96, 97–100, 103, 117, 154–155, 158–159, 163, 190–194, 197–203, 215–216, 218–220. *See also* Baptists and Millennium

Discussion of the Doctrines of Endless Misery, 118. *See also* Debates (Campbell-Skinner)

Dissertation on Miracles, 137, 138

Divine Legation of Moses, 141

Divinity schools. *See* Theological seminaries

Doctors of Divinity, degrees and titles, 16, 20, 24, 26–28

Doddridge, Philip, 31

Dwight, Timothy, 193

EARLY RELATION AND SEPARATION OF THE BAPTISTS AND DISCIPLES, 47, 67, 226

Ecclesiasticism. *See* Alexander Campbell

Education, 3–4, 17, 29–30, 60–61, 66, 69–70, 75, 88, 94, 95, 111, 131, 165, 196–202, 207, 211. *See also* Bethany

College and Millennium and Theological seminaries

Edwards, Jonathan, 193, 227

Election and reprobation, 32, 192

Emotionalism, 23, 31, 53, 109, 182, 189

Encyclopedia of Christianity, 143

Enlightenment, vii, viii, 7, 10, 46, 53, 66, 105, 218; and deists, skeptics, and infidels of, 58–65, 105

Enthusiasm, 7, 10, 24, 109

Episcopalians, 10, 17

Essay Concerning Human Understanding, 224

Evidence and Authority of Divine Revelation, 141

Evil. *See* Nature of man and Problem of knowledge

Experience, 80, 91, 98, 100–104, 170

FAMILIAR LECTURES ON THE PENTATEUCH, 200

Facts. *See* Problem of knowledge

Faith, types of, 32, 43, 97–99, 114, 136–137, 154, 175. *See also* Problem of knowledge

Fall of man. *See* Nature of man

Ferguson, Jesse B., 117

Fourth of July, 3–6, 203

Fowler, O. S., 124

Franklin, Benjamin, 4, 37, 61, 157, 158

Franklin, Elder Benjamin, 102

Frazee, W. D., 228

Freedom, of man and of religion, 3, 18, 48, 63, 157. *See also* Human Nature and Religious liberty

Free Inquirer, 118

Free speech. *See* Speech

Free thought, vii, 35, 47, 49, 63, 64, 101–102, 143

Free will. *See* Nature of man

French Revolution. *See* Revolution

Frontier, vii, ix, 3, 23, 46, 49, 50, 164, 181, 223

GARRISON, W. E., 47, 50, 146, 179

Gates, E., 46, 47, 226

Gibbon, 46, 199

Godwin, William, 46, 51, 52, 76, 116, 225

Graham, James, 115–116

Greatlakes, Lawrence, 45

Great Revival, vii, 222, 227

HAGGARD, RICE, 229

Haldanes, Robert and Alexander, influence of, 45, 46, 47, 141, 220, 221, 225

Haley, J. J., 67

Herbert, Bishop, 46, 107, 108, 150

Historical criteria, 72, 138–139

History, genuis of Christianity in, 85–86, 101, 151–159, 171; Alexander Campbell's stages of, 141–142, 151–152, 165, 171–176, 183, 215, and Robert Owen's, 86–87, and Walter Scott's, 169–170. *See also* Millennium and Primitive Christianity

Hobbes, 46, 62, 113, 199, 221

Holingbroke, 117

Holy Spirit, call of, 10; and conversion, 11; influence of, 11, 136–137, 147, 154, 218

Hopkinsville Female Institution, 116

Howe, E. D., 184

Hume, David, 46, 62, 63, 64, 76, 92, 93, 101, 144, 221, 225. *See also* Miracles and Prophecy

Hyde, Thomas, 151, 221

ILLUSTRATIONS OF PROPHECY, 166

Immersion, 38, 39, 40, 43, 59, 99, 142, 191. *See also* Baptism

Infidelity, vii, 7, 26, 45, 48, 50, 57, 58, 59, 60, 64, 116, 129, 144, 163, 199–200, 211, 213

Internal View of the Evidence of the Christian Religion, 146

JACKSON, ANDREW, 18

Jefferson College, 27

Jefferson, Thomas, 3, 4, 61, 205

Jenyns, Soame, 146, 155, 221

Jesus Christ, confession of, 11, 15, 31, 35; character and mission of, 60, 61, 64, 96, 122, 136, 140, 142, 151–155, 158–159, 214–216, 218; and prophecy, 140, 214–216; as ruler of the world, 203

Jones, Abner, 228, 229

KEITH, ALEXANDER, 66

King James Translation of the Bible. *See* Bible

Kinkade, William, 229

Knowledge, 24, 29–30. *See also* Problem of knowledge

LAITY, 3, 7, 9, 11, 13, 16, 23, 25, 26, 27, 30, 48

La Place, 148

Last Will and Testament of the Springfield Presbytery, 227–228

Law, profession of, 20, 22, 87, 196; enforcement of, 81, 87, 195, 205

Laws, natural. *See* Miracles, Natural science, and Nature of man

Leslie, Charles, 66, 138–139, 146, 221

Letter to Alexander Campbell in Reply to an Article in the Millennial Harbinger, 45

Letters to a Skeptic, 58

Living Oracles, 27, 31, 33, 121

Locke, John, 46, 61, 92, 93, 100, 110, 111, 112, 158, 197, 198, 215, 220, 221, 224, 225

Lord, David Nevins, 166

Lord's Supper, 15, 117, 142, 188, 190, 226

Luther, Martin, 19, 43, 44, 47, 173, 186, 200, 207, 208

MACCALLA, WILLIAM, 66. *See also* Debates

Macknight, James, 31

Madison, James, 202–203

Malthus, T. A., 171

Man. *See* Nature of man

Marshall, John, 202

Memoirs of Alexander Campbell, 67, 179, 183, 196, 223

Memoirs of Elder Thomas Campbell, 223

Mesmer, Frederic Anthony, 126. *See also* Spiritualism

Methodists, vii, 10, 14, 30, 35, 44, 183, 222; Conference, 33; Discipline, 37; enthusiasm of, 109; and influence upon Barton W. Stone, 227

Millennial Harbinger, 3, 5, 39, 51, 58; objectives of, 165–167, 178, 179, 187, 190, 194–195, 211–212, 215, 220, 221, 224, 225

Millennium, 32, 45; Alexander Campbell's views of, 163–184; and Anglo-Americanism, 202–211; and the Disciples of Christ, 164, 167–170, 178–179, 185–194, 210, 211, 213; introduction of, 164–210; Millerite views of, 177–181; postponement of, 211–217; Robert Owen's views of, 86, 177–178; and role of education, 165, 196–202, 211, 212; and role of foreign missions and interdenominationalism, 163–165, 201–202, 207–208, 211, 213; and role of Roman Catholicism, 179, 194–196, 211; and role of sectarianism, 164–165; and Walter Scott's views of, 169–170

Milton, John, 50, 158, 197, 224

Mirabaud, M., 84, 85, 108, 114–115

Mirabeau, Gabriel, 63

Miracles, and Christianity, 134–144; and David Hume, 137; evidences of, 10, 135–144, 148, 159; faith of, 32; and George Campbell, 137–138; and Mormonism, 183; and natural religion, 106, 108, 133–134, 136–138; and redemption, 156. *See also* Roman Catholicism

Mission of America, 202–211

Missionary societies, 12, 13, 17, 38, 46. *See also* Millennium

Money, and support of the clergy. *See* Clergy

Monroe, James, 202

Montgomery, G. W., 119–120

Moore, W. T., 179, 183, 200

Mormonism, 183–184

Mormonism Unveiled, 184

NATURAL LAW, 72, 87, 137, 191. *See also* Miracles, Natural science, and Nature of man

Natural religion, 46, 58, 91, 112, 124–126, 130–134

Natural science, 93, 106, 125, 127, 129–135, 138, 197, 199

Natural theology, 91, 108, 112, 124–125, 130–133, 199

Nature. *See* Bible, Natural theology, Nature of man, and Problem of knowledge

Nature of man, analysis of, 66, 113, 121, 125–127, 173–176, 197–200; Christian view of, 63, 85, 88, 152–153; free will and determinism, 69, 72–82, 88, 98, 109, 115, 157, 197; and society, 79–82, 86–88, 94–95; and spiritual capacity, 33, 80–82, 88, 94–104, 153, 155, 198. *See also* Problem of evil, Problem of knowledge, and Sin

New Harmony Gazette, 67–68

New Jerusalemites, 17

New Testament, Christianity, vii, 186, 226; editions, 5, 31, 33, 47; and ordinances, 33, 142, 190–191, 212, 226; and organizations inferred, 14, 185–189. *See also* Bible, *Campbell's Translation*, and Primitive Christianity

Newton, Isaac, 61, 95, 106, 148, 158, 198, 220, 225

Newton, Thomas, 169, 221

Nicaea, Council and Creed of, 33, 36, 42

Novatians, 49, 57, 64

ORDINANCES, OF THE CHURCH, 43. *See also* Baptism, Disciples of Christ, Lord's Supper, and New Testament

Owen, Robert, 39, 57, 63. *See also* Debates, History, Millennium, Nature of man, and Problem of knowledge

Owen, Robert Dale, 106, 118

Owenism, 115–116, 176, 199, 213. *See*

Owenism (*continued*)
also Debates, Robert Owen, and Social System

PAINE, THOMAS, 47, 50, 51, 61–64, 84–85, 95, 107, 108, 117, 121, 125, 145, 157, 221
Paley, 132, 200, 221
Parker, Daniel, 33
Pedobaptists. *See* Baptists
Pelegian, 45
Perfectionism, 87, 88, 115, 178, 187
Philomathesean Society, 50
Phrenology, 123–126
Pittsburgh Recorder, 22, 23
Plato, 105
Politics, 7–8, 19, 20, 202–204; and duties of Christians, 205–210; and Presbyterian influence, 17–18, 29–30; and Roman Catholic influence, 60–62, 195
Popular Lectures and Addresses, 4
Prayers, 12, 20, 21, 24, 126; as evidences of revelation, 108, 126, 136, 149–150
Presbyterianism, 10, 16, 17, 18, 28, 29, 35, 44, 49, 110, 111; and Barton W. Stone, 227–228; General Assembly, 17–18, 24; Seceder or Antiburgher Church 67, 223–225, 229. *See also* Politics
Prideaux, Humphrey, 141
Priesthood and priestcraft, 7, 9, 12, 30, 62. *See also* Clergy
Primitive Christianity, 11, 12, 13, 14, 167, 188; divine origin of, 61; and restoration of the ancient order of things, 13, 18, 166, 167, 173, 185, 187, 211, 218; as true Christianity, 36, 51, 61, 136–137, 157, 185–191. *See also* History, Millennium, and New Testament
Princeton Theological Seminary, 23
Problem of evil, 67, 69; and atheism, 113, 156–157; and the Campbell-Owen Debate, 79, 83–88, 153; and deism, 109–110; and determinism, 69; and the Fall of man, 84–85, 117, 123, 126, 172, 174–176; and natural

evils, 84; and natural man, 152–153, 173–175. *See also* Nature of man, Perfectionism, Problem of knowledge, and Sin
Problem of knowledge, and atheism, 113–115; and belief, facts, knowledge, opinion, and truths, 34–35, 72–79, 82, 113; and Bible facts, 102–104, 136–148, 159; and credulity, 95, 96, 103, 114; and deism, 107–112; and evidences of Christianity as divinely founded, 136–150; and faith and reason, 57, 77, 95–100, 106, 132, 159, 175; and methods of proof, 72–74; and miracles, 136–144, 148; and natural science, 129–135; and necessity of revelation, 58, 90, 91, 94–97, 100–102, 105, 114, 132–134, 148, 173, 218; and origin of ideas of the material world, 90, 92–93; and origin of spiritual ideas, 69, 80–83, 140, 218; and speech and language, 94–95, 97, 98, 102–104, 114. *See also* Experience, Historical criteria, Miracles, Owenism, Phrenology, Revelation, and Spiritualism
Prophecy, 87–88, 136, 161, 166, 169, 170, 182, 211, 214–215; and David Hume, 144; and Mormonism, 183
Protestantism, 7, 40, 41, 43, 44, 49, 51, 123, 165, 180, 186, 195, 196, 199, 200, 205, 208, 209, 213, 220, 223. *See also* Reformation
Purcell, Bishop, 36–37, 41, 185, 186. *See also* Debates
Purivance, David, 229

QUAKERS, 17, 30, 67, 121, 128

RACE PREJUDICES, 13. *See also* Slavery
Randolph, John, 202
Rationalism, 10, 52, 53, 98–100, 154, 218
Reason, vii, 30, 48, 57, 68, 78, 87, 91. *See also* Problem of knowledge
Reformation, Protestant, 41, 43–44, 107, 146, 173, 207

Reformers, Disciples of Christ, 6, 35, 40, 155, 229

Regeneration, 10, 11, 14, 17, 49, 60, 97, 98, 153, 193

Reign of Terror, 62

Religion Follows the Frontier, 47, 50, 179

Religious Education of Alexander Campbell, 47

Religious liberty, vii–viii, 4, 7, 9, 11, 13, 15, 19, 48, 203–204; and the press, 4, 52; and theological opinion, 3–4, 18, 29, 30, 35, 52. *See also* Speech

Reminiscences and Sermons, 228

Restoration of the ancient order of things. *See* Primitive Christianity

Revealed religion, vii, viii; defense of, 57–164, 200, 213, 218. *See also* Problem of knowledge

Revelation, 10, 33, 46, 57, 59, 66, 74, 87, 90, 94, 95, 98, 136, 218. *See also* Bible, Nature of man, Prayers, Problem of Evil, and Problem of knowledge

Revivals, 181. *See also* Great Revival

Revolution, the new, 3–6, 203–204; American, 4, 48, 203, 227; French, 8, 47, 48, 49, 59, 63–65, 116, 221

Rice, N. L., 10, 11, 35, 39, 40, 46, 191. *See also* Debates

Richardson, Robert, 67, 179, 196

Rigdon, Sidney, 183, 184

Rights of man, 3, 18, 48, 50, 52

Rogers, John, 227

Roman Catholicism, 10, 17, 20, 35, 47, 57, 138, 163; and claims of divine right, 7; and the clergy, 7; and despotism, 50, 61–62, 195; millennial role of, 164–165, 172, 194–196; as the "mother of sects," 40–44, 59–62, 186; and special miracles, 137, 191; and transubstantiation, 61, 191

Rousseau, 46, 63, 64, 144, 198, 221, 225

SACRED AND PROFANE HISTORY OF THE WORLD, 141

Sacred Writings of the Apostles and Evangelists of Jesus Christ, 31. *See also Living Oracles*

Salvation, by faith, 43, 98–99, 136, 191; and election and reprobation, 192; by human nature, 79, 125; in human history, 88, 165; by merit, 43; by prayer, 150; and Universalism, 116–121, 128

Sandemanians, 45, 46, 220, 221, 225

Sciences, 86. *See also* Natural sciences

Scott, Walter, 169–170, 181, 183, 185, 187, 220, 228, 229. *See also* History

Scriptures. *See* Bible, New Testament, and Primitive Christianity

Sebellian, 45

Second Great Awakening, vii, 222

Sectarianism, and creeds, 13, 37–38, 44; early and medieval, 186; and orthodoxies, 17, 18, 30–40, 53, 57, 87, 165, 167, 201, 226; and ranks, titles, and conceit, 25–28; and Roman Catholicism, 40–48, 65, 186. *See also* Millennium

Shaftsbury, Earl of, 46

Shakers, 17

Shannon, Joseph, 209

Short and Easy Method with Deists, 66, 138–139, 146

Shuckford, Samuel, 141

Sin and sins, 32, 43, 47, 79, 88, 155–156, 159, 191, 206; and the Fall of man, 84–85, 123, 126, 142, 155, 171–172

Skepticism, 52, 53, 91, 139, 153; classical, 57–66, 116; in London, 213; types of, 53, 74, 87, 105–107, 121, 129, 143–144, 177. *See also* Bible and Clergy

Skinner, Dolphus, 118–120

Slavery, 166, 202–204, 213

Smith, B. L., 9, 47, 179

Smith, Elias, 178

Smith, Joseph, 183, 184

Smythe, Alexander, 167

Socialism, 87, 157, 213

Social system, 67, 68, 86–88, 115–116, 153, 157

Socinian, 45, 111, 122
Socrates, 105
Sources of Alexander Campbell's Theology, 47, 146
Spaulding, Solomon, 184
Speech, free, 4, 18; and pure speech, *see* Creeds. *See also* Americanism, Problem of knowledge, and Religious liberty
Spinoza, 113, 199
Spiritualism, 126–129
Stages of history. *See* History
Stephen, Leslie, 169
Stiles, Joseph, 45
Stone, Barton W., 39, 40, 220, 226–229. *See also* Baptists and Methodists
Sunday School, 12, 13, 17

TAMMANY HALL, 59, 106
Taylor, John, 51, 185
Theocracy, 87, 176, 177
Theological seminaries, 8, 19, 20, 23, 28, 51–52, 196; and false training of, 19–25, 41; Princeton, 23, 24
Theology, 31, 36–40, 42, 43, 46, 52, 117, 163. *See also* Disciples of Christ and Natural theology
Towers, Joseph Lomas, 166
Tract societies, 13, 17
Transylvania University, 26, 111
Trinitarians, 35
Trinity, 32, 36, 117

UNDERHILL, SAMUEL, 68, 106
Union Literary Society of Miami University, 63
Unitarianism, 35, 45, 116–117, 121, 122, 155
United States, 7, 138, 188, 189, 204, 205, 206, 209
University of Glasgow, 3, 223–225
Universalism, 45, 116–121, 128

VIEW OF THE INTERNAL EVIDENCE OF THE CHRISTIAN RELIGION, 146
Volney, 46, 63, 64, 117, 150, 199
Voltaire, 46, 51, 63, 64, 117, 125, 198, 199, 221

WALDENSES, 16, 186
Walker, John. *See* Debates
War, 13, 34, 87, 156, 177, 209, 221; Civil, 122, 214, 216
Warburton, William, 141
Washington, George, 4
Watson, Richard, 145
Western Reserve College, 29–30
Westminster Confession of Faith, 36, 111, 227
Whitefield, George, 50
Williams, Roger, 15
Wright, Frances, 61, 106, 117
Wycliffe, John, 173, 207

YALE STUDIES IN RELIGIOUS EDUCATION

I. A History of Religious Education in Connecticut to the Middle of the Nineteenth Century by George Stewart, Jr.

II. A History of Religious Education in the Episcopal Church to 1835 by Clifton Hartwell Brewer.

III. Horace Mann and Religion in the Massachusetts Public Schools by Raymond B. Culver.

IV. Presbyterian Parochial Schools, 1846–1870, by Lewis Joseph Sherrill.

V. Community Organization in Religious Education by Hugh Hartshorne and J. Quinter Miller.

VI. Case Studies of Present-Day Religious Teaching by Hugh Hartshorne and Elsa Lotz.

VII. Church Schools of Today by Hugh Hartshorne and Earle V. Ehrhart.

VIII. Children and Puritanism by Sandford Fleming.

IX. Standards and Trends in Religious Education by Hugh Hartshorne, Helen R. Stearns, and Willard E. Uphaus.

X. The Church Follows Its Students by Clarence Prouty Shedd.

XI. From School to College. A Study of the Transition Experience, conducted by Lincoln B. Hale, D. W. Bailey, G. H. Menke, D. DeK. Rugh, and G. E. Schlesser. Hugh Hartshorne, Editor.

XII. The Presbyterian Doctrine of Children in the Covenant by Lewis Bevens Schenck.

XIII. Tennant's Philosophical Theology by Delton Lewis Scudder.

XIV. The Rise of the Social Gospel in American Protestantism, 1865–1915, by Charles Howard Hopkins.

XV. Millhands and Preachers by Liston Pope.

XVI. The Social Gospel of Walter Rauschenbusch and Its Relation to Religious Education by Vernon Parker Bodein.

XVII. The Moral Theory of Evolutionary Naturalism by William F. Quillian, Jr.

XVIII. Religion in Higher Education among Negroes by Richard I. McKinney.

XIX. The Mother's Role in Childhood Education. New England Concepts, 1830–1860, by Anne L. Kuhn.

XX. The College Seeks Religion by Merrimon Cuninggim.

XXI. Alexander Campbell and Natural Religion by Robert Frederick West.

During the last three decades of the eighteenth century the religious faith of America was challenged by the vogue of deism—the natural religion of the Enlightenment. Advocates upheld deism as the only true religion. They appealed to the freedom-loving Americans in the name of "free thought"; but the churches, prizing freedom just as much, called the movement "infidelity." By the first few years of the 1790's deism had become fashionable in certain academic and sophisticated circles in American society, but during the last few years of that decade and during the early part of the nineteenth century, America experienced a marked recovery from the threat of deism and atheism. Three Christian movements—the "Second Great Awakening," "The Great Revival," and the Methodist Movement—have been customarily described as contributing greatly to this recovery, but a fourth, known as the Primitive Gospel Movement, needs to be stressed for its contribution. Among the leaders of this movement Alexander Campbell (1788-

Continued on back flap